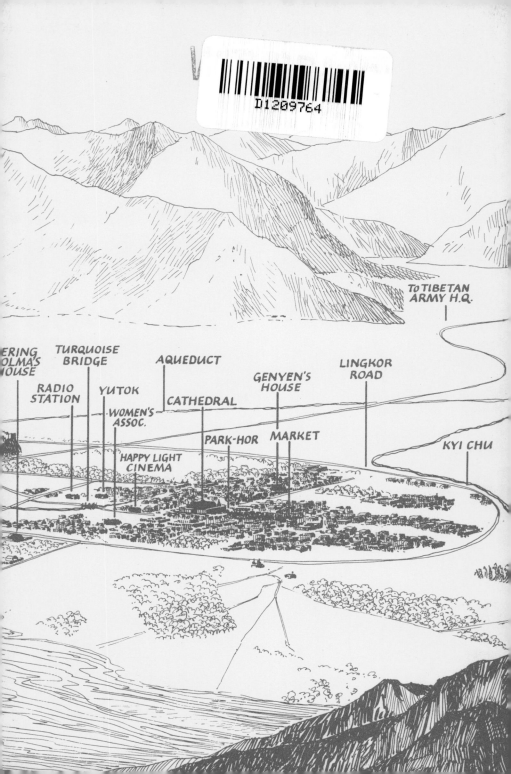

To TIBETAN
ARMY H.Q.

ERING
OLMA'S
HOUSE

TURQUOISE
BRIDGE

AQUEDUCT

GENYEN'S
HOUSE

LINGKOR
ROAD

RADIO
STATION

YUTOK

CATHEDRAL

WOMEN'S
ASSOC.

PARK-HOR

MARKET

KYI CHU

HAPPY LIGHT
CINEMA

From the Land of Lost Content

Into my heart an air that kills
From yon far country blows.
What are those blue remembered hills,
What spires, what farms are those?

That is the land of lost content,
I see it shining plain,
The happy highways where I went
And cannot come again.

A. E. HOUSMAN

Also by Noel Barber

The Black Hole of Calcutta

A Sinister Twilight
The Fall of Singapore 1942

From the Land of Lost Content

THE DALAI LAMA'S FIGHT FOR TIBET

Noel Barber

Houghton Mifflin Company Boston

1970

For
ESMOND and MARY

Acknowledgements

It would never have been possible to compile the facts in this book without the unstinted co-operation of a great number of people, whom I visited in many corners of the earth, and I am most grateful to them all for their help. His Holiness the Dalai Lama not only gave me his precious time, but was directly responsible for leading me to many of the main characters who held important positions in 1959, such as the remarkable Thondup of the Lhasa City Council, who masterminded the defence of the Cathedral during the revolt; General Kusangtse, then Commander-in-Chief of the Army; Phala, the Dalai Lama's Court Chamberlain, now in Geneva; Surkhang, the Prime Minister, who had to be interviewed in Seattle, Washington; Luishar, the Foreign Secretary, now retired in Trenton, New Jersey. All these and many others gave me their wholehearted help; though I should make it clear that the opinions expressed by me may not necessarily be shared by them.

Among those not in the Tibetan government, I would particularly like to thank two ladies—the Dalai Lama's mother for the many delightful hours I spent in the company of this remarkable woman, and the equally fascinating Tibetan now called Mary Taring, who runs a school for Tibetan orphans at Mussoorie in Northern India. It was Mary who helped me to discover many of the ordinary men and women who patiently endured hours of interrogation and who are too numerous to mention personally.

Among Tibetologists I should like to thank my old and trusted friend George Patterson, a Tibetan-speaking scholar, now living in Hong Kong, who gave me sage advice which was invaluable.

ACKNOWLEDGEMENTS

was faced with one serious difficulty in the preparation of this book—where to obtain Chinese corroboration of dates, a point on which the Tibetans tend to be rather casual. While I was interviewing and writing abroad, the problem was solved for me by my colleague Donald Dinsley, whose help with research in four of my books I gratefully acknowledge. When the British Foreign Office kindly opened some of its archives of monitored Chinese broadcasts, newspapers and magazines to us, Mr Dinsley spent several painstaking months in a small room under the shadow of Big Ben, analysing every single Chinese utterance relevant to the period. Quite apart from obtaining vital corroboration of many dates and events, Mr Dinsley discovered two invaluable documents which he copied and airmailed to me. One was the diary of a Chinese who was in Lhasa during the uprising; the other was a detailed account given by a Tibetan traitor, describing among other things his meetings with the Dalai Lama just prior to his escape. Only by the exercise of great diligence were these documents unearthed.

Mr Dinsley was greatly helped by the Tibetan Society of the United Kingdom, and our thanks are due to its secretary, Mrs Catherine Sawle Daly for her unstinted assistance.

Lastly I should also like to acknowledge the invaluable help of my Tibetan interpreters, Rintack and Miss Chambra in Mussoorie, Samden in Dharamsala, Miss Yangchen Surkhang in Seattle, and Sonam Rapten and Phintso Thonden in New York.

An alphabetical bibliography of books and papers consulted appears at the end of this volume, and I should like to express my gratitude to those authors and publishers who have kindly permitted me to use extracts.

I have taken one liberty with the rather complicated Tibetan names. Though Tibetans do not normally have surnames in the manner that we do, they usually possess several names or honorific titles. Some are extremely difficult to pronounce. In order to make it easier for the reader to follow the adventures of the various characters, I have (with their permission, of course) called them by their 'main' names only, a habit which I noticed was practised by the Dalai Lama in his book on Tibet. Thus the Prime Minis-

8

ACKNOWLEDGEMENTS

ter, whose full name is Wangchin Gyilek Surkhang is referred to throughout as Surkhang (not Mr Surkhang as it is not his surname); and the Tibetan traitor Ngabo Ngawang Jigme becomes the much easier Ngabo. It seemed to me the simplest thing to do.

NOEL BARBER
Dharamsala, India,
February, 1969

9

Contents

PART ONE: THE UNEASY TRUCE

1 February 13, 1959   17
2 February 14-15   32
3 February 16-24   48

PART TWO: THE INCREDIBLE REVOLT

4 March 3-16   67
5 March 17   103
6 March 18-19   122
7 March 20   133
8 March 21   154
9 March 22   173
10 Up to March 25   185

Epilogue   208
Historical Appendix   221
Bibliography   227
Index   229

Maps

The Plain of Lhasa
front endpaper

Tibet and Surrounding Countries
page 18

The Dalai Lama's Escape Route to India
page 29

The Battle for the Cathedral
back endpaper

List of Principal Characters

The Tibetan 'Court'

HIS HOLINESS THE DALAI LAMA
PHALA, his Court Chamberlain
SURKHANG, the Prime Minister
LUISHAR, the Foreign Minister
THONDUP, member of the Lhasa City Council
GENERAL KUSANGTSE, Commander-in-Chief, Tibetan Army
KUSUNG, Commander of the Dalai Lama's personal guard and married to the Dalai Lama's sister

The Ordinary People

GYALYUM CHEMO, the Dalai Lama's mother
CHIME YOUNGDONG, an Incarnate Lama
JIGME TARING, a close friend of the Dalai Lama's
MARY TARING, his wife, secretary of the Lhasa Women's Association
JAMYANGLING, a Tibetan noble
GENYEN, his ten-year-old daughter
KUNCHOK, a Khamba, in love with
TSERING DOLMA, his fiancée
GURGUR, a hunchback policeman
JAMYANG, a member of the Dalai Lama's bodyguard
LOBSANG, a government clerk

The Traitors

NGABO, a member of the Tibetan Cabinet, in the pay of the Chinese
PHAKPALA, a pro-Chinese Tibetan monk official

GYAMTSO, a Tibetan close to the Dalai Lama, also in the pay of the Chinese

The Chinese

GENERAL TAN KUAN-SAN, Commander at the time of the revolt

GENERAL CHANG HWA-TING, the pro-Tibetan Commander of the Artillery in Lhasa

BRIGADIER FU, Military adviser

SHAN CHAO, a diarist

Part One

THE UNEASY TRUCE

I

Friday, February 13, 1959

On this particular morning—a day the citizens of Lhasa would never forget—dawn broke across the city with an almost exaggerated Oriental splendour. As the first daubs of pink lit the skies behind the mountains circling the capital, the throb of drums and the low, mournful boom of ceremonial trumpets seemed to linger and tremble high in the air before swooping down to earth, to the city far below. Everyone knew from where the sounds came—the gilded roof of the white and russet Potala, the greatest building in all Tibet, towering high above the Plain of Milk on which the city stood twelve thousand feet above sea level. The heavy trumpets were between ten and twenty feet long, so the lamas in their saffron robes rested them on golden supports as they blew notes which carried far beyond the edge of the plain, fifteen miles distant.

In a way the trumpets were Lhasa's alarm clock. Within a few minutes the first wisps of smoke were trailing upwards as dutiful wives lit their fires of yak dung and brewed the morning butter tea. In air made cold with the tang of the mountains, lamas and monks shuffled through the streets to their morning devotions, shadowy forms in the uncertain light of dawn. The first carts trundled past. The pathways leading south to the broad River Kyichu—where the houses quickly gave way to countryside—were alive with small boys fetching water or with girls milking yaks or goats.

It was perhaps at dawn more than any other moment of the day that Lhasa displayed to perfection its enigmatic and remote mysticism. Certainly in the last weeks before revolt shattered the

17

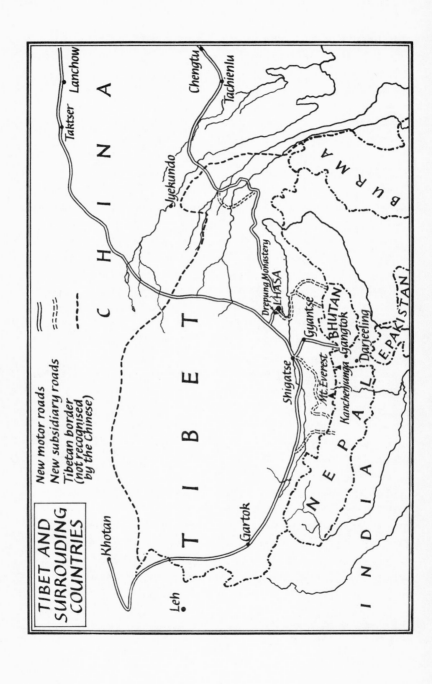

TIBET AND
SURROUDING
COUNTRIES

New motor roads
New subsidiary roads
Tibetan border
(not recognised
by the Chinese)

C H I N A

Lanchow
Taktser
Chengtu
Tachienlu

Jyekundo

T I B E T

Khotan

Leh

Gartok

Shigatse

Drepung Monastery
LHASA
Gyantse

BHUTAN
Gangtok
Darjeeling

Mt. Everest
Kanchenjunga

N E P A L

I N D I A

E. PAKISTAN

B U R M A

city in three days of slaughter, there was no capital in the world like it. Locked in by the endless contours of mountains carved throughout the ages, aloof and apart from the world, it was a city of yesterday uninterested in tomorrow. Wrapped in an aura of mysticism, of devotions, of tinkling bells and fluttering prayer flags, its religious life spilled out into every street—pilgrims spinning their prayer wheels, the chanting monks, the panoply and colour of each new procession with its clashing cymbals and gigantic drums shaking the air, with the Tibetan army band invariably playing 'God Save the Queen' (which a Tibetan bandmaster trained in India in the distant past had liked, learned and passed on). No wonder the weavers of romantic novels had found it irresistible as a setting for fiction, and had added their own mystique, so that to the Western world Lhasa was not only remote and unattainable, but had somehow achieved a peace and serenity denied to ordinary mortals in the frenetic world outside.

Much of this was true, and there was a dream-like quality about the tales which had reached the West from the few travellers who had penetrated the country—stories of devout mystics who could see to the heart of the human spirit, animals and insects treated with loving care because they might house the souls of humans; lamas who lived in solitary meditation for years, praying simply for their fellow-men; of a country with no concept of time as the Western world knew it. And as if this were not enough, the very isolation of Tibet doubled its mystery to those who read about it, with perhaps an uneasy feeling that here, in this timeless tranquillity, lay the secret of life as it was meant to be lived.

Yet Lhasa was a city of bewildering contrasts. As the streaks of dawn gave way to the clear, sharp mountain air, the first of the pious pilgrims were making their ritual tour of the Ling-kor, the five-mile sacred walk round the city; another caravan was preparing to set off across incredibly hostile country to China. Already the fretting ponies, the stoic yaks, the placid mules were being loaded with yakskins of frozen butter, saddlebags of barley, bricks of tea, haunches of dried yak meat. And yet now and again this almost Biblical scene—one enacted without change for thirteen centuries

19

—was snapped by a sinister note as a Chinese staff car, embellished with Communist signs, hooted imperiously in the narrow streets, a sign the people of Lhasa could never forget—that for eight years their capital had been the headquarters of Mao Tse-tung's army of occupation.

With the presence of China, 'civilization' had reached the city. Endless processions of praying monks might still fill the streets, bricks of tea might still be popular (both to drink or as a convenient form of currency), but in Shagyari Street the city's first traffic policeman had been installed on a dais, and one could buy anything from a Chinese torch or a Japanese kimono to an Indian doll or a Bing Crosby record barely two years old. The dark glow of candles or hissing pressure-lamps might still be the only light in most houses, but some streets already glared with electricity. And though the monk doctors still distilled their potions (while jealously guarding their dwindling power), anyone could get a jab of penicillin at the Chinese Hospital, and nobody any longer gave a second glance at the old plaque let into a wall by the Cathedral with its warning against smallpox, which as late as 1925 had killed seven thousand in Lhasa.

Already the streets were crowded. In one, every basement shop sold nothing but bales of untearable Tibetan cloth, silk from China, cotton from India; round the corner all the shops were owned by Nepalese selling necklaces of semi-precious stones, charm boxes in gold filigree or the turquoise earrings so popular with men. In the broader Shagyari Street, there was the nearest thing to a general store, with its assortment of torches, sunglasses, mirrors, toothpaste, soap, sugar (in yellow and white balls), boiled sweets from India, a few tins of American corned beef (pre-1950 vintage), sewing-machines, and even the occasional dusty jar of beauty cream. Shagyari Street had another attraction— the Chai Tsonkang, an up-to-date café which served 'English' tea (as distinct from butter tea). One long plastic-topped table stretched the length of the single room, and the tea was served already poured into cups, with yak milk and sugar added whether one liked it or not. To scores of Tibetans the Chai Tsonkang represented the ultimate in the sophistication with which the Tibetans had inevitably come in contact since the Chinese invasion.

The higgledy-piggledy shops, the garish colours, the women shopkeepers in their brightly coloured aprons—all in the pure, almost dazzling air of a mountain city—lent a beauty to Lhasa which made one forget the hovels and the dirt, and remember only the Oriental splendour, which was if anything stronger when one turned out of Shagyari Street into the fruit and vegetable market, with its mounds of tart-tasting russet apples mingling their perfume with that of peaches and grapes from the south, next to barley, peas, cabbages, radishes three feet long, all spilling on to the ground near trays of walnuts, chillies, curry powder, cloves and nutmegs.

This year the winter had been mild, and by the spring every balcony on the white-painted, flat-roofed houses was edged with the first pots of spring flowers. In the heart of the city the pointed, gilded roofs and shining cupolas of the Chokhang, or Cathedral— the holiest place in Tibet—dominated the smaller houses that hemmed it in, and looked down on the cobbled square in front which always seemed to be jammed with lamas or monks, pre-occupied on their mysterious errands, pilgrims prostrate on the dirty ground, scrofulous scavenging dogs, beggars by the score, piles of rubbish ; for the square was part of a warren of unpaved streets circling the Cathedral, and bearing the collective name of Park-hor, or 'Inner Ring', a sacred circle (with a few bumps in it) around which the pilgrims felt obliged to walk in clockwise fashion if they were not robust enough to take the longer Ling-kor around the city.

The ominous date was February 13, 1959; the day was the second of the Tibetans' three-day celebration of their New Year, a day of destiny in the fortunes of Tibet, though the people of Lhasa could not yet realize its significance. For it was on this New Year's morning that a remarkable man was reaching journey's end —a journey which had taken him across half Tibet, had exacted a fearful toll of life, a journey with only one end in view: to see the Dalai Lama, the spiritual and temporal leader of the country,

21

and beg his help in fighting the Chinese atrocities in eastern Tibet.

By noon, under a hot sun, the ragged caravan of five hundred monks, guerrillas, old and infirm had passed Sera Monastery to the north of the city, where the plain curved in a great arc between two mountain ranges. It was in a pitiable state, yet at its head rode a man sitting straight as a ruler on a large tan-coloured horse; a man of almost incredible beauty and taller by a head than any of the bodyguard clattering close on his heels. This was Chime Youngdong, undisputed king of two hundred thousand people in the Jyekundo area near the Chinese border in the east. He was, however, much more than that, for at the age of two he had been proved to be the ninth incarnation of Chime Youngdong of Benchen Monastery,* on the outskirts of Jyekundo. Granted the title of Rimpoche ('Precious One'), he had assumed the name of Chime (pronounced as in chimney) Youngdong and become one of the élite of Tibet, living and studying in Benchen and wielding much the same sort of power in his local kingdom as the Dalai Lama did over all Tibet.

Aged eighteen, he was very slim, startlingly good-looking, with long slender hands and a sense of humour showing in sudden smiles revealing dazzling white teeth. He bore few traces of his arduous training, which had included a period of three years in solitary meditation. Nor did his face betray his anguish at the way in which the Chinese, barely two months previously, had abducted his father, who had never been seen since. This, and the increasing Chinese atrocities, had made him decide to seek the Dalai Lama's help. It was a decision which, because of the distance, passed quite unnoticed in Lhasa at the time, but, because every man who followed Chime was a guerrilla spoiling for a fight, it was to break the uneasy truce of eight years and change the fortunes of Tibet in the weeks that lay ahead. Chime had barely got away, for the evening before he planned to flee Chinese troops had fired on the

* Incarnate lamas are the vehicle of the spiritual power of the originators of their line, whether human or (as in the case of the Dalai Lama) divine.

monastery. He had escaped during the night, dressed as a servant, and the next morning he had taken a last look through binoculars at the monastery which had been his home for almost all his life. Quite clearly in the overlapping circles of the glasses he could see a splash of scarlet against the leaden, snow-filled sky. The Chinese flag was flying over Benchen.

That had been two months ago, but to Chime, preparing to enter Lhasa—he could already see the gilded roofs flashing in the distance—'it seemed more like two years, a different world, a different age.'

The flight of Chime Youngdong from Jyekundo had been the signal for a great exodus from the east. Chime's father and several other local kings had vanished—languishing in dungeons or possibly executed; many monasteries had been desecrated; and their God—Chime—was on the way to Lhasa. And so, with a sort of collective instinct, thousands of eastern Tibetans from the areas of Kham and Chamdo seem to have decided to march westwards and carry on the fight. Perhaps for the first time in its history, Lhasa became a goal, a focal point, not for pilgrims but for men of war. Chime estimates that nearly twenty thousand flooded from the east across the central plateau of Tibet—ironically at a time when the Dalai Lama in Lhasa was doing everything in his power to prevent resistance to the Chinese from getting out of hand.

No one but the occasional Chinese pilot in his spotter plane can ever have seen a total picture of this extraordinary flood of human beings, hundreds of different groups—sometimes a thousand or more to a group—straggling in long ink-black lines against the snow; sometimes many miles would separate two columns; sometimes they would be close together; not all had started at the same time or from the same district, so the columns, each moving at much the same pace, were scattered like giant black snakes over a white belt fifty miles wide and perhaps a hundred miles long. All moved slowly in the same direction across flat deserts, sometimes snow, sometimes grass; to each man the goal was the same—the distant rim of white-clad peaks, the treacherous tracks leading to the next pass, which would lead them to yet another plain, at the end of which they could see the next mountain barrier.

At first all went well with Chime and his party, which numbered nearly a thousand (including an escort for Chime of nearly 800 guerrilla fighters) though from time to time they were held up by natural barriers. Sometimes the plain gave way to terrifying gorges littered with the debris of the last avalanche—rocks as big as motor-cars which blocked the way, forcing the column to find another route up to the pass above.

Sometimes they slept in the open, sometimes on higher, safer ground they would see in the distance the forest of prayer flags on tall lances that heralded a solitary village with a small monastery; usually it consisted of a central lamasery with its gilded roof, and a series of buildings glued like white stamps to the mountainsides and linked by a honeycomb of narrow streets, gardens, balconies, cells and shrines. Here they would be greeted by the sonorous rhythmic throbbing of ceremonial trumpets, followed by the dream-like music of the acolytes singing their hymn of welcome, the sad, pure, haunting Tibetan music which seemed to Chime 'to tell me at the same time all about the suffering of our people and yet hold out the promise of peace to come'.

For more than a month they trudged across the central plateau without serious incident, and it was not until they were within striking distance of Lhasa that they scored a spectacular victory.

The straggling party had spent three days resting in a small village on the edge of the plain, for the strain on the older members was beginning to tell. Chime remembers the village—a compact square of dun-coloured, flat-roofed houses, 'as sharply rectangular as shoeboxes', linked by alley-like streets surrounded by a wall not only for military defence, but as a windbreak; so that the village offered a cosy snugness in marked contrast to the bitter whistling winds of the plateau. On the far side of the village lay the route ahead—a leaden-coloured river backed by tiers of eroded cliffs below the grey and white contours of the next mountain range.

After crossing the river in coracles made of yakskins, the party started to climb the last mountain barrier before the plain due north of Lhasa, where they could expect the protection of friendly guerrillas. In the mountains towering above them Chime caught glimpses of the path ahead, bend after bend etched in brighter colours in the empty sky, each horseshoe higher than the last until the track was lost in snow.

On the third day they were spotted by a Chinese aircraft. It did not bomb them, but returned several times as though to keep track of their route as they traversed a narrow, twisting ravine, a deep cut sliced into the mountains like a wedge. The climbing, turning shelf of rock was so narrow that even the hardiest climbers hugged the rock face like flies crawling slowly upwards. Several yaks plunged into the chasm thousands of feet below. Across the other side of the narrow ravine, equally high bare mountains blotted out the sky except for a narrow, grey, snow-filled band above their heads.

Without warning, two Chinese aircraft came roaring along the ravine, their wings almost scraping the sides. As machine-gun fire echoed along the gorge, scores of men, women and children 'toppled like dummies off the edge of the path'.

The guerrillas had had no time to fire before the planes were at the end of the ravine. But then the Chinese made a mistake. They came tearing back. This time every guerrilla was gripping his rifle or sub-machine-gun as the aircraft approached, flying at almost the level of the flinty track. They were not quick enough to hit the first plane, but as the men opened up with every weapon, they did hit the second one. 'I didn't know anything about engines,' Chime remembers, 'but the sound changed into a sort of cough and then someone shouted that it was on fire, and before our eyes the plane went spinning down, just like a shot bird.'

This heady victory was, however, to have a terrible consequence. The remaining plane flew off, and when Chime's party reached the pass two days later, several hundred Chinese troops were lying in wait.

The battle could have only one ending. The Tibetans were exhausted. They could not match the modern Chinese weapons with their ill-assorted collection of arms. Somehow they did manage to hold out for a day, but towards the evening Chime realized that once it was dark they would have to return to the shelter of the narrow pass up which they had first travelled, for at least they would be safe from frontal assault on the narrow ledges of rock. It was, however, a frightening journey to be undertaken at night. They had electric torches, but could use them only sparingly until they were hidden in the ravine.

The Tibetan losses had been fearful. Nearly five hundred guerrillas had been killed, and the remnants cowering in the gorge had only enough animals left to carry the food supplies. Splitting into smaller groups, they now faced a week of hiding like hunted beasts in the mountain ravines. 'We did not dare to take any of the normal tracks,' says Chime, 'because we knew the Chinese would be looking for us. We moved along the tops and sides of mountains that few Tibetans had ever seen.' It snowed almost all the time. On some narrow paths the drifts were so deep that Chime remembers trudging through snow up to his knees, the snow tugging and sucking at his boots with each step. But it was the animals which fared worst. There was virtually no fodder. Horses and mules were sometimes trapped shoulder high. They could move neither backwards nor forwards and some were frozen to death. Food was so short that as each animal died of cold or exhaustion the carcass was cut up for meat. Several animals plunged over the edge of the precipice with saddlebags containing the last remnants of tsampa, the staple food of Tibet, made of finely ground barley.

After four days almost all the food had gone. The women and children were rationed to a little tsampa and half a cup of tea a day. For the guerrillas (and Chime) the diet was even more spartan: an iron-hard ball of tsampa which each man kept in his chuba* so that when he could no longer bear the pangs of hunger he would lick the ball of barley.

* The universal male dress in Tibet; a loosely-fitting belted blouse and skirt, which incidentally makes a warm 'nightshirt' when the belt is taken off.

Finally the tattered remnants of the once-great party of a thousand—now reduced to half that number—stumbled over an unknown pass into a broad plain hemmed in by distant mountains. Chime had barely added a stone to the cairn (as all good Tibetans do) when someone cried out that Chinese were approaching. Across the white plain Chime could see a moving grey smudge.

As the guerrillas loaded and prepared to fight, Chime brought the indistinct blur into focus with his binoculars—the same binoculars with which he had seen, so long ago it seemed, the Chinese flag flying above his monastery of Benchen. One glance told him that these were not foes. At long last they had reached friendly territory, and the way to Lhasa lay open.

By midday Chime had reached the outskirts of Lhasa, and the 'welcoming committee' must have provided a remarkable sight. The Tibetans are among the most generous people on earth, and soon men, women and children with baskets of food and fruit were surrounding the slow procession—the horses hardly able to move, the guerrillas in rags, the wounded and the old carried on litters. Slowly they rode or walked through the colourful streets of Lhasa, swarming with monks and pilgrims, until they reached the Cathedral, where Chime stopped for a few moments to pray. Then the procession set off through the imposing stone Lubok Gate by the city walls—and moved into another world, one of such extravagant contrast, of such natural beauty, that it never ceased to astonish men like Chime seeing it for the first time, who could not believe that such 'arcadian luxuriance' was possible at such an altitude and in such hostile conditions.

Their road led (past Lhasa's only cinema) under the Turquoise Bridge, with its roof of Chinese tiles and its golden dragon heads at each corner, until it reached the Vale of Lhasa—the heart of the great plain fifteen miles long—which opened out like a garden, its fence the distant grey mountains. To Chime, after two months, it must have been like a dream. Willow-warblers, thrushes and

27

even occasionally the very English kingfisher darted in and out of the groves of poplars and willows, now in bud. In the lingkas, as the public parks were called, children were playing in gardens already coloured with first flowers, while (as though to heighten the illusion of a rural English countryside) occasional white butter-flies or painted ladies fluttered overhead.

It was now the season for kite-flying, and as Chime looked for a place to camp, every boy was concentrating on the sport, trying to cut down other kites with his line of twine treated with glue and powdered glass. Little girls played a strange and skilful game in which they kicked a homemade shuttlecock, sometimes keeping it in the air for ten minutes at a time. Much of the Vale was carpeted with tents of all kinds, for picnicking was Lhasa's most irresistible New Year pastime. Huge tents, their coarse cloth covered with gay stitched-on decorations, had been erected near the dunes of the river—tents littered with sheepskins, brightly woven rugs, carpets, cushions, wooden altars and pots of flowers. 'At first I could not believe my eyes,' Chime confessed, 'it was all so beautiful.'

And there was something else. Chime's journey had been made for one reason only—a burning passion to help his subjects, to seek the aid of the Dalai Lama. And now, looming high above Chime's tent, dominating the Vale, dwarfing the surrounding houses, was the greatest, the most dramatic building in Tibet, perhaps in all the world: the Potala. And inside, just below the golden roofs, was the Dalai Lama in one of its thousand rooms.

Chime remembers standing there for several minutes in silence, overawed by the massive bulk of this white and russet building—nine hundred feet long, four hundred and forty feet high—and all it stood for. For this was the seat of power, spiritual and temporal, and it was here that the Dalai Lama and his cabinet had for eight years been trying to find a way of living with the Chinese who were now their masters.

Chime could be excused for being overawed by a vastness so overpowering that even the Dalai Lama, after living in it for years, confessed that he 'could never know all its secrets'. No traveller

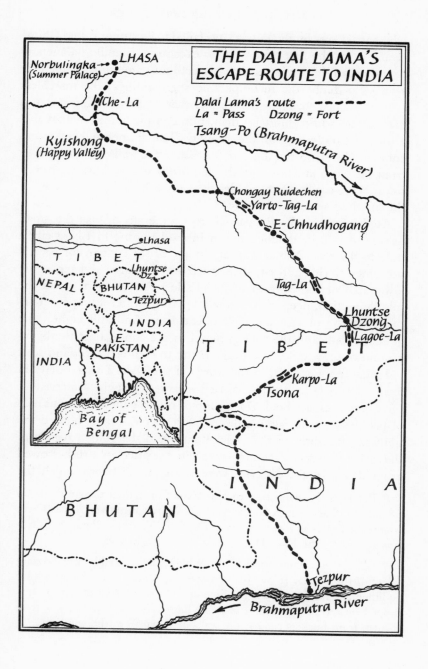

THE DALAI LAMA'S
ESCAPE ROUTE TO INDIA

Norbulingka
(Summer Palace)
LHASA

Che-La

Dalai Lama's route
La = Pass   Dzong = Fort

Kyishong
(Happy Valley)

Tsang-Po (Brahmaputra River)

Chongay Ruidechen
Yarto-Tag-La

E-Chhudhogang

Tag-La

Lhuntse
Dzong
Lagoe-La

T I B E T

Karpo-La
Tsona

I N D I A

BHUTAN

Tezpur

Brahmaputra River

TIBET

Lhasa

Lhuntse
Dz.

NEPAL   BHUTAN

Tezpur

INDIA

E.
PAKISTAN

INDIA

Bay of
Bengal

who has set eyes on the Potala* has failed to be stunned, and Chime seeing it for the first time, was no exception. Standing alone and proud on a hill, it was 'as near perfection as anything I have ever seen'. No doubt the incomparable surroundings, the matchless setting, helped to make Chime feel that he was looking not at a great stone edifice built by man, but at a phenomenon that had grown naturally out of the ground. The immense height was enhanced by an optical illusion, for each of the walls sloped inwards from its base, and each of the hundreds of windows narrowed towards the top, so that the higher one raised one's eyes, the more the building seemed to recede.

At the foot of the Potala, where Chime stood, was the small hamlet of Sho lying along the main road leading to Lhasa city a mile to the east. Above Sho, 250 steps, broad enough for several horsemen to ride abreast, sliced their way upwards and across the lower half of the colossal white façade.† Above them stood the middle section, deep russet in colour, from which hung an enormous curtain of yak hair eighty feet deep. And still higher, the golden cupolas on the roof glittered in the sun against the background of grey and white peaks rising to eighteen thousand feet.

Inside there existed, in the words of the Dalai Lama, 'a city in itself'. There were thirty-five richly carved chapels; a monastery for 175 monks; a school. One group of rooms contained thousands of priceless scrolls, some a thousand years old; others housed the immense treasures of the Dalai Lamas and the golden regalia of the earliest kings of Tibet, together with the priceless gifts bestowed upon them. In the libraries were some of the books which the

* Potala is the name of a rock at Cape Comorin at the southern tip of India. Indians believe that the God of Mercy once lived there. There is another Potala in eastern China. The building of the Potala in Lhasa was started by the Fifth Dalai Lama, who died in 1680.

† All travellers appear to have been highly impressed by the dazzling white of the Potala. It was painted every September, though in rather rudimentary fashion. A bag of lime at the end of a yakskin rope was dipped into a well, turning the water into whitewash, which was then thrown from buckets against the walls or down from the windows.

Dalai Lama studied from time to time—seven thousand enormous volumes, some weighing eighty pounds and written on palm leaves brought over the mountain passes from India centuries before. Near-by rooms housed two thousand illuminated volumes of the Scriptures. No books in all the world could ever match their beauty, for each line was written in a different coloured ink, which the monks had made of powdered gold, silver, copper, turquoise and coral.

This was the self-contained world which dominated not only the green countryside, not only Lhasa, but all Tibet: nineteen storeys of dark passages and steep ladder-like stairs leading to rooms housing priests, politicians, books, treasure, stocks of food, caches of arms, while far, far below, in dungeons hewn out of the rock, prisoners whose lives could not be taken for religious reasons mouldered in black captivity until they had slowly rotted away.

Chime, however, strained his eyes upwards, for he was looking at only one set of windows—the four simple rooms that comprised the private apartments of the Dalai Lama on the top storey, four hundred feet above the Vale, and Chime, almost in a trance, remembers that 'I stood looking at those windows until they started moving before my eyes.' Then he went inside his tent. He wanted to think clearly, to catalogue the incidents and Chinese atrocities, to make notes of the grave news he had brought—news from a land so distant that it had taken two months to reach Lhasa, and which would come as a terrible shock to the Dalai Lama.

2

Saturday, February 14-Sunday, February 15

The Dalai Lama's favourite room in the Potala was about twenty-five feet square, its walls covered with historical paintings so detailed that no individual portraits were more than an inch high. Facing south (like all important buildings in Tibet), it overlooked the carpet of the Vale with the city of Lhasa a collection of dolls' houses a mile to the east.

Here one of the world's most extraordinary men lived, prayed, studied and ruled. Tall and slim, he was now twenty-three, with closely-cropped black hair (shaved for certain religious ceremonies) and wearing glasses as a result of years of study in the ill-lit rooms of the Potala. He was a man not only of great piety, but of remarkable learning and a certain peasant shrewdness inherited from his farmer parents. (Perhaps unfortunately he had also learned the art of tolerance to such a degree that he found nothing amiss in remaining on friendly terms with those plotting against him.) Nearly twenty years of intensive study had fashioned him into a leader with interests far more wide-ranging than those of his predecessors. He had an insatiable thirst for knowledge of all kinds. Quite apart from his formal education, he had taught himself to speak tolerable English. He had mastered astrology, and something of the art of medicine. By the age of thirteen he had learned by heart the 302 pages of a learned treatise on the Perfection of Wisdom, for his spiritual education was of the highest importance. Yet in marked contrast, he was equally fascinated by mechanical things, and 'though there was nobody who could tell me anything about them', he had unlocked the secrets of electricity, while in order to study the principles of watch-making he would take his watch to pieces and put it together again.

By February 1959 the Dalai Lama—despite eight years of Chinese occupation and the problems of Communist domination—was preparing for the hardest examination of his life, the final test for his doctorate of metaphysics, which he was due to take early in March. It was an entirely oral examination in which he would debate with Tibet's most learned scholars before an audience of several thousand. In the morning thirty monks would interrogate him in turn on congregational discussion. In the afternoon another fifteen would oppose him in a debate on 'The Perfection of Wisdom'. And finally in the evening, when the normal student would be exhausted, the Dalai Lama would face thirty-five scholars testing his knowledge of monastic discipline and the study of metaphysics.

There was only one way to prepare for what the Dalai Lama thought of as 'battles of intellect' and that was to practise debating with his tutors. Now, as on every day, he spent several hours in his favourite room being peppered with questions which demanded rapid-fire answers. When he was asked, 'Which is the more important—the mind, the body or speech?' the Dalai Lama had to reply instantly, 'Mind. Body and speech are servants of the mind.' A tutor would dart out, 'But does your mind exist or not?' 'One cannot say,' was the Dalai Lama's reply, 'because it has no shape or colour.'

In any ordinary mortal this profound dedication to learning would have been staggering, but the Dalai Lama was no ordinary mortal. He was unique in the world, both a God and a King, and his extraordinary intellect becomes even more incomprehensible when one considers the astonishing manner in which he had been 'found' as a baby of two, after answering a series of tests; for each Dalai Lama represents the return to earth of Chenrezi, a Living Buddha, the patron God of Tibet, and this young man studying so earnestly was the fourteenth incarnation.

When a Dalai Lama dies—or, as the Tibetans say, when he departs to the Honourable Field—it is believed that his spirit

33

enters the body of an infant who becomes the next Dalai Lama. This infant must be discovered; the search for him is undertaken as a solemn religious act, for the doctrine of incarnation is so deeply ingrained in Tibet that no man entertains even the slightest doubts.

Naturally the Dalai Lama cannot remember the manner in which he was chosen, but one highly-placed Tibetan who took part in the search is still alive. He is General Kusangtse, Commander-in-Chief of the Army until March 1959,* when he escaped from the Chinese. Kusangtse remembers that after the thirteenth Dalai Lama had died in 1933, his body sat in state in the Potala, looking towards the south. 'One morning,' says Kusangtse, 'the head had turned towards the east.' How or why, nobody has explained. Since signs and portents were needed before the search for a new Dalai Lama could begin, the State Oracle was immediately consulted. During a trance he threw a traditional white scarf in the direction of the rising sun. Time means so little in Tibet that, as Kusangtse puts it laconically, 'for two years nothing really happened.' Then the Regent visited the sacred lake of Lhamoi Latso, ninety miles south-east of Lhasa. Looking into the mirror of water, he saw a three-storeyed monastery with golden roofs close to a humble Chinese peasant house with carved, turquoise-coloured gables. This was enough to start an intensive search by several groups. Each group journeyed to the east taking weeks to make the trip;† each carried objects which had belonged to the dead Dalai Lama.

Kusangtse's party, led by a high-ranking lama, reached the village of Taktser near the Tibet-Chinese frontier. There, after many abortive searches, they found the three-storeyed monastery with the golden roofs. Near-by was a small farm with turquoise gables. Kusangtse and the monks changed clothes with their

* General Kusangtse now lives in northern India and kindly gave the author a great deal of assistance.

† The Tibetans have no sense of distance, but usually measure it by the number of days' ride. Significantly, the Tibetan word for distance is *Tha-ring-thung*, meaning literally 'way-long-short.'

servants. If there was a child, they argued, it would probably be playing in the kitchen. And high-ranking monks attracted too much attention anyway. So the servants drank ceremonial tea in the best parlour, while the monks, together with Kusangtse, made for the kitchen. Almost as they entered, a two-year-old boy toddled towards them and seized the skirts of the disguised lama who was wearing the rosary of the previous Dalai Lama. He tugged at it. The lama said he could have it if he could guess who he was. The boy instantly replied 'Sera Lama!' The lama did in fact come from Sera Monastery near Lhasa.

A few days later the search party returned. This time they were not disguised. They explained to the boy's father and mother that their son might be an incarnation, though they did not suggest that he might be the next Dalai Lama. The boy was awakened, and taken by four monks to an altar-room. Here, out of large selections, he without hesitation picked out a rosary, a drum, a walking stick, all of which had belonged to the Dalai Lama. In addition the boy bore certain marks for which the monks were looking—large outstanding ears, and moles on his trunk.*

Though Taktser was a Tibetan village (and these events took place, of course, before the Chinese invasion), the south-eastern part of Tibet was under some sort of loose Chinese jurisdiction at the time, so the Chinese governor had to be consulted. Sensing the possibility of ransom, the governor summoned the boy of two together with several others and submitted them to a simple test: he offered them a box of sweets. Those who were frightened refused to take any. Those who were greedy grabbed a handful; 'but I—I am told—took one and ate it discreetly.' Convinced, the Chinese governor demanded a ransom of a hundred thousand

* This is the briefest of accounts. As Miss Lois Lang-Sims rightly says in her paper on 'The Function and Status of the Dalai Lama': 'The outward methods adopted are fairly generally known . . . what is not so generally recognized is that these outward methods are but the exterior forms of a process based upon the deep intuitions, meditations and prayers of the highest lamas in Tibet. This, rather than the actual tests employed, is the true safeguard against a mistaken choice.'

Chinese dollars which the Tibetans were forced to pay before the boy could be permitted to leave for Lhasa.

By the late summer of 1939—six years after the death of the thirteenth Dalai Lama—the boy was on his way to Lhasa, and as Kusangtse remembers, 'From the moment he arrived there, he was distributing blessings as if he had done this all his life.' He was four years old.

The morning session of mock debate on metaphysics was abruptly terminated as a court official warned the Dalai Lama that a delegation of Chinese generals would shortly be arriving. From long experience, the Dalai Lama knew that it was bound to be an unpleasant meeting, in which he would be faced with a battery of bitter Chinese protests. For eight years, since the date the Chinese had invaded his country, the Dalai Lama had been striving, as a man dedicated to a policy of non-violence, to reach some compromise with the Chinese who were now the masters of Tibet. 'I tried my best to discourage violence, even at the risk of displeasing some of my own people.' But all attempts had failed, and now the Dalai Lama knew that as 'the oppression of the invaders throughout the country became intolerable,' the patience of his people was reaching breaking-point.

Everything had started on the morning of October 7, 1950 when Tibetans in the Kham and Chamdo areas in the east had awakened to find Chinese troops pouring across the ill-defined border. The first local reaction had been one of bewilderment rather than fear, for to these people the frontier had little more significance than a line drawn on a map. Many Tibetans had Chinese blood in their veins. Many had never stirred beyond the next rim of mountains— the edge of their world. To these peasants growing barley and peas, distant Lhasa had all the romantic (and unattainable) connotations of a dreamlike city inhabited only by the privileged. The local kings—such as Chime's father—were all-powerful, and though they respected the spiritual leadership of the Dalai Lama, some were not entirely displeased when the Chinese arrived with promises that they would not interfere with their religion, but would at the same time bolster their independence from the central government in Lhasa. And so, when the Chinese invasion was launched, many Tibetans tacitly welcomed the troops and in some parts there was little or no fighting.

Not in all areas, however; for eastern Tibet was not only the home of thousands of devout monks in the monasteries or peasants tilling the fields. It was also (in marked contrast to the generally accepted picture of all Tibetans as gentle peace-loving people) an area inhabited by bands of warlike brigands; superb horsemen, utterly fearless when attacking with their big flat swords or the Mannlicher rifles they had smuggled in from India. Not for the Khambas—as they were called—the doctrine of non-violence. To them the Chinese presented new opportunities for loot, for the acquisition of arms—and for the actual pleasure of fighting. These were the men who were to become the legendary heroes of Tibetan resistance.

The reactions in Kham and Chamdo were, however, purely local, with fighting in some areas and a tolerant acceptance in others. None—or so it seems—realized that these first Chinese attacks were to change the future of Tibet. In Lhasa, however, the reaction had been totally different. The Potala at this time had a radio link with the east, and when the news was flashed across the central plateau, the Tibetan Regent (who would normally rule Tibet until the Dalai Lama reached the age of eighteen) realized instantly that this latest invasion bore no resemblance to any past Chinese frontier incidents. The threat was not only more powerful, it was of a totally different nature. In the past there had always been some religious sympathy between the two countries, but now Tibet was threatened with more than military domination; it was being attacked by an alien materialistic creed abhorrent to every Tibetan belief.

The Cabinet—or Kashag as it was called—immediately despatched telegrams to Britain, the US, and India begging for armed help to repel the invaders, and announcing the imminent departure of Tibetan delegations to the three governments. In Lhasa, political leaders prepared to set off on horseback across the mountain passes to India, from where they would fly to Delhi, Washington and London.

Then came the replies to the cables. To the dismay of the Tibetans, Britain and the US bluntly said that there was nothing they could do. Worse—both politely declined to receive the delegations. The Indian government made it clear it would give no military aid, and advised Lhasa not to offer any armed resistance.

The Dalai Lama was at this time a boy of sixteen, without any temporal power. But now, as the leaders of Tibet realized the country stood alone—and as the pitifully small detachments of the Tibetan army in the east were beaten back—the Cabinet came to the Dalai Lama in the Potala with a solemn request: that he should take over the responsibility of the government from the Regent.

The Dalai Lama was filled with alarm. He knew nothing, he protested, about the world, and had no experience of politics. He insisted that he was too young—though, despite his modesty, he had enough political awareness to realize that, as so often happens under Regencies, 'Most people were anxious to avoid responsibility, rather than accept it.' It was an awareness that was to be demonstrated time and again in the years of crisis, and it was enough to make him agree, though with trepidation. So, at an age when most boys were still at school, 'I had to put boyhood behind me, and immediately prepare myself to lead my country against the vast power of Communist China.'

Though the Dalai Lama may have thought of himself as politically immature, his first action demonstrated forcibly a grasp of statesmanship unusual in a boy of sixteen. The West had let Tibet down. There was only one course to take. Without delay, the Dalai Lama appealed on November 7 to the United Nations to debate the Tibetan question before the General Assembly. The United Nations took a month before replying, and during the period of waiting grave news reached the capital: the Chinese armies were planning to advance into central Tibet, and might even fall on Lhasa.

The immediate reaction among the Tibetan cabinet ministers
would have been unpalatable to any healthy boy of sixteen; they
demanded that the Dalai Lama should leave Lhasa immediately
and set up a temporary government at Yatung, conveniently near
the Indian frontier. With all the fire of youth, the Dalai Lama told
the cabinet that 'I did not want to go— as a young and able-bodied
man, my instinct was to share whatever risks my people were
undergoing.'

It was a personal conflict that was to be dramatically repeated
years later—but in the end the Dalai Lama, knowing that 'to
Tibetans the person of the Dalai Lama is supremely precious',
had to agree to go. And once again he revealed traces of shrewdness
which more than offset any unworldliness, for—possibly with an
eye to future disaster—he took one precaution. Across the mountain trails leading to the Sikkim frontier, just south of Yatung,
his yaks were loaded with an assortment of boxes and cases. Each
one contained gold dust or bars or silver from the Dalai Lama's
personal treasure. Quietly he arranged for it to be placed in a
vault safely across the frontier. There it lay for nine years.

Now shock upon shock followed. First, the United Nations
curtly decided to 'postpone' indefinitely any discussion of the
Tibetan appeal. They did not even reply to Tibet's request for a
Commission of Enquiry. A little polite sympathy was drummed up,
but that was all. Britain, which had implied her recognition of
Tibet's independence by concluding treaties with her as a sovereign
power, smoothly said that the legal position of Tibet was not very
clear. To the Dalai Lama's dismay, the attitude of the Indian
representative was equally equivocal. Despite the close religious
and geographical ties, he insisted that a peaceful settlement was
possible, but (with a logic difficult to understand) felt that peace
would be easier to come by if the United Nations abandoned the
idea of discussing the Tibetan question in the General Assembly.
No wonder the Dalai Lama felt that 'Now we had to learn the
bitter lesson that the world has grown too small for any people to
live in harmless isolation.'

There was only one hope—or so the Dalai Lama thought. He

would send a negotiating team to Peking 'on the firm condition that the Chinese armies would not advance any further into Tibet'. The result was disastrous. The mission was headed by a high-ranking monk official called Ngabo, later to become a Tibetan traitor of the first magnitude.* His actions in Peking certainly seemed in character with those of a man prepared to sell his country. The Dalai Lama had sent him trustingly to try and find a formula to limit any Chinese dreams of expansion. Without informing the Dalai Lama, Ngabo, on May 23, 1951, signed the now notorious Seventeen Point Agreement in Peking. Since no agreement could be valid unless the great Seal of Tibet was affixed, a duplicate was conveniently forged in the Chinese capital.

The unsuspecting Dalai Lama knew nothing of what was happening until a message reached the monastery at Yatung warning him to turn on his radio and listen to an important announcement. In the small spartan cell which he had chosen, he turned on a cheap battery set. To his horror, he heard the voice of Ngabo. Still in Peking, Ngabo had gone to the microphone himself, and the Dalai Lama would never forget 'the terrible shock' as he first heard the terms of the agreement. 'We were appalled at the mixture of Communist cliché, vainglorious assertions which were completely false,' he remembers. 'The terms were far worse and more oppressive than anything we had imagined.' Above all, the Chinese made it clear that 'the Tibetan people shall return to the big family of the Motherland—the People's Republic of China.'

Now the Dalai Lama insisted on returning to Lhasa—and it

* Despite a role which, as the reader will see later, leaves no room for equivocation, it is only fair to say that several leading Tibetans are still not certain that he was a traitor, but wonder if Ngabo (now openly working with the Chinese) was not merely acting realistically. One does not wish to be biased, but the Tibetans, by the very nature of their isolated, religious existence, tend to be extremely naïve, as will be seen, and to the author there is no doubt that Ngabo was, and still is, violently pro-Chinese.

was not long before the Chinese came out in their true colours. By July 1952, General Chang Chin-wu was installed in the capital as 'Chinese representative'—and was quickly complaining that he had not been greeted with sufficient deference. Within two months three thousand Chinese troops marched into the capital. They were followed shortly afterwards by another eight thousand, while others occupied key points throughout the country. They requisitioned houses, land, built camps, raided the Tibetan granaries for food until the Dalai Lama found that 'for the first time in memory the people of Lhasa were reduced to the edge of famine.'

Before long, the Chinese were contravening their own Seventeen Point Agreement which had guaranteed the maintenance of the existing political system and the status and power of the Dalai Lama. They demanded the dismissal of two leading Tibetan politicians; they created a 'Preparatory Committee for the Tibet Autonomous Region', in which Chinese influence predominated. While the Dalai Lama tried to compromise, the Chinese carved Tibet into three regions, thus reducing his prestige. They announced publicly that if the Dalai Lama did not follow their advice he would be removed. But as the Chinese stranglehold on the country inexorably tightened, they reserved their real spleen for the monasteries. They attacked monastic institutions, they sent thousands of lamas to forced labour camps. Others were degraded publicly. Many were executed. Raids on the monasteries became commonplace—with the excuse that the monks were hiding caches of arms.*

Before long the Chinese-controlled newspaper, the *Karzey Nyinrey Sargypur*, published in eastern Tibet, was screaming that 'We must destroy completely the forces of these monasteries.

* This was often true, and if it seems incongruous for peaceful lamas to be hiding arsenals, there is a simple explanation. The monasteries were also frequently granaries storing food (which would keep in the refrigerated atmosphere for up to thirty years)—and arms caches had originally been sent there in case it became necessary to guard the food reserves. The habit had grown.

If we scatter this great mountain of self-appointed potentates who tread on ordinary folk, we shall be able to establish the final happiness of ordinary Tibetan people under Communist guidance.'

On the military side, the Chinese were manœuvring into a position of great strength in central Asia,* busily constructing airfields, strategic strongpoints, all leading to the frontiers of Tibet's southern neighbours—all leading, in effect, to India, perhaps remembering a phrase which the percipient Lenin used to enjoy rolling round his tongue, 'The way from Moscow to Paris lies through Delhi.'

Throughout all these years, the Dalai Lama struggled to preserve what he could of Tibet's great heritage. Quite apart from his dedicated policy of non-violence, he knew that his country had no chance of staging a determined uprising. And he knew, too, that whatever else happened, Lhasa must not be the scene of bloodshed. He not only had to consider what would be the fate of Lhasa itself, what would happen in the crowded streets and the tumbledown poorer quarters of ramshackle buildings if the machine-guns opened fire. Lhasa was the centre of all Tibetan affairs, religious, political and economic, and, in a country with no railways and few roads, there was no other city to replace it; so that the fall of Lhasa would in effect mean the fall of the country.

And yet nothing the Dalai Lama could do could stop the insatiable Chinese colonists. By late 1956 the Chinese were even sterilizing males in some areas, and forcing Tibetan women to bear children fathered by Chinese. Any opposition to Communist orders was punished with the utmost brutality and almost always in public. The inhabitants of a remote village called Patung Ahnga were assembled and forced to watch twenty-five wealthy people being publicly burned to death. In another village called Jeuba men and women had to watch twenty-four parents being killed by

* The Chinese army's greatest construction feat was to build the highest road in the world—1413 miles from Chengtu in China's Szechuan province to Lhasa. It crossed twelve rivers and fourteen mountain ranges at an average altitude of thirteen thousand feet.

having nails driven into their eyes—because they had refused to send their children to Chinese schools.*

Inevitably the warlike Khambas sought revenge for these and other atrocities. By 1957, they were in open revolt in the East, and many thousands had fled to southern Tibet with their swords and their guns. Relentlessly they attacked lonely Chinese outposts and barracks, slaughtering every man they could find. Roads and convoys were disrupted. And this in turn brought still more ferocious Chinese reprisals, such as the abduction of Chime's father at the end of the year—an event which had been a signal for tens of thousands of Khambas to stream across the central plateau and march on Lhasa, doubling its population. And every one of them was spoiling for a fight.

The three Chinese generals reached the foot of the Potala and prepared with some distaste for the gruelling ascent to the Dalai Lama's apartments on the nineteenth floor.† They heartily disliked audiences in the Potala, with its interminable flights of worn stone steps and narrow corridors in a building so vast that Phala, the court chamberlain (who lived there when the Dalai Lama was in residence) needed fifteen minutes to walk from his quarters to the Dalai Lama's private apartments.

Leading the 'delegation' was General Tan Kuan-san, a hard-core doctrinaire Communist of sixty, who had been a private in the Chinese army during the Long March of 1935, and who had just assumed complete command in Tibet, after being second in command to a general who had been recalled. His most marked characteristics were a pair of stooped shoulders, yellow teeth,

* From statements by witnesses called before the International Commission of Jurists.

† In typical Tibetan fashion, which takes little account of time, no Tibetan officials are certain of the precise date of this meeting, and Chinese sources which have corroborated many dates in this volume do not mention it. It was certainly in the first half of February, shortly after Chime's arrival in the city.

extremely thin hands, and a habit of reeking with perfume. He was utterly ruthless and the picture we have of Tan is that of the dedicated party member who is also the complete boss—storming, ranting, raving, a hard, tough, professional soldier, his authority buttressed by his spies everywhere. But if the Dalai Lama had the 'failing' of tolerance, Tan had one which was even more deadly. He was a heavy drinker, and under the influence of whisky he could (and did) issue orders which he would never have done had he been sober.

No two leaders could have been more different than the Dalai Lama and General Tan, yet if reduced to its essence the destiny of Tibet in the coming weeks—the lives of ordinary men, women and children caught up in events beyond their control—resolved itself in a highly personal duel of wits and differing ideologies between these two men.

Puffing slightly, the three Chinese generals reached the door of the long narrow conference room. Phala ushered them in and offered them tea. Two sat down on the low chairs facing the Dalai Lama's throne at the end—a low Tibetan sofa of gilded, carved wood covered with rugs and flanked by a small altar on the Dalai Lama's left. General Tan, however, did not sit down at first. He walked up and down the room which was nearly forty feet long. He drew aside the muslin curtains covering the windows and peered out at the magnificent view of the River Kyichu in a great curve beyond the Vale. Not until the Dalai Lama arrived did he sit down.

The Dalai Lama took his place on his throne facing the Chinese. He knew that more and more Khamba attacks were being launched against the Chinese, but he knew also that like all invaders the Chinese 'had totally lost sight of the sole cause of the revolt against them: that our people did not want them in our country, and were ready to give their lives to be rid of them.' He knew of the presence in Lhasa of Chime and the Khambas—in fact, he had already agreed to receive Chime. But spiritually he was aghast at what was happening, for he knew that the thousands of Khambas who had followed Chime to Lhasa could spell nothing but trouble.

44

Not only was he dedicated to a policy of non-violence (however ironic it may seem in view of the aggressive nature of some of his subjects), but all his religious teaching told him that violence could not be suppressed by equally brutal violence, though his dilemma was made even more acute since 'part of me greatly admired the guerrilla fighters.' They were, as he admitted, brave people putting their lives at stake to save their country and their religion, and the Dalai Lama was human enough to realize that 'when one heard of the terrible deeds of the Chinese . . . it was a natural human reaction to seek revenge.' And yet, 'however great the violence used against us, it could never become right to use violence in reply.'

To his surprise, however, General Tan appeared less testy than usual. After enumerating several complaints, the Chinese general announced, somewhat to the Dalai Lama's astonishment, that he had been in touch with Peking, where the Chinese leaders were convinced that the Tibetan government was in league with the Khambas. To this allegation the Dalai Lama was able to reply that he had sent a five-man mission to the largest guerrilla head-quarters south of Lhasa to tell the Khambas not to provoke reprisals. (What the Dalai Lama did not mention was that the mission of two lay officials and three monks had never returned. Its five members had joined the guerrillas, and even the Dalai Lama admitted to himself that 'it was difficult to blame them.')

Unaware of this, General Tan seemed mollified, giving the Dalai Lama the opportunity to complain that the Chinese were exacerbating the situation by arming their civilians and reinforcing their barricades in Lhasa. General Tan promised that these were only for the protection of Chinese nationals.

Then the General came to the crux of his visit. The Chinese government was so deeply alarmed that it felt a high-level confer-ence in Peking was necessary. He therefore extended on behalf of Comrade Mao Tse-tung a formal invitation to the Dalai Lama to visit the Chinese capital. Very shortly the Chinese National Assembly would be holding its spring meeting, and this, it had been suggested, would be an opportune moment for the Dalai Lama to honour China with an official visit.

The Dalai Lama was appalled. He realized immediately that it was not General Tan who had been in contact with Peking, but Peking which had given instructions to General Tan. A visit to the Chinese capital was, however, unthinkable. 'Knowing the mood of the people', the Dalai Lama realized immediately that he must try to avoid the invitation. Tactfully he replied that he would be honoured to visit Peking, but begged to be excused from making a firm arrangement until he had discussed the matter with the Kashag. What really alarmed the Dalai Lama was not the very real prospect that the Chinese might not allow him to return from Peking, but that his own people might refuse—even physically— to permit him to go. If this were to happen, the reaction among the Chinese generals would be appalling.

If this thought crossed General Tan's mind, he said nothing. With more politeness than usual, he said that he quite understood, and after a few more formalities the meeting broke up and the occupation generals left for their headquarters at Yutok, an old house near the Turquoise Bridge.

To the Dalai Lama that meeting—however unruffled it might have appeared on the surface—heralded imminent danger, and he not only admitted to himself that 'I was very near to despair,' but within a few minutes was unburdening his soul to his mother, for it happened that on this day she had her regular weekly lunch with her son, and after she had struggled up the worn steps of the dark stairways, resting to regain her breath on each floor, the two ate alone, a frugal meal of vegetables and butter tea.*

Gyalyum Chemo,† the Dalai Lama's mother, was a handsome clear-eyed lady of sixty with fine bones. She had moved to Lhasa after her son had been 'found' and was comfortably installed in a

* The Tibetans make butter tea by crumbling a handful of brick tea into boiling water. It is stewed for up to five minutes. A pinch of salt (never sugar) is added. Finally, a big dollop of butter, sometimes rancid, is added into a man's tea bowl, then he stirs the tea with his finger.

† 'The Great Mother'.

large house at the foot of the Potala, opposite Sho. Though she
was suffering severely from rheumatism in one knee, she rarely
missed her weekly lunch with her son, for 'I knew that perhaps I
was the only person to whom he could unburden his soul.' And
his mother, certainly more than any other person, knew the tor-
ment which for eight years had tugged at the two differing sides
of her son's character—on the one hand the religious beliefs so
deeply instilled that the thought of taking life was abhorrent; on
the other, the natural instincts of any boy born in the land of the
Khambas, to feel a sense of pride in the deeds of those defending
his country to the death against the hated oppressors.

The Dalai Lama had already arranged to receive Chime Youngdong in the near future, but now he asked his mother to tell him
something about the Khambas crowding Lhasa. One has the
impression of an almost wistful curiosity, if not envy, on the part
of this young man denied any contact with the outside world. All
who talked to him in those troubled days were struck with his
almost pathetic eagerness to learn more about the ordinary people
who were his subjects but whom he was never allowed to meet.

With his mother, however, it was different. Her son might be
hemmed in by officials, but she was able to move about the city
unhindered by protocol. The capital, she told him, was becoming
'more and more like an armed camp'. Guerrillas from the east
were flooding the city. They were openly insulting the Chinese.
Scuffles or minor fights were nightly occurrences. And all the
Khambas from the east had sworn allegiance to the unnaturally
tall, handsome lama who was their king, and who had sworn
revenge for the murder of his father.

As she was preparing to ask her son's blessing before leaving,
the Dalai Lama turned to his mother and she would never forget
his words, uttered with a sad simplicity that made them all the
more ominous. 'I don't know when it will come,' he said, 'but
one day the Chinese will take away everything we have—and they
will kill every Tibetan who has seen anything of the outside
world.'

3

Monday, February 16-Tuesday, February 24

The stories circulating in Lhasa about Chime Youngdong and his Khamba followers might have been exaggerated, but there was some truth in them, for certainly he was the spiritual and temporal ruler of two hundred thousand subjects demanding action; and so, by no means for the first time in Tibet's history, a man like Chime, a believer in non-violence, found himself pushed into a position where his greatest value to his people lay in helping them to fight. To many Western eyes, accustomed to the picture of a serene, peace-loving Tibet isolated behind its mountain barriers, the contradictions in personal behaviour may seem puzzling. In fact, a Khamba from the east was as different from a citizen of Lhasa as a Londoner would be from a Scot or a New Yorker from a New Mexican. And, too, one has the feeling that the different sides of the average Tibetan's character were always struggling against each other. Chime certainly believed in non-violence; but he also believed passionately in defending the rights of his people. It was one thing to attack. It was quite a different matter to defend. (It was equally illogical for a man like Chime to regard the killing of an animal as abhorrent yet to sit down contentedly to a meal of meat slaughtered by men conveniently labelled as outcasts.)

The Chinese were also largely to blame for Chime's involvement, for as Chime waited for his audience with the Dalai Lama, he lived the life of a hunted man. While the Khambas were openly boasting that a nation wide revolution would soon burst into flames, the Chinese discovered that Chime had reached Lhasa and they immediately put a price on his head, dead or alive. To the Chinese he would be a prize capture. He was the son of a king who had been liquidated and was thus best out of the way. But most of all, he was—whether he liked it or not—the rallying-point for thousands of Khambas. To Chime the days of waiting must have been nerve-wracking. He had to leave his tent and go into hiding. After a lifetime spent in the placid environment of his monastery he had suddenly become the slightly bewildered central figure in an intrigue utterly alien to his nature.

The Chinese wasted no time. Within days of Chime's arrival they were burrowing into every house where they thought he might be lodging, and soon the simplest problems of food and shelter became acute. Time after time Chime escaped detection only, it seemed, by a miracle. One night he was warned not to return to the house where he had been staying. It belonged to a family from Jyekundo, who were therefore his subjects. Dressed in an old, stained chuba, Chime and another monk watched the building. Armed Chinese lolled near the front door, and Chime discovered later that all the inhabitants had been taken away for questioning. From that moment Chime slept in a different house each night. Each day he wore a different chuba, in some elementary attempt at disguise. Some days he did not dare to venture out. He was not afraid, but to Chime it was of paramount importance to keep out of harm's way until he had seen the Dalai Lama. He had to tell the Dalai Lama all that was happening in the east. He had to ask for assistance—not only food for the peasants, but for troops whose very presence would help to restore order. And above all, he was hoping to persuade the Dalai Lama to approach Peking urgently and beg the Chinese to stop their wanton attacks on the monasteries. Chime felt that if this could be achieved, he might in his turn be able to persuade the vast majority of his Khambas to return to the Jyekundo region, and thus stave off open revolt.

'After that,' he remembers thinking, 'it would not matter much what happened to me.'

His audience with the Dalai Lama took place at nine o'clock in the morning, in a small room with brown walls and orange curtains. It was simply furnished. It contained no butter lamps, not even a Buddha. Apart from one small table, a divan and a few cushions scattered on the carpeted floor, the room was bare. The Dalai Lama sat on the divan, flanked by two red pillows. Chime presented the customary white scarf before sitting cross-legged on a cushion on the floor.

The exchange of views started pleasantly enough. One must remember that if the Dalai Lama was the undisputed leader of Tibet, Chime also held an exalted rank in his vast and distant region. This, therefore, was no meeting between king and commoner. Though not, of course, the Dalai Lama's equal, Chime at least spoke with the authority of one whose Khamba subjects were among the most fearless in the land. And because of this, his views commanded respect.

The Dalai Lama asked Chime for details of his journey. To Chime, the adventures, the brutality of the Chinese, the number of his followers who had been killed, seemed to provide the ideal point at which to start his pleas for help. As dispassionately as possible he told of the disasters which had engulfed the Jyekundo area; of the repression of the peasants whose crops were being ruthlessly seized, of the desecration of the monasteries, and of the abduction of prominent citizens.

The Dalai Lama listened impassively, but as Chime warmed to his subject, the Dalai Lama began to interrupt from time to time when points were not clear, and from the nature of these interspersions Chime realized with a sense of dismay that his instinct had been right: this was perhaps the first time the Dalai Lama had heard such detailed evidence of the fighting in the east.

'I told him,' Chime remembers, 'that I did not think his cabinet ministers realized just what the Chinese were doing to us, and I felt that he should know what the ordinary people were saying and feeling.'

Without doubt the Dalai Lama was deeply shocked. He demanded more details. He cross-questioned Chime, displaying a local knowledge of the terrain that was astounding. And yet Chime began to realize that he was getting nowhere with his arguments. True, the Dalai Lama agreed that the Chinese atrocities were intolerable. Yet in his careful, modulated voice, he warned Chime of the dangers if the Khambas took reprisals. They could, he said, do nothing but lead to yet another set of Chinese reprisals against the Khambas and, even worse, innocent peasants.

Not only would such a course be wrong from the point of view of the peasants who would inevitably suffer most, but the Dalai Lama also made it clear that however much he admired the Khambas, 'I am strongly opposed to any resort to arms.' For over eight years, he pointed out, he had tried to discourage violence because such a course was immoral and could lead only to havoc.

From the theological point of view Chime had to agree, but he could not see what this had to do with his appeal to the Dalai Lama to make a formal protest to the Chinese government about the desecration of the monasteries. The Dalai Lama hesitated. He was deeply upset at the Chinese interference with religious beliefs, but he did not feel it wise to lodge a written protest. He had, he told Chime, been asked to visit Peking, and when he went he would raise the matter personally with the Chinese leaders. 'The Dalai Lama could not give me a date for his visit,' Chime remembers, 'and I had the distinct impression that he did not want to go.' Though Chime had hoped the Dalai Lama would agree to send a formal Note immediately, he had at least gained his point, and had to be content with the rather vague assurances.

When he raised the question of a token force of regular troops for the Jyekundo area, however, he was met with a firm refusal. Chime did not seem able to make the Dalai Lama understand that sometimes the mere presence of a small force of regular troops would calm simmering passions, could prevent sporadic fighting from spreading. Yet the Dalai Lama insisted that such a move would bring nothing but harm. 'The Central Government is trying to make the Chinese occupation forces behave more reasonable,' added the Dalai Lama, 'and it would be unthinkable to send troops and increase the hostility.'

In vain Chime argued that in his view Tibetan troops would have exactly the opposite effect. He was convinced that if troops of the Tibetan army were to parade in the Jyekundo area, it would help to calm the temper of the Khambas. Without troops they would riot whenever they felt like it. There was another point. As he told the Dalai Lama, tens of thousands of Khambas had followed him across the central plateau to Lhasa. He had not asked them to come. They had swarmed across half the country, motivated by a blind instinct. Would it not be in the best interests of everyone if Chime could persuade them to return to the east? They were now so near breaking-point that he could give no assurances, but if he could tell his followers that Tibetan troops were on the way to Jyekundo, he might be able to persuade many of the Khambas to return. Indeed he, Chime, would lead them back. The Dalai Lama appeared to hesitate, and Chime added guardedly, 'I would not be true to my people if I did not tell Your Holiness that many feel the Central Government does not really care what happens to them.'

Chime had the curious sensation that, while the Dalai Lama secretly admired the Khambas in many ways, he might also be thinking that if only there were no Khambas in Tibet, the task of working with the Chinese might be much easier. And this feeling was intensified after Chime had said, 'But, Your Holiness—you cannot expect my people to do nothing while the Chinese kill our women and children and plunder our monasteries.'

There was a moment's pause, 'as though the Dalai Lama were carefully weighing every word'. Finally, he said very simply, 'There is nothing I can do. I think your people should show a little more tolerance and try to abide by the Seventeen Point Agreement.'

Chime was aghast. Of course he had realized full well the difficult position in which the Dalai Lama was placed, but he had hoped at best for the promise of a token force of troops, or at worst a promise that the Dalai Lama would lodge a stern protest with the Chinese in Peking. Instead nothing was going to be done.

Almost without thinking, Chime blurted out, 'Perhaps, Your Holiness, you do not know the full truth. Perhaps you are only getting the stories your cabinet wants you to hear.'

The Dalai Lama 'did not take offence at my presumption'. He gave Chime 'a grave, sad smile', and told him that he knew about the influx of Khambas who had followed Chime to Lhasa, but hoped Chime would realize that 'I am very near to despair' and that Chime would be doing his country the greatest service if he could persuade his followers to contain their anger while the government tried to work out a compromise with the Chinese.

'I may admire the bravery of the Khambas,' the Dalai Lama added, 'but their actions often do great harm to those of us who are trying to find a way of living with the Chinese.'

It had been a powerful plea. But though Chime realized the force of the Dalai Lama's arguments, he knew that he could make only one reply. Admitting that he understood the Dalai Lama's reasoning, Chime felt that he had to warn him that no man in Tibet could hold back the Khambas much longer. It needed only one spark—one small insult, real or imagined—to start a revolution that could sweep the country.

'What will you do then?' asked the Dalai Lama as Chime rose from his cushion to leave.

'If we can't get any help', Chime replied, 'I must return to the east and help my people in their fight.'

The Dalai Lama seemed 'very upset', but then for the last time he turned to Chime and said, again simply and quietly, 'Don't do that, stay in Lhasa and pray. Pray so that what you fear may not come about.'

Lhasa was changing—and for the worse. Life assumed a crazy, often dangerous pattern. Food was becoming increasingly scarce. Though there was no curfew, trigger-happy Chinese patrols made all but the hardiest remain in their homes at night. The Dalai Lama received disturbing reports that the Chinese were forcing Tibetans to attend meetings where they were warned 'that the Cabinet was in league with the reactionaries and would be dealt with accordingly—not merely shot, but executed slowly and publicly.' Sometimes life was stupidly illogical, particularly with the shifting population, for while more and more Khambas streamed in from the east, some inhabitants were fleeing, making for the jagged mule paths leading to the bleak mountain wilderness south of Lhasa where all men and women—those in rags, those in silks—were reduced to equality by a ferocious nature.

To many of the ordinary men, women and children of Lhasa, unaware of the catastrophe that was shortly to engulf them, there seems to have been, for each of them, one particular incident during those last weeks which (though they did not realize it at the time) pin-pointed the precise moment when their destinies were about to be changed.

For Genyen, the ten-year-old daughter of Jamyangling, a Tibetan noble, it came one night when she was awakened by the sound of horses treading the courtyard of their large house in the northern sector of the city. The dull thudding, the jangle of harness metal, was followed by the sound of the bolts of the massive wooden gates being drawn home as the gates were closed. She jumped out of bed and peered down into the enormous courtyard. Half a dozen servants with pressure-lamps were guiding a throng of men and at least fifty horses into the stables flanking the house. Dimly, as the pools of light rested first in one corner and then in another, she could see the glint of steel from swords, make out guns strapped across men's backs, and not until the last man had disappeared did she creep back to bed, hugging her favourite doll— an Indian girl who blinked her eyes.

Genyen's mother had died at sixteen, giving birth to her first child, and leaving Genyen's father a widower at eighteen. In the vague way that children form pictures of the past, Genyen remembers her father as tall, grave, beautifully dressed, but inevitably she was left very much to her own devices, so that in a way she was closer to the servants, especially 'Ma', her nurse, who had brought her up from birth and was now almost a member of the family.

Ma came into Genyen's room sharp at six-thirty the next morning, carrying a silver jug of water. As Genyen brushed her teeth she blurted out, 'Who were all those men in the night?'

Ma wheeled round, darting questions at her. How did Genyen know? What had she seen? How dare she get out of bed in the dark? She must have gone straight to Genyen's father, for later in the day he sent for her.

Her father could never be angry, but he told her that the bitter fighting in the east was spreading westwards. More and more Khambas were moving into Lhasa. And as her father explained gently, no true Tibetan would ever refuse hospitality to people who had been forced to flee their homes leaving all they possessed behind. But she must promise him never to divulge their secret. And she remembered exactly his final warning, 'If the Chinese ever find out, we might never see each other again.'

There were forebodings too in the Women's Association in Lhasa, whose four hundred members were endeavouring to help the less fortunately placed. The secretary of the Association was Mary Taring, whose husband Jigme was a close friend of the Dalai Lama's (their names had been Westernized while schooling in Darjeeling) and one day, during a discussion in the plain room decorated with the inevitable picture of the Dalai Lama and rows of kitchen-type chairs,* five Chinese women in the blue uniforms of the political branch entered the hall, and one started haranguing the audience. The Chinese women were joined by a gang of Chinese teenagers, members of the Chinese-sponsored Society for Tibetan Youths. There was some heckling and the ladies were shocked to see one man in particular. He was Phakpala, a monk who acted as liaison officer with the Chinese, and whose pro-Chinese activities were common knowledge. Perhaps it was as well for Mary Taring's peace of mind that she did not realize she had been watching a Judas who was even then laying his plans to betray the Dalai Lama.

For Kunchok, trader and guerrilla, there were moments of happiness etched against the dark background of mounting tension.

Kunchok was twenty-two, a burly man with close-cropped hair

---

* To be more precise, 'non-honorific' chairs. In the amusingly derivative Tibetan language, such a chair is called a *kup-kya*, meaning literally 'bottom prop'.

and an infectious grin, who had built up a fine business in Lhasa as a wholesale trader, mostly in wool and yak butter, and who now and again—more to amuse himself than to make money—would set up a stall outside the house north of the Cathedral where he lived with his uncle.

From time to time, Kunchok would disappear mysteriously from his old haunts, vanishing without a word to his friends. Then he would return, laughing off all questions. In fact Kunchok was a highly placed guerrilla fighter, operating with forces in the south, whose business in Lhasa served as a convenient blind for him to return to organize recruiting among the Khambas arriving from the east.

He was back now, looking quite unlike a Khamba warrior, for most of his friends say Kunchok was something of a ladies' man, though, as he remembers, 'Marriage wasn't for me. I was getting too much fun out of life.' So he thought—until the day in late February when a beautiful girl stopped at his stall for some butter. Goggle-eyed, Kunchok pressed the small packet into her hands and refused all payment. The girl was tall for a Tibetan, very slim, and she accepted the gift prettily. And then, while Kunchok was trying to think of an excuse to detain her, she was gone. Leaving his stall, he ran among the crowds, jumping up on his toes, trying in vain to catch a glimpse of her ahead.

It was a day or two before he saw her again—and this time it was, of all places, outside the Women's Association building where she had been attending a meeting. Kunchok had been to the cinema near the Turquoise Bridge, an ugly, squat building, which now showed virtually nothing but Chinese propaganda films instead of the good old Indian singing and dancing films to which every-body with a spare coin had flocked.

She strolled towards the Inner Ring by the Cathedral with an old lady, no doubt her mother, so Kunchok did not like to ap-proach the girl, but he followed the pair discreetly as they made their circular tour, and then passed through the Lubok Gate, walking to a small house set in poplars near the River Kyichu.

After that it was comparatively easy. He knew she would have to go and fetch water at the well, and he lay in wait for her the next morning. Her name was Tsering Dolma, she was twenty-one and Kunchok thought she was the most beautiful creature he had ever seen. Within a few days he asked if he could approach their parents for permission to marry.

The Dalai Lama's Prime Minister at this time was Surkhang, a tough, stocky man of forty-nine whose thoughts were often conveniently masked by a pair of hooded eyes. Surkhang had borne the brunt of the Chinese spleen. Time after time he had been called to the Chinese headquarters in Yutok and forced to listen to the interminable harangues about the 'reactionaries' in league with the Khambas. Every time the old familiar Communist catch-phrases were trotted out as the Chinese demands on Surkhang became stiffer. One day General Tan would suggest that Tibetan troops should help to stamp out guerrillas—an impossible request because, as Surkhang knew full well, the army would have deserted to the Khamba cause. The next, Tan wanted the Chinese flag to be flown on all Tibetan army barracks—a request which was equally impossible. By the spring of 1959 Surkhang realized that the Chinese would have to be placated, and so he had hit on a plan which he hoped would mollify them, yet secretly arm him with all the available information about the Khambas—just in case the increasing number of isolated incidents became merged into a nation-wide revolt.

Ostensibly he formed a committee 'to discuss Khamba activities and report to the Chinese'. In fact this Committee was a blind. 'We kept telling the Chinese we were working hard to solve the Khamba problem,' Surkhang remembers, but instead the Committee was making Tibet's first attempt to co-ordinate on a national basis 'every aspect of Chinese oppression and what steps might be necessary to deal with it'. For the first time the committee received reports of dispositions of Khamba groups, monasteries in which the arms were hidden. Throughout the spring a trickle of Khamba leaders had made secret visits to Lhasa. Communication channels had been organized, guns and ammunition distributed, and secret centres had been set up to deal with volunteers. While this was happening, Surkhang had paid regular visits to the Chinese generals and fed them with false and hopeful stories of what they were doing to control the 'rebels'.

Without warning, the Chinese, in the middle of February, discovered the truth; as Surkhang admits ruefully, 'We never discovered who told them, but with a big committee like this, the secret discussions were bound to leak out.'

Surkhang knew nothing of the leak, even when he was summoned to the Chinese headquarters at Yutok to hear a propaganda lecture. Quite unaware of the storm about to descend on him, Surkhang put on his broad-brimmed Western felt hat—considered the height of fashion in Lhasa in 1959—and proceeded to the beautiful old house by the Turquoise Bridge which had been requisitioned by the Chinese. Once there, he sat with other Tibetans on one side of the long table. Opening a small turquoise-studded silver box, he offered a pinch of snuff to Luishar, the Foreign Minister, who was sitting next to him.* Tea was served, and an unknown lecturer droned on. As the propaganda talk ended, General Tan stormed in. He was grasping a slip of paper, and Luishar remembers that his face was beetroot red and 'he looked as though he was going to have a stroke.'

Banging a fist on the table, General Tan cried that the Tibetan government was collaborating with the Khambas. As Surkhang sat there aghast, the Chinese general recited detail after detail of the secret committee meetings. Then, turning to the Prime Minister, he pointed a finger and shouted, 'Look at that man Surkhang! He's the man behind this plot!' Though everything Tan said was true, Surkhang rose to protest, for 'I felt I must pretend to be insulted.' General Tan waved him down, and turning to the other

---

* Since smoking was frowned upon (though tolerated), many Tibetans found refuge in snuff. Surkhang always made his own mixture and the first thing he would do when meeting a friend was to exchange a pinch.

Chinese cried, 'Watch him! From now on, we shall watch Surkhang every hour of the day and night.'

Not content with this outburst, General Tan was the central figure in another extraordinary incident, for without warning the head of all the Chinese in Tibet—in effect the most powerful man in the country—took it upon himself to pay an unannounced visit to Mary Taring's Women's Association and address the ladies.

It was a normal quiet meeting, called to try and devise a means of looking after Khamba wives whose husbands had gone south to fight, when General Tan, flanked by two aides, burst into the room and harangued the startled women for half an hour. The nub of his argument came when he shouted, 'Where there's rotten meat, the flies will gather. Get rid of the meat, and the flies will cause you no more trouble.' (The Dalai Lama's wry comment when he heard of this outburst was, 'The flies, I suppose, were the guerrilla fighters. The rotten meat was either my cabinet or myself.')

Then, on the night of Tuesday, February 24, an event occurred which none could have foreseen. A high-ranking Chinese general defected to the Tibetan cause. Chinese troops in their sprawling camp south-west of Lhasa were assembling and marching across the ruler-straight unpaved streets into the camp cinema. Following the weekly ritual, they filed into the rows of seats filling the long, one-storey building. The officers followed, sitting in the front rows, until every seat except one was occupied. The chair reserved for General Chang Hwa-ting, Commander of the Artillery, was empty, for he had sent a message to say that he was unwell. In fact, as the film show started, the General was in the best of health and very busy. He was packing his few personal belongings and preparing to flee.

The decision had not been made hurriedly. By all accounts—and they come mostly from Phala, the Dalai Lama's senior chamberlain, who became directly involved—General Chang was an introspective, deeply unhappy man, unable to reconcile his conscience with Communism; but even so, he must have passed many agonizing months before reaching the gravest decision of his life—to toss aside an unblemished military career, to leave for ever his homeland and his family, and to cast his lot with the Tibetans who, reason told him, could never be free.

He had planned carefully. The camp was always 'at ease' on film nights, with only a few sentries on guard, for though the Khambas might be active in isolated areas, there had never been so much as a skirmish near the camp. Thus it had been a simple matter for the General to leave his jeep near the camp perimeter, and once he was certain the cinema show had started, he walked to the gates and got in. To the sentry, he was of course a general, and generals are not questioned. However, this was Communism, so Chang announced that he had been summoned to army head-quarters at Yutok. The gates were opened without demur, and soon he was bowling along the road that skirted the hamlet of Sho below the Potala. Here he turned left, leaving Lhasa City on his right as he struck across the Plain of Milk, with the great snow-capped granite mountains facing him. He was making for the main Tibetan army camp near Sera Monastery, where the mountains met the plain, four miles north of the capital. There was very little in the way of a road, but a straight aqueduct helped to guide him in the dark and he reached the camp in under half an hour.

It must have been a startling moment for the sentry on duty when, hearing the sound of a vehicle screeching to a stop, he shone his torch—and found himself facing a fully-fledged Chinese general. Chang confessed afterwards that he half expected to be shot on sight. He could speak only a little Tibetan, but as he clambered out of the jeep, holding his hands above his head, he cried, 'General Tasha Paran!'—the name of the camp comman-dant. In a few moments vague shadows and the blink of swinging pressure-lamps materialized and the Chinese was taken to a small hut under guard.

We might never have known the details of this extraordinary

defection had not General Tasha Paran instantly realized that this was a problem which might have far-reaching political implications. Certainly it was too serious to be left to a soldier, especially when the Chinese general, sipping ceremonial tea, announced that he wanted to join the Tibetan guerrillas.

'Why this change of heart?' Tasha Paran asked him. General Chang put down his bowl and said with a terrible finality, 'Under Communism I have no liberty. The Communists treat all human beings like animals, and I don't believe we Chinese have any right to be in Tibet.'

Tasha Paran was a man who made up his mind quickly. Ordering his horse to be saddled, he placed the General under arrest, and at eleven p.m. set off alone for the Summer Palace where he knew that Phala, the Dalai Lama's chamberlain, had moved to prepare for the Dalai Lama, who would leave the Potala in just over a week. Half an hour later, a nervous sentry at the main gate was asking the General if he would mind waiting until Phala had been awakened.

Phala was destined to be one of the central figures in the extraordinary diplomatic manœuvres immediately preceding the uprising. He was a strongly built man with the frame of a football player, and he must have looked very handsome in his ceremonial robes. Unswervingly loyal, the thing one noticed most about him was the way in which his rugged face, beneath close-cropped greying hair, would light up with a spontaneous, warm smile. Unmarried, he lived in the Potala when the Dalai Lama was in residence, and also had a comfortable house in the grounds of the Summer Palace. Soon, over the inevitable cups of butter tea and biscuits, Tasha Paran was telling the Chamberlain what had happened, repeating the reasons the Chinese had given him for defecting.

Both men agreed that the Chinese general could be trusted. Phala liked Chang and had frequently felt that something like this might happen. Now that it had, he made his first decision: they would accept him as a guerrilla. In the south, his knowledge of Chinese military tactics could be invaluable; if, on the other hand,

Chang was playing a double game, a spy hemmed in by those lonely mountain barriers would never be able to get any information back to base; and anyway, the Khambas would soon find out.

'What do you think His Holiness will say?' asked Tasha Paran.

Phala remembers squeezing out of his seat, standing over the General, and saying slowly, 'His Holiness mustn't know. If he did, he would be placed in an impossible position. In fact,' Phala added, 'it would be better if we didn't even inform the Kashag.'

His decision was based on three factors. He did not want to embarrass government leaders in their meetings with the enemy; no political capital could be made out of the defection; and, perhaps most important, if Chang were to be of use, it was essential to get him out of Lhasa this very night before the Chinese realized he was missing. So there was no time to tell anybody—and no point in telling them when all had been decided and the Chinese general was scores of miles distant.

Tasha Paran had one last point to make: Chang had asked if he could see Phala, but to this request Phala gave an emphatic 'No'. Secrecy was as essential as speed. Already enough men would be wondering—and talking—about Tasha Paran's midnight gallop. If Phala were to ride in the dead of night to the Tibetan army camp, it would only increase the suspicion.

'But tell the General,' said Phala, 'that I admire his courage, and that one day, when I'm in the south, I will be sure to meet him.' It was a promise that would be kept in a moment of high drama.

Before dawn the General had been kitted out with a chuba and guerrilla arms. He had also been given a new Tibetan name—Lobsang Tashi. With a small party of Khambas he set off—and he had crossed the Tsangpo river forty miles to the south before an angry General Tan was accusing mystified Tibetan political leaders of abducting a senior Chinese officer.

Grimly he warned the Tibetan Kashag that this latest outrage, following the increased Khamba uprisings, was 'the last straw'.

In vain the Tibetans—who were completely in the dark—denied all knowledge of what he was talking about. Finally General Tan leaned forward, tapped the green table at Yutok with his thin hand, and said, 'I will give you one week to return the Chinese general. Otherwise . . .' He left the sentence unfinished.

The week would be up on March 3.

Part Two

THE INCREDIBLE REVOLT

4

Tuesday, March 3-Monday, March 16

The inner courtyard of the Chokhang, the cathedral of Lhasa, was crowded with nearly five thousand monks, all eagerly witnessing an astonishing spectacle. Attired in their finest yellow or maroon robes, they filled every inch of the vast open space ringed by cloisters. Lucky ones nearest the centre sat cross-legged on bright cushion seats or mattresses. Behind them stood row upon row of monks, those at the back craning their necks for a better view. A sea of faces crammed the parapets and balconies above the cloisters, while some monks were even perched on the high, gilded cathedral roof. As in a boxing arena—though the simile may be irreverent—all eyes were watching the small central stage, for there sat the Dalai Lama, engaged in public debate with a relay of monk teachers. It was Tuesday, March 3, and he was in fact engaged in his final burst of swotting on the day before taking his oral examination as a doctor of metaphysics.

Among the Tibetan monks on the stage with the Dalai Lama was one called Gyamtso Ling—a name to be noted, for he was not only in the pay of the Chinese, but has left us an invaluable, if pro-Chinese, account of some of the events of the next few days. Gyamtso was a monk tutor in his forties, 'fat, fidgety and nervous'. It is beyond question that he was a brilliant scholar much admired by the Dalai Lama for his learning, though there is equally no doubt that the Dalai Lama must have known of his pro-Chinese proclivities. (The Dalai Lama's tolerance of known Tibetan traitors provides one of the many untidy inconsistencies in this story. It cannot be put down to naïvety alone. More possibly the

Dalai Lama, in his efforts to preserve religious freedom, thought it wiser to avoid open clashes with these Quislings.)

Just before midday, Gyamtso left the dais and thrust his way through the ranks of the audience towards the main gates. A few minutes later he returned and held a whispered conversation with the Dalai Lama who, after a moment's hesitation, left the platform.

What had happened to cause this interruption? Two junior Chinese officers had arrived at the cathedral demanding to see the Dalai Lama in person—an event 'so unusual', as the Dalai Lama mildly commented, that it 'immediately aroused suspicion among my people.' The Dalai Lama was not, after all, the sort of person to be approached in such casual fashion. Nevertheless, he surprisingly agreed to see them in an ante-chamber, though he found that 'this visit was curious'.

The two officers came straight to the point. General Tan was arranging a theatrical performance in the main Chinese army camp, and wanted the Dalai Lama to name a date when he could conveniently attend. Slightly taken aback, the Dalai Lama pointed out that arrangements of this nature were handled by his court chamberlain. In any event he could not, he said, possibly make a decision while preparing for the most difficult examination of his life. 'I really could not concentrate on anything else just then,' he recalls, 'so I told the officers I would arrange a date as soon as the ceremonies were finished.'

To the Dalai Lama's astonishment, the officers refused at first to take no for an answer. 'They kept pressing me to decide on a date at once.' The Dalai Lama, however, replied firmly that in no circumstances would he discuss the matter before the examination, and finally, after some argument, the two officers left to take this message to General Tan.

Apparently innocuous, this was the meeting which led in a matter of days to open revolt, and several questions concerning it remain unanswered. Was it merely chance that lit the fuse of the long-simmering Tibetan hatred, or was it a Chinese plot, following the well-known Communist technique, to 'force' the Tibetans into violent action, and so give China a convenient excuse to take over the country completely? It is a technique which is distressingly familiar to many small nations, and the Dalai Lama admits that he does not know whether it happened 'by accident or design'. There is, however, one intriguing (and at first sight unrelated) incident which tends to indicate that the Chinese were preparing for a coup of some sort. Within a few hours of the Dalai Lama's meeting with the Chinese officers, Peking Radio announced without warning that he had agreed to visit the Chinese capital. The report was completely without foundation, for though it is true that the Dalai Lama had been asked to visit Peking, he had carefully avoided accepting the invitation. The immediate reaction in Lhasa was that the broadcast was a clumsy Chinese ruse to force the Dalai Lama to fly out of Tibet against his will.

The most puzzling question of all, however, is: How were the two junior Chinese officers able to enter the closely-guarded cathedral and approach such an exalted personage? The massive gates were heavily guarded by the Dalai Lama's personal bodyguard. And in a country of such Oriental protocol, it would be unthinkable for two men to stroll in and demand to see the ruler. The Dalai Lama merely says he was told that 'two Chinese officers wanted to see me' and they were shown in, which gives the impression that the visit came as a surprise to him. But even so, how did they pass the guards? A member of the Lhasa City Council called Thondup says he heard that the officers had previously arranged the appointment by letter; but that seems extraordinary, for why should the Dalai Lama agree to see them on this particular day when years of intensive study were about to be climaxed by the actual examination? It would have been a simple matter for him to receive them a couple of days later, with the examination behind him.

There is, however, a third alternative—that Gyamtso, the monk debater, let them in on orders from the Chinese. As one of the six debaters who had been practising for weeks with the Dalai Lama, he had come to know him well, and was certainly in a position to suggest various plans for 'keeping the Chinese generals calm'. What in fact probably happened is that Gyamtso arranged in advance for the Chinese to call at a given time. He then left the debate and ordered the guards (in the name of the Dalai Lama) to admit them. It would then have been easy for him to suggest to the Dalai Lama that it might be wise for him to spare them a few moments since they came from the General. This theory is supported by the knowledge that Gyamtso did leave the debating platform at the time the Chinese arrived, and he was certainly seen (possibly while the officers were cooling their heels in the outer courtyard) to hold a private conversation with the Dalai Lama.

Nothing happened—nothing on the surface, that is—for the next couple of days, though Lhasa was simmering with a vague feeling of unrest and distrust. The city was filled not only with monks attending the Monlem Festival,* but with thousands of Khambas, all quick to take offence at any insult directed towards their ruler. The Chinese officers' breach of protocol had quickly become common gossip; so had the Peking Radio broadcast. But these were nothing compared to the studied insult which General Tan now decided to administer to the Dalai Lama, presumably as a mark of his displeasure at the treatment of his junior officers.

On the day following the examination (which he passed with flying colours) the Dalai Lama made his way in a state procession from the Cathedral to the Norbulingka, or Summer Palace, west of the city and south of the Potala. It was a fairy-tale procession of Oriental splendour, attended by all Lhasa, which camped out in gaily-coloured tents by the side of the three-mile route. Led by two hundred bobbing cavalry on richly caparisoned horses, and with two bands—one inevitably playing 'God Save the Queen'— and with the Dalai Lama perched high on a gilded throne, this was the greatest annual spectacle in the capital, in which every man seemed to vie with his neighbour to be more colourful. There were lay officials in purple wraps edged with yellow silk, their fur hats

* An annual religious festival attended by high-ranking monks from all over Tibet, which this year had been timed to coincide with the Dalai Lama's examination.

crowned with silk of the same colour; others wore robes of saffron, and hats with matching crowns. The outriders, servants and grooms were resplendent in uniforms which at times outshone their masters'. No wonder that by custom Lhasa's small diplomatic corps was always invited, together with high-ranking Chinese. This year, however—for the one and only time since the invasion of 1950—General Tan ordered the Chinese to boycott the parade, and though the sophisticated Mary Taring found it 'refreshing not to have any Chinese around', the ordinary Tibetans were stunned at the deliberate slap in the face.

To Western eyes, the reaction of Tibetans to these infractions of protocol may seem exaggerated (though one can imagine the hullabaloo in London if an invited diplomat chose to boycott the State Opening of Parliament). But one has to remember that the Tibetans had been smarting under occupation for eight years, and if their emotions were exaggerated, then that is what happens when simple, devoutly religious people feel they have been affronted.

If the Dalai Lama felt any annoyance, it was not betrayed on his serene face as the parade disbanded on the edge of the meadows surrounding the Summer Palace. He blessed the large, good-natured crowd pressing on either side of the main gates and took no notice of the more unruly youngsters throwing stones at the savage, growling, long-haired guard mastiffs, each chained with yak-hair leashes to granite kennels set in the wall at regular intervals, and each wearing a bright red woollen ruff to protect its throat if attacked by wolves.

This was the home he loved most of all, for it had none of the prison-like atmosphere, the dark corridors and dimly-lit rooms of the Potala. It was not a palace in the accepted sense of the word, but an amorphous collection of buildings, more like a village than a palace, set in glorious parkland, square in shape, surrounded by four ten-foot walls, each half a mile long. The Dalai Lama passed under the portico of the main gate with its glazed tiled roof, grinning demons, and golden medallions on a dark red background, and made his way through the grounds, with orchards of peach and pear just bursting into blossom, along a beautiful avenue of

71

straight white poplars, past the stables for five hundred horses and barracks for his personal bodyguard. After passing two enormous prayer barrels cunningly set over streams so that they revolved by water power, he reached his private apartments, in an enclosure two hundred yards square and surrounded by an inner wall, always known as the Yellow Wall. In his small private sitting-room his jade teacup on its golden stand awaited him, as always.

This was perhaps the only place the Dalai Lama could really call home for, despite the golden pagoda-like roofs of the temples, his private apartments were simple to the point of being spartan, and set in grounds with trees overhanging a small lake with two summer pavilions on islands, and peacocks strutting on immaculate lawns. And his summer palace was not only private, it was more practical than the Potala, with its hundreds of offices and scurrying figures filling the corridors. The Chinese had laid on a direct telephone line to their headquarters at Yutok; there were villas for his cabinet ministers and senior officials; and the Dalai Lama even had a bath imported from a well-known English firm and a flush toilet—in marked contrast to his sanitary arrangements in the Potala, which consisted of an airless room with a hole in the floor open to a cesspit four hundred feet below.

Now the scene is set. For the moment all is well. Having moved to the Summer Palace, we have a picture of the Dalai Lama holding court, strolling through his private gardens, holding tea ceremonies each morning with high-ranking lamas, and, generally speaking, hopeful that the immediate future presented no insoluble problems. But complications were to follow, largely due to Tibetans in the pay of the Chinese.

There were three key figures, at this very moment working with General Tan in the Chinese headquarters. Gyamtso we have already met. He was aided by Phakpala, the lama from Sera Monastery whom Mary Taring had seen at the Women's Association. He was something of a fool; but the master mind was Ngabo, who had signed the Seventeen Point Agreement in Peking;

a man later to be elevated to the status of Chinese general. Ngabo was an extraordinary man. Tall, very thin, he was without doubt one of the prime movers in the plot to strip the Dalai Lama of his powers, and yet, incredibly, he was a member of the Kashag, with special responsibility for maintaining liaison with the Chinese; and again one is puzzled why such a known traitor was not dismissed from the post of cabinet minister. Possibly the Dalai Lama felt that he could not exercise enough power to dismiss the most important liaison officer in the country without precipitating a fresh Chinese outburst, or giving the Chinese an excuse to increase their hold on Tibet. The Dalai Lama may also have hoped that a man like Ngabo would in the end be able to help Tibet by mollifying the enemy.

On March 7—two days later—events moved forward, when General Tan again asked the Dalai Lama when he could visit the Chinese camp. The Dalai Lama promptly agreed to go on March 10, though oddly enough no practical arrangements for the visit seem to have been discussed until March 9. Then at eight o'clock in the morning, Jamyang, a member of the Dalai Lama's personal bodyguard, was on duty at the main gate as a jeep tore up and two Chinese officers jumped out.

Jamyang was twenty-five, and from this moment onwards was to be deeply involved in the unfolding drama. Dressed in his special ceremonial dark green chuba with its striped collar and a bronze medal announcing his enviable status, Jamyang was the son of a soldier, and had been in the army since the age of thirteen. Though paid only the equivalent of £10 a month (which stopped during his annual leave) he revelled in the British-style army life, with the bugle-call at six each morning, an hour's physical jerks before breakfast, and the discipline of camp with its parade ground, bands, football and netball pitches.

The two Chinese banged imperiously on the heavy, creaking, wooden gates, grabbing the metal knockers—each one a ring held in the jaws of a lion—and when Jamyang opened one door, they curtly demanded to see General Kusung Depon, Commander of the Guard (who as it happens was married to the Dalai Lama's

73

sister). Jamyang told the Chinese that the General was breakfasting, but they were so insistent—even trying to brush past him—that eventually they were shown in. They had, they explained, come from Brigadier Fu, the Chinese Military Adviser, who wished to see the Tibetan general immediately. Pointing to his unfinished breakfast, Kusung mildly suggested that he would present himself at the Chinese headquarters in two hours. The Chinese officers left.

Within the hour they were back, 'curt and angry' and demanding to see Kusung—'without the loss of a minute'. Jamyang took them to the General, and what happened after that we know from Kusung himself. The Chinese insisted that he must come at once 'as the Brigadier was waiting impatiently', and the Tibetan general (having anyway finished his breakfast) decided that for the sake of peace and quiet he had better go.

By all accounts, Brigadier Fu was a man of extremely short temper. An old hand at the business of dealing with conquered countries (as apart from doing the actual conquering), he disliked intensely any form of criticism. He was a heavy man, with horizontal brows over a waxen skin as smooth as a girl's. Disdaining even the normal courtesies which a man of Kusung's rank might have expected, Fu hardly gave the Tibetan a chance to sit down before he blurted out, 'The Dalai Lama is coming here tomorrow to see a dramatic show. There are some things to settle. That is why I have sent for you.'

Since no arrangements had been discussed in the Summer Palace, Kusung knew nothing of any dramatic show, and asked in all innocence, 'Has the date been fixed?'

'Don't you know?' Fu snapped. 'The Dalai Lama has accepted the General's invitation and he's coming on the tenth.'

Then Brigadier Fu dropped a bombshell.

'I want to make this clear to you,' he said curtly. 'There will be none of the ceremony you usually have. None of your armed men are to come with the Dalai Lama. No Tibetan soldier is to come beyond the Stone Bridge.*

Kusung was flabbergasted, for never in the history of Tibet

* The Stone Bridge marked the limits of the Chinese army camp.

had a Dalai Lama moved in public without a ceremonial escort of at least twenty-five guards, even on the most normal errands. For him to venture into the Chinese Military Area Command without a guard was unthinkable.

All this flashed through Kusung's mind as he listened, stunned, to Brigadier Fu, and then he asked the obvious question: since bodyguards had always escorted the Dalai Lama in the past (and could be no threat to the Chinese anyway) why was the custom suddenly being changed? His question seemed to enrage Fu, whose voice rose in a crescendo until he was almost screaming, 'Will you be responsible if someone pulls the trigger?'

Kusung might have wondered who would pull the trigger unless it were the Chinese, for in the past every meeting between the Dalai Lama and the occupation leaders had taken place with decorum. The possibility that the Chinese were hoping to make trouble might have taken deeper root in Kusung's mind after Fu's next remark, which was sinister in the extreme.

'The whole thing is to be kept strictly secret,' said the Chinese brigadier softly.

This was not only an incredible stipulation, it was an impossible one, for the Dalai Lama's every move was 'public property', as he puts it. However, some sixth sense warned Kusung to keep these thoughts to himself. Not for the first time, he found himself in the position of so many Tibetan leaders who had discovered that (for some unfathomable reason) even the most innocent remarks seemed to enrage the Chinese. He drove back to the Summer Palace and sought out the Chamberlain. Phala was in no doubt what to do, and within a few minutes, Kusung 'in a state of distress' was re-telling his story to the Dalai Lama.

The Dalai Lama was not entirely surprised by Kusung's story, for while the General had been at the Chinese headquarters, the Dalai Lama had been holding a curious conversation with the traitor Phakpala, whose appearance in this tangled story is a brief but bloody one.* Phala remembers him as being about twenty-five,

* The Dalai Lama describes him as 'notorious in Lhasa because of his close association with the Chinese occupation forces'.

fair, short, thin, 'and looking very Chinese'. Though a lama, with a brother even more illustrious, Phakpala had been co-operating with the Chinese for over two years, and among other peculiarities he kept a wardrobe of Chinese clothes at Yutok and changed into them during his frequent visits to Chinese parties.

Despite all this, however, he was a lama of distinction, and as such was one of nearly two hundred who held a brief tea ceremony with the Dalai Lama every morning at nine o'clock, and on this particular morning, Phakpala, in his loose-fitting maroon habit and saffron blouse, managed to draw the Dalai Lama aside after the meeting and tell him that General Tan's theatrical performance would be of such an informal nature that 'in the interests of good relations it would be best if the Dalai Lama went without his Kashag ministers or armed bodyguard.'

The Dalai Lama does not appear to have been greatly disturbed, nor afraid. But he was concerned about what others would think, for the Tibetans are sticklers for protocol and the manner in which the invitation had been presented was a direct breach of Tibetan manners. However, he said nothing to Phakpala.

Now, however, as he listened to Kusung's story of Brigadier Fu's insistence on secrecy, the invitation took on an ominous overtone. 'No one could help feeling that the whole of the Chinese invitation was suspicious,' the Dalai Lama felt, 'and their wish to keep the visit secret made the suspicion worse.' It was also ridiculous, for 'the moment I prepared to go out, the word always went round and the whole of Lhasa turned up and lined the route to see me.'

But what was to be done? After discussing the problem with Surkhang, the Prime Minister, Luishar, the Foreign Minister, and Phala, the Dalai Lama rather trustingly insisted that he would go to the Chinese camp unescorted if this was their wish. But secrecy being impossible, what excuse could he give to the citizens of Lhasa, who knew all about the invitation, and would be horrified if he ventured into Chinese hands unescorted? After talking round the problem for some time, the Dalai Lama hit on what he thought was an ingenious plan. He arranged for a police announcement

76

that on the following day 'there would be special traffic restrictions and nobody would be allowed beyond the [Stone] Bridge.'

It was a fatal mistake. It was naïve to the point of absurdity to expect the already suspicious people to swallow such a thin story in a city which had hardly any traffic anyway, and the result was exactly the opposite of what the Dalai Lama had hoped. Within a matter of hours a rumour swept the capital that the Chinese were planning to kidnap the Dalai Lama.

The result was astonishing. By sunset on March 9 thousands of men, women and children started to gather outside the walls of the Summer Palace. As so often happens in spontaneous demonstrations, people's thoughts seem to have been communicated to each other by instinct, so that all knew why they were there. It was to prevent the Dalai Lama leaving the palace. While most people made for the Summer Palace, one party demonstrated outside the Indian Consulate, petitioning the Consul to cable New Delhi for help. Others besieged the Nepalese. and Bhutanese Consulates. The surge of humanity caught up people from all walks of life. Lundok, a priest who had come into Lhasa from Sera Monastery, had finished his shopping and remembers being borne along by a tide of people singing patriotic songs and crying 'Tibet for Tibetans', until they reached the main gates. On the other side of the gates, an apprehensive Jamyang was on sentry duty, 'wondering what I should do if the crowd burst in. That's what I thought they would do.' Kunchok, who had planned to see Tsering Dolma that evening, had his leave cancelled, and was assigned with his Khamba colleagues to mingle among the crowd in case fighting broke out. He found 'everyone tense and determined', and was soon busy clearing a passage for two Chinese officers who were nearly torn out of their jeep by the mob. Troops were rushed out to help, but several Tibetan civilians were injured before the shaken Chinese were pushed through the gates, where Jamyang watched them brush down their uniforms with their hands before being taken to the Dalai Lama.

They were bearing the formal invitation cards to the party—but not, as was customary, for all the high Tibetan officials of the court. To the astonishment of the Kashag members, only six officials were invited; noticeable among those who were not invited was Phala, though as the Dalai Lama remembers, 'by custom, my Senior Chamberlain always accompanied me wherever I went, as the Chinese knew very well.' The cards were accepted in stony silence, broken only when one Chinese made a highly unusual request: that the six who had been invited should not bring more than one servant with them.

No sooner had the Chinese departed than Surkhang, Luishar and Phala urged the Dalai Lama to cancel the visit. Quite apart from the affront to protocol, every single move of the Chinese pointed to trickery. The demand for secrecy, the outburst of Brigadier Fu, the total refusal to allow a bodyguard, surely meant, said the Kashag ministers, that the Chinese were planning an abduction. There was another point. Ngabo, the traitor member of the Kashag, had refused point blank to leave the Chinese head-quarters when summoned to the Summer Palace. Surely he would never have dared to take such a stand had he not been convinced that the Dalai Lama would shortly be removed from power? The Dalai Lama, however, was obdurate. Though aware of the rising tension among the crowds outside, he felt the only hope of calming the Chinese lay in falling in with their wishes. He did agree to one concession, however. Instead of making their way separately to the camp (as they would normally have done) those who were invited would accompany the Dalai Lama 'because they felt that if anything unpleasant happened, they would at least have the satis-faction of not having left me alone.' With that, the Dalai Lama retired to bed, though his ministers talked far into the night. They had one problem to discuss—one they preferred to talk about behind the Dalai Lama's back. It was the possibility of flight, not necessarily to India, but perhaps to Khamba-controlled territory south of the River Tsangpo.

Two other people received invitations that night to the Chinese party. The Dalai Lama's mother, whose rheumatism was still

troubling her, had gone to bed in the family house at the foot of
the Potala when the telephone rang and General Tan's interpreter,
a man called Li, invited her and her youngest son Choegyal, aged
eleven. The Dalai Lama, he said, had agreed to go. So had her
eldest daughter, the wife of General Kusung Depon who had spent
such an uncomfortable time that morning with Brigadier Fu.
(They were living in the Summer Palace so that Kusung could
keep an eye on the Dalai Lama's bodyguard.)

There could be no question of the Dalai Lama's mother attending the Chinese performance. As she explained, her knee was
causing such pain that she could hardly walk, so she begged to be
excused; nor could she answer for her youngest son who was at
the moment studying at Drepung monastery. General Tan's
interpreter said he quite understood, and the old lady retired to
bed without a thought of what the next morning would bring.

The Dalai Lama had slept badly, and on the morning of March 10
—which he feels was 'the most momentous Lhasa had ever seen'—
he rose at five and made immediately for the peaceful, familiar
prayer-room with its butter lamps and altar bowls filled with
golden-coloured saffron water, the perfume mingling with the
fragrance of incense. Here he prayed and meditated before partak-
ing of what had become a daily ritual—a long, solitary stroll in the
private gardens inside the Yellow Wall. This early morning walk—
quite alone, apart from a sentry at the gate—was his most enjoyable
moment of the day, and though at first the Dalai Lama was pre-
occupied with his worries, 'I soon forgot them in the beauty of the
spring morning.' In a cloudless sky the sun was rising over the
mountains behind the city. A faint breeze stirred the air, and
everything—the poplars and willows in bud, the unfolding lotus
leaves, even the new grass 'was fresh and gay in spring.' The Dalai
Lama made the most of it, still unaware that he was savouring
'the last brief moment of peace of mind I was to know.'

That peace of mind would have been rudely shattered had he
been aware of what was happening at that very moment at his

mother's house, for two jeeps clattered past the front gates and
six Chinese soldiers—two of them women—tumbled out. Through
an upstairs window, the Dalai Lama's mother could see them
brandishing guns. All wore bandoliers across their chests. She
could also hear them clearly. The soldier in charge brusquely
demanded to see her. She heard her servant tell them she was ill.
They had to see her, insisted the Chinese, for they had come to
take her to the Chinese camp to see the theatrical performance.

Fortunately her eight servants, alarmed at the sound of the
jeeps, had rushed to the front of the house and stood firmly on the
steps, blocking the Chinese as they tried to push their way past.
There was a minor scuffle. All her servants, however, were Khambas—and the Chinese certainly knew this. They were also probably
aware that each man carried a pistol hidden in his chuba. After
twenty minutes or so—and some more jostling—the Chinese
finally left.

A frightening thought now struck the Dalai Lama's mother. If
they could try (in effect) to abduct her, what could they not do to
Choegyal, her youngest son? She sent a servant on horseback to
Drepung to make sure the boy was safe. Within the hour he had
returned with grim news. Chinese troops had visited Drepung
at dawn and had 'invited' the youngster to the concert. He
was already a prisoner behind the barbed wire of the Chinese
camp.

'Now I began to be really afraid,' the Dalai Lama's mother
remembers, but considering that she was sixty and suffering badly,
she kept her head magnificently. Time after time she tried to get
through to the Summer Palace on the telephone. It was impossible
—as she had half expected, for Lhasa's primitive telephone system
had a habit of working only when the Chinese were on one end of
the line. She sent servants to the palace—only to discover that it
was impossible for them to get through the crowds. She did,
however, send relays of servants to keep watch outside the Chinese
camp, and though they could not enter, they were able to catch
occasional glimpses of the boy when he went under guard to an
outside toilet.

Her eldest daughter in the Summer Palace knew nothing of this; indeed, she and her husband felt at this stage that her mother would be safer away from the crowds which were becoming increasingly belligerent. No doubt the Dalai Lama was also unaware of what had happened to his youngest brother; and in any event, he was quickly immersed in deep troubles of his own.

He had just about finished his morning walk when the silence of the gardens was shattered by shouts from outside the palace walls—a cacophony so discordant that the Dalai Lama could not make out the words before hurrying inside to find out what was happening.

Phala went to the gates to see for himself. The main gate and portico contained steps leading up to a platform, and when Phala peered over the wall, he gasped with astonishment. A sea of faces seemed to stretch 'all the way back to the city'. In the pellucid mountain air, the vast concourse stood patiently chanting slogans. All over the Vale wisps of blue smoke trailed upwards from the hundreds of yak-dung fires on which butter tea was being warmed up. Here and there the glint of swords was caught in the early sun, while the colours of the different clothes, tents and cushions 'made the Vale look like a flower-bed.' The crowd of the previous night had been huge, but now it had increased, certainly to more than ten thousand. From dawn onwards thousands had surged out of the capital's warren of streets and streamed towards the palace. And every chanted slogan made their collective resolve abundantly clear: they were determined to prevent the Dalai Lama from visiting the Chinese camp. Nothing like this had ever happened before in Lhasa, as Phala told the Dalai Lama. The Tibetans had always enjoyed (and, really, that is the word) popular manifestations which at times crowded the puny police force off the streets; but this was something of a different order; now the people were not only defying the forces of law, they were even defying the decision of the Dalai Lama himself. It was an extraordinary phenomenon.

The great danger was that the crowd might get out of hand—

and there was soon evidence of this. Around nine o'clock, Luishar and Shasur, another member of the Cabinet, had difficulty in reaching the palace when they drove up in the Chinese army jeeps allotted to most government officials. Fortunately they were known by sight, but a few moments later a newly-elected Minister, Samdup Phodrang, drove up escorted by a Chinese driver, and the crowd, thinking the Chinese had come to take the Dalai Lama away, lost control. One man threw a stone, and, as though a signal had been given, the crowd surged forward. The jeep was overturned. As more stones were hurled one hit the Tibetan minister on the head, knocking him unconscious. It was, of course, the sight of Chinese jeeps which had infuriated the crowd, and when Surkhang arrived in a similar vehicle shortly afterwards and found his way blocked, he had the intelligence to leave his jeep and walk to the palace.

Surkhang sent another summons to Ngabo, but once again it was refused, though Surkhang could hardly know at the time that Ngabo was probably conferring with General Tan at Yutok on how to spirit the Dalai Lama out of the palace. Shortly after nine o'clock, however, a Tibetan spy planted as a cleaner in the Chinese headquarters arrived with information making it clear that 'some sort of abduction was being discussed at Yutok.' Outside the palace there was near rioting as the crowd warned government leaders that in no circumstances would the Dalai Lama be allowed to leave the palace grounds. Surkhang wasted no time. He and Phala confronted the Dalai Lama, telling him bluntly that they felt he should not visit the Chinese camp.

Though it was now barely three hours before the theatrical performance was due to start, the Dalai Lama agreed that it would be impossible to go, but still hesitated to inform General Tan, and told Phala to say nothing of his decision to the monks now arriving for the daily assembly. Thus Phakpala, who was present, left after the brief meeting under the illusion that the Dalai Lama still intended to visit the Chinese camp. He had a more than usual interest in the visit, for he had been picked by General Tan and Ngabo to escort the Dalai Lama, no doubt because Phakpala's high monastic rank would make it easier for him to 'persuade' the Dalai Lama to go if his ministers tried to dissuade him at the last moment.

Phakpala made straight for Yutok to receive his final briefing from Ngabo, who was comfortably installed in the Chinese head-quarters together with Gyamtso. For the moment, there was nothing for the traitors in Yutok to do but wait; and this they did without alarm, for everything seemed to be going according to plan. What they did not, of course, know, was that the Dalai Lama had already decided to cancel the visit. The bombshell burst in Yutok about eleven o'clock, after Phala had telephoned General Tan's interpreter with the news.

No one will ever know the stunned reactions of men like Ngabo who had plotted this coup. It is not difficult to imagine their dismay, to say nothing of the scorn of General Tan as he confronted the Tibetan traitors; but we do know one thing. The thwarted Phakpala seems to have been seized by a brainstorm, and though there are no precise details of what occurred in the next fateful minutes at Yutok—such as possible altercations between the traitors—the evidence makes it abundantly clear that Phakpala determined to try and assassinate the Dalai Lama, for we do know that he changed out of the monk's robes which he had worn at the morning meeting into a Chinese quilted jacket, dark glasses, and even put on a Chinese-style motor-cyclist's 'dust mask' which concealed the lower half of his face. Finally he stuck a pistol in his belt and set off back to the Summer Palace on a bicycle. Presumably he wore the dust mask in the hope of passing the gates unidentified. But if so, why wear a Chinese jacket? It seems absurd. He did manage to reach the main gates, where Jamyang stopped him. The crowd was not certain whether he was Tibetan or Chinese until someone tore the mask off his face and a man recognized him and yelled, 'It's Phakpala, the traitor!' The crowd started to man-handle him. To Jamyang, Phakpala was a revered monk, and ironically he was in the act of trying to drag him inside the palace grounds to safety, when Phakpala panicked and drew his pistol. It was the last conscious action of his life, for in the mounting bedlam the crowd fell on him. Horrified, Jamyang saw a Khamba's sword flash as men pulled the monk away from his bicycle. As he fell, the crowd started stoning him. 'He took a long time to die,' but when he was dead, someone sent for the Ragyapa, the outcasts who dispose of the dead. Even they would not actually handle the body. Instead, five men of the Ragyapa took off their chuba girdles and tied them to Phakpala's feet, using them as ropes to drag him through the streets.

By chance, Lundok, a monk who had often shared the early morning tea ceremony with Phakpala at Sera, was trying to make his way back to the monastery when he saw the corpse being dragged past Sho. 'The crowd had gone mad with hysterical religious ecstasy. The body was roped round the legs and dragged along head down, while the crowd ran along yelling and cheering. It was terrible—especially when I thought of the times we had prayed together.'

Later Phakpala's body was paraded through the streets of Lhasa on a horse, and we know this from a Chinese who kept a diary during this period.* Shan Chao appears to have been either a Chinese journalist or broadcaster, and naturally he put his own interpretation on what he witnessed. 'We saw a group of mounted soldiers. A bloody corpse was slung over the back of a horse,' he wrote. 'The rebels [sic] had knifed and stoned Phakpala to death and now they were going to expose his corpse in the main street to terrify the people.'

The news of Phakpala's death shocked the Dalai Lama profoundly. Such a murder by his own people was against every tenet of his religious beliefs, but Phala, who was much more down to earth, was more concerned with the deterioration in public morale. If the crowd could go wild like this, they would soon be stoning Chinese, and that would mean punitive reprisals. Now the possibility of military action could not be ruled out. With these sombre thoughts in mind, Phala, General Kusangtse, Commander-in-Chief of the Tibetan army, and Surkhang started to discuss the advisability of moving in reinforcements. Kusangtse was a man of

* 'A Lhasa Diary', published in the *Peking Review*, May 5, 1959.

fifty-seven—a typical 'army' man, spare and straight, with a trim moustache on a handsome face, who had achieved miracles with inadequate materials and lack of training facilities.

The main body of the eight thousand or so Tibetan troops was stationed north of the city where the Vale of Lhasa was dominated by a range of massive granite mountains which also sheltered Sera Monastery. Kusangtse had no illusions that 'a big row was going to blow up' which could possibly result in the flight of the Dalai Lama; to protect him in this event, two thousand troops were ordered to move south of the River Kyichu. They would cross in coracles under cover of dark. Another three thousand would file across the Vale that night—guided by the canal—and take up positions south of the Summer Palace, in case the Chinese to the south-west of the palace started fighting. Others would reinforce key positions in the city, including the police barracks near the Cathedral, while a small detachment was detailed to climb the Iron Mountain—a rocky excrescence south of the Potala—and occupy the Medical College on its summit. Kusangtse also decided to issue Sten guns to government workers in the Summer Palace who were members of the Volunteer Guards—a move which spies rapidly reported back to the Chinese, so that we find the North China News Agency reporting:* 'On March 10 it was decided that for the sake of the Dalai Lama's security, government officials and People's Volunteers should be stationed in the Summer Palace as a garrison in addition to the garrison regiment.'

As the trifling original incident—the visit of the Chinese to the Cathedral—became magnified out of all proportion and then forgotten, it is hard for us, perhaps, to understand the misery in which the Dalai Lama now found himself. All around him the forces of law and order were being taken over by the crowd, which was even issuing orders (of a sort) to his cabinet ministers. The Dalai Lama was dedicated to a policy of non-violence, and yet he was surrounded by violence, so that he felt 'as if I were standing between two volcanoes, each likely to erupt at any moment.' On the one side were his people, who had left him in no doubt as to

* In a delayed despatch, dateline Lhasa, which appeared on April 23.

their feelings; on the other was the armed might of a ruthless foe. And to the Dalai Lama only one thing mattered—to prevent a clash between the two, because if that clash came 'the Lhasa people would be massacred in thousands.' He was under no illusions about the almost impossible task that faced him: 'I must try to calm the anger of the people and pacify the Chinese, who would certainly be even angrier.' But how could he do it? How could he please both sides?

The first thing was to cool the temper of the crowds and the Dalai Lama asked Surkhang and Luishar to speak to them from the platform over the main gate.

Laboriously the Premier and Foreign Secretary—both a little tubby—climbed the steep, ladder-like steps from the gate-room— only to find that the microphone and speakers had not been properly linked up. 'It took me ten minutes to fix the speakers,' Surkhang remembers; and then he looked down on the sea of upturned, expectant faces. Surkhang was a skilful orator—and he commanded respect because of his known hatred of the Chinese— but even he found it difficult to calm the crowd, which insisted on chanting the inevitable slogans. He asked them to return to their homes 'but no one moved.' He promised that the Dalai Lama would not visit the Chinese camp. 'I told them they were serving no useful purpose in shouting outside the palace,' but still no one made a gesture.

Then Surkhang had a brainwave. 'If you have any grievances,' he cried to the crowd, 'why don't you choose some men as your representatives and I'll let them inside the palace to talk with us— and work with us.' Thus was born—out of desperation—the Freedom Committee of about sixty workers, peasants, traders, and businessmen. It was destined to work with the Kashag throughout the crisis.

At last the crowds had been pacified a little, and Surkhang and Luishar now sought an audience with the Dalai Lama. They felt they should go personally to see General Tan, apologize and explain just why it had been impossible for the Dalai Lama to visit the Chinese camp. The Dalai Lama was standing in the small,

simple sitting-room of his private apartments talking to Phala as
the two cabinet ministers were ushered in. Phala withdrew—
this was a 'cabinet problem'; he kept within earshot, however,
in case the Dalai Lama needed him. (They had their own 'code':
whenever the Dalai Lama wanted Phala to join in a discussion,
he rapped sharply with his knuckles on the small table by his
throne.)

The Dalai Lama's only question to Surkhang was, 'Aren't you
afraid of the danger to yourselves?'

Both men were, and frankly admitted it, but as Surkhang said,
'If we don't go, there'll be terrible trouble.' They had to try and
make the Chinese understand, Surkhang explained, that it was the
people and only the people who would not let the Dalai Lama go,
but that the government was striving to resume the cordial relations
which had existed before the crisis. It was a cogent argument, and
after some misgivings the Dalai Lama agreed.

It was now about one p.m.—and for Surkhang and Luishar
the troubles of the day had barely started, for they found it almost
as difficult to leave the palace as it had been to enter it. The crowds
immediately surrounded their car, forced them out of it and
searched it, 'saying that we were taking the Dalai Lama to the
Chinese camp'. In vain Surkhang insisted that they were going to
Yutok to tell General Tan why the Dalai Lama was *not* going. After
some delay, they were finally allowed to leave.

From the moment they entered the conference room at Yutok
everything went badly. Ten Chinese officers—but not General
Tan—were sitting on one side of the long table, talking and drinking tea. And there was an eleventh man sitting on the Chinese side
of the table—none other than the saturnine Ngabo. This was
astonishing, for invariably at these conferences the opponents were
ranged on opposite sides of the green table, but now Ngabo made
no attempt to join the Tibetans as they sat down. Though it had
been Ngabo's task to act as a go-between at the Chinese headquarters, this was the final insult. Presumably Ngabo thought the
time for keeping up pretence had passed. For nearly ten minutes
the Tibetan cabinet ministers stood there. No one looked up to

acknowledge their presence until the conference between the Chinese broke up, and 'one of the officers politely asked after our health.'

At that moment Tan entered the room—and any hopes of an amicable discussion vanished. General Tan was in a foul temper. His shoulders were more stooped than ever, and (to the Tibetans anyway) 'it seemed that he had been dipping into his stocks of whisky.' When he sat down at the head of the table, 'he almost bared his yellow teeth' as the Tibetans rose nervously from their seats as a mark of courtesy. Surkhang says that for at least a few minutes—a long time at a conference table—he was literally speechless with anger. He could not even mouth the normal words of greeting demanded by protocol. Surkhang explained apologetically just why the Dalai Lama had been unable to keep his appointment. While the other ministers added their apologies, General Tan remained grimly silent. The interpreter finished, and then the General, 'visibly red in the face', rose from his seat and started pacing, enraged. No man in the long conference room spoke until at last Tan managed 'after a great appearance of effort' to control his anger. He sat down and deliberately started the inevitable harangue against 'Tibetan reactionaries'. The Tibetans, with their inbred respect for good manners, listened appalled as Tan's voice rose and 'his simmering anger burst out in rude and abusive language', using barrack-room words never spoken in polite Chinese society. Shouting and swearing, he hurled allegations at the Tibetans which were so ridiculous that no sane (or sober) man would have dared to utter them. The Dalai Lama, he said, was secretly arming the Khambas. He was urging the Khambas to attack the Chinese. He had told the police to shoot any Chinese on sight. Surkhang stole a glance at the other Chinese generals during this tirade, and may have gleaned a moment of satisfaction at their obvious embarrassment.

Finally, hunching his shoulders and spitting out the words, General Tan came to the crunch with this warning: if the Tibetan government did not take immediate action to restore order in

Lhasa (something they clearly could not do at the moment) 'drastic measures would be taken to crush the opposition to Chinese rule.'

Surkhang remembers particularly the way Tan thumped the table and 'shouted almost incoherently'. Finally, looking directly at Surkhang and Luishar, Tan cried, 'The government is supporting the Khambas. You have killed several of our people. We will take Tibetan blood for this—and you two will pay.'

Both Surkhang and Luishar were convinced they would be thrown into jail then and there, the more so when the other generals started shouting. Brigadier Fu screwed up his beetle brows and yelled, 'Our government has been tolerant so far, but this is rebellion. This is the breaking-point.' And then Fu, who seemed to have a penchant for the 'punch line', added in the suddenly soft, sinister voice that seemed to match his waxen skin, 'We shall act now, so be prepared.' To the Tibetans, this could mean only one thing—military action if the Lhasa demonstrations did not cease immediately. General Tan now directed his wrath at Luishar, who also held the post of head of security.

'You are responsible for security', shouted Tan, 'but you haven't prevented Chinese being killed.' Stamping his feet (a sign of great rage in China), Tan added to Luishar, 'You are responsible for all this. I order you to produce within three days the people who killed Phakpala. If you don't, you will be publicly hanged.'

Luishar was certain 'we would never get out of the meeting alive. They would put us in the cells before hanging us in the street.' But then a curious thing happened. A Chinese soldier passed a slip of paper to General Tan, who read it, re-read it carefully, then abruptly announced, 'For today neither of you has anything to fear. You are not going to be arrested. But remember this—when this is all over, we will take your blood after a trial in the people's court.' Neither Surkhang nor Luishar ever discovered the contents of the message on that fateful slip of paper.

Late in the afternoon they left Yutok 'convinced the prospect was dangerous and involved the safety of the Dalai Lama'. The meeting had lasted more than two hours. And during all that time Ngabo had not once opened his mouth.

Any hopes of an improved situation were quickly dashed when the ministers reached the Summer Palace. The demonstrations were growing. One crowd had publicly denounced the Seventeen Point Agreement which they claimed the Chinese had broken, ceremoniously burning copies in front of the Cathedral. Inside the palace grounds, members of the Dalai Lama's personal bodyguard had held a demonstration of their own, which Jamyang remembers was also attended by about seventy junior government officials. They also announced that 'we will take no more orders from Chinese officers, and we refuse to wear Chinese uniforms any longer.'*

The meeting with General Tan had one immediate effect, however. Convinced there would soon be bloodshed, the Kashag ministers called a hurried conference in the house allotted to them in the palace grounds, which they used when they had to be in close contact with the Dalai Lama. It was well equipped with bedrooms, kitchens, servants and a long rectangular council chamber decorated with thankas, statues of Buddha, and with windows overlooking a grove of poplars.

The object of the meeting was simple: to discuss practical ways for the escape of the Dalai Lama should such a course become necessary. At this stage the ministers were thinking only in terms of fleeing to Khamba-controlled territory in southern Tibet—they had the town of Lhoka in mind—and there was no mention of flight to India. The talks dragged on for hours. All protocol went by the board. Though normally the Kashag members sat on special cushions according to rank, now they just sat down at the nearest vacant place. There was no time for a proper supper. Servants brought in tea, home-made steamed bread, dishes of cold meat. They talked as they ate.

* Though the bodyguard had ceremonial uniforms, it wore Chinese uniforms for normal duties.

Some ministers were spoiling for a fight, but Surkhang, though bitterly anti-Chinese, counselled against a showdown. 'Don't forget,' he warned them, 'that these people beat eight million Chiang Kai-shek troops. What chance would we have?' (One Kashag member—Surkhang forgets which—interrupted drily, 'A very interesting point. Better not repeat it outside. It would be bad for the morale of our people.')

All were agreed, however, that it was no longer possible to work under the Chinese. 'We knew,' Surkhang remembers, 'that they wanted to get the Dalai Lama and use him as a puppet.' Surkhang himself was convinced that if ever the Dalai Lama went to the Chinese camp he would be spirited to Peking, where he would be taken ill, forced to have specialist treatment, 'and we all knew what that treatment would be.' So all decided that it was now necessary to inform the Dalai Lama to prepare for escape, and the unenviable task fell naturally to Surkhang as senior minister. He left the meeting, went to the Dalai Lama's private apartments, and told him bluntly that it was the advice of his government that the Dalai Lama 'should be prepared if necessary to set up his government outside Lhasa until help could come from India or the Western countries.'

The Dalai Lama gave no indication of whether he expected any help from the West, which so far had shown an almost brutal indifference to Chinese activities in Tibet. 'He looked very grave, very sad,' Surkhang remembers, 'and he stood there for a few moments.' Finally the Dalai Lama said, 'I didn't think it was as serious as that. I don't want to leave my people, but I do agree that I may have to.'

This was the assurance—however vague—which the Kashag required. Swiftly Surkhang returned to the meeting. And late that night the Kashag came to an historic—and secret—decision. In order to bypass red tape they gave Phala complete power to make any plans he thought fit—even down to deciding the date and the hour. Phala may still have shared his master's hope that a crisis could be averted, but all the same he quietly sent for his personal tailor and instructed him to make up a set of ordinary

soldier's clothes. He would keep the disguise handy for the Dalai
Lama—just in case.

The gloom of the evening was relieved by one piece of good news.
The Dalai Lama's mother was reunited with her youngest son.
Since the theatrical performance had been cancelled, the Chinese
presumably thought there was no point in keeping the boy in the
camp, and so he was packed off back to Drepung in a military jeep.
His mother's servants were waiting outside the monastery gates.
They had little difficulty in persuading the boy to return to his
mother for the evening—not only because he might have wanted
to see her, but because he was bursting to tell her of the wonderful
day he had had. 'They let me pretend I was a soldier for the whole
day,' he told her.

For one man the time had come to escape. Chime had failed in his
pleas, and during the time since he had seen the Dalai Lama, he
had, without quite realizing what was happening, become a central
figure making contacts with guerrilla leaders, channelling fighters
into various groups, making sure the wives and children left
behind were cared for. From the monasteries he had begged arms.
From the government he had begged barley, trading always on his
exalted rank. Soon Khamba leaders were approaching him, knowing that he controlled a huge pool of men.

All this had had to be done in the most dangerous circumstances.
He had changed his address daily, for Lhasa was not only filled
with Chinese, but had its quota of Tibetan Communist sympath-
izers. 'Everywhere spies were looking for me,' says Chime, who
day after day dodged Chinese soldiers—even praying in small
unimportant temples in order to evade Chinese guards watching
out for him. He realized the Chinese had not given up the search
for him after his first visit to the Chokhang, the Cathedral, for as
Chime, in ordinary clothes, entered the temple, he saw a Chinese
official who had known him dressed as a monk. The man was lolling

by the door of the temple. He moved forward as though to speak. 'I stared hard and walked on without stopping,' Chime remembers. 'Once inside the Chokhang I hurried out by another door and said my prayers elsewhere.' On another occasion Chime's rooms were searched by Chinese only a few moments after he had left in the morning—and it was only by chance that the Khambas found him and warned him not to return.

Finally, on the evening of the tenth, he met several Khamba leaders in one of the dozens of small monasteries scattered within a few miles of the city. And there, by the light of the butter lamps, his Khamba leaders begged him to flee. Much as he wanted to stay, Chime could not argue. Like the Dalai Lama years previously, he had to obey the wishes of subjects who regarded his life as sacrosanct.

As the final plans for his departure were being laid, a Khamba leader presented Chime with a parcel—something wrapped in old rags. 'As I opened it, I did not have the faintest idea what it contained,' says Chime.

It was a revolver.

'Since you are a man of peace,' said the Khamba leader, 'you do not need to attack anyone. But at least learn how to defend yourself.'

Chime set off for the south almost immediately.

One last act of drama remained to be played out on this fateful March 10. During the evening, Gyamtso, the third of the Tibetan traitors, arrived at the Summer Palace bearing a personal letter from General Tan. This was the first of three letters which, together with the Dalai Lama's replies, have caused something of an entertainment for historians seeking to understand what at first sight appears to be direct appeasement by the Dalai Lama. As it happens, we have some fascinating details of this episode from four sources—the Dalai Lama, Gyamtso himself, Phala and even Jamyang, who was on duty at the gates.

It seems that General Tan had agreed with the Dalai Lama that it would be unwise to send any Chinese messengers to the Summer Palace because of the mood of the crowds, so after consultations with Ngabo, Gyamtso was chosen to bear the letter. Gyamtso says* that after he was given the letter, he went by car to his house 'where I got a horse [probably because his Chinese jeep would have been stoned] to ride to the Norbulingka. I found armed rebels everywhere along the roads to the Norbulingka, which was tightly surrounded.'

Jamyang was on duty at the gates with explicit orders to allow no one in the grounds except members of the government and the Freedom Committee. This doubtless accounts for Gyamtso's complaint that he was kept waiting an hour and a half before being permitted to enter, despite the fact that he was the bearer of a vital letter.

Eventually he was ushered in to the Dalai Lama's presence where he was warmly received for, after all, only a few days had passed since they had been debating together. 'The Dalai Lama,' said Gyamtso, 'looked very worried, sitting in a chair with his head in his hand.' According to Gyamtso, 'The Dalai Lama said to me in deep grief, "The rebels say it is for my safety, but in fact they are endangering me." The Dalai Lama told me that he had heard a monk had been killed and asked me whether I knew what the reason was. He also asked me if I had the courage to go again to the Chinese Military Area Command and asked me to tell them of his situation and what I had seen both inside and outside the Norbulingka.'

Somewhat naturally, the Dalai Lama's memory of the meeting is at variance with Gyamtso's. He read General Tan's letter, which he found to be 'written in friendly terms which would have seemed more sincere if I had not already been told of his rage by my ministers.' In the letter, Tan said he was concerned for the Dalai Lama's safety and urged him to take refuge in the Chinese camp. Though the letter was delivered with calculated indifference to Tibetan protocol (directly to the Dalai Lama instead of through the cabinet), the Dalai Lama felt it demanded a conciliatory answer

* In a long interview in the *Peking Review*, April 14, 1959.

and he sat down to reply 'in a way which would calm him down'. Argument, he decided, would be pointless, and so in his reply the Dalai Lama even spoke of his shame at the actions of his people. This and subsequent letters were later used as propaganda weapons by the Chinese with remarkable effect, and it is not difficult to understand why, for the Dalai Lama wrote, 'I intended to go to the Military Area Command to see the theatrical performance, but I was unable to do so owing to the obstruction by people, ecclesiastical and secular, who were instigated by a few bad elements and who did not know the facts. This put me to indescribable shame. I am greatly upset and worried and at a loss what to do.'

Certainly to Western eyes this is a curious letter, but the truth is that the Dalai Lama was playing for time—time for the anger on both sides to abate. And above all he feels that 'even if I had thought at the time that these letters would be quoted against me later, I would still have written them, because my most urgent moral duty . . . was to prevent a totally disastrous clash between my unarmed people and the Chinese army.'

It is not clear whether the Dalai Lama asked Gyamtso to deliver the message, though one would have thought this the natural thing to do, particularly as, according to Gyamtso, 'I had been asked by the Dalai Lama to inform the Military Command of the situation.' But Gyamtso did not leave the Summer Palace for several days. According to him, Tibetan troops refused to allow him to leave, and 'all I could do was to send my servant to the Chinese headquarters to return my theatre ticket indicating that I was now unable to leave the Norbulingka. My servant hid the ticket in his hat, so it escaped the close search by rebels as he left the grounds.'

Phala, however, has a different story to tell, for he was waiting in an ante-room when a highly agitated Gyamtso appealed for sanctuary. He was afraid that the crowds outside might lynch him in the same way they had killed Phakpala. Phala counselled him, 'It would be wiser for you to keep quiet and stay here for a few days.' And that is just what Gyamtso did. He was allowed rooms in one of the many government houses that dotted the park, and

Gyamtso's insistence that he was prevented from moving about the grounds of the palace and 'was repeatedly threatened' is proved nonsense by his own admission (in the interview) that he had no difficulty in seeing the Dalai Lama again a few days later.

For the second day in succession the Dalai Lama's mother was awakened by the sound of a jeep tearing up the road through the gates and crunching to a halt in front of the steps of her home. But this time it was a friendly jeep and she could hardly stem the tears when her daughter, accompanied by two members of the Dalai Lama's personal bodyguard, clambered out, waving a piece of paper. It was a pass from the Freedom Committee. Her daughter had come to take the old lady and her youngest son into the Summer Palace. Speed was essential. The crowds were getting more unruly. Another hour and the jeep might not be able to get through, despite the pass. After hurriedly dressing, they all crammed into the jeep. They had no time to take any personal belongings—not even the small Buddha which the Dalai Lama's mother had had in the old farm-house before the lives of simple peasants had been so drastically changed.

Inside the Yellow Wall in the Summer Palace the Dalai Lama's mother had a small four-roomed villa. Indeed, apart from the Dalai Lama's apartments, and a few rooms for servants and gardeners, hers was the only building within the walls. It was built on a patch of green on the opposite side of the small ornamental lake.

That evening, as dusk fell, mother and son met alone, and she has a very clear memory of their conversation. She even remembers that it was not too cold, though she slipped a cardigan over her shoulders before walking out to meet the Dalai Lama who was waiting for her on the lakeside. His very first words were an attempt to reassure her. 'I'm happy you've come to the Norbulingka,' he said, 'but don't be frightened—things will calm down in three or four days.'

They strolled for half an hour or so. He wanted to know the

answers to scores of questions: had it been difficult getting through
the crowds? Were the people behaving themselves? What was it
like outside the palace walls? ('I wish I could go and see for
myself,' he added.) Over and over again he insisted that there was
nothing really to worry about, 'but,' as she remembers, 'I knew
him better than anyone else and he was always calmer than usual
in times of trouble. I think he was afraid to say too much of what
he really thought in case it excited the people around him. I sensed
that he knew we were moving towards a terrible crisis.'

Only once did he make a remark of ominous foreboding. It was
when she said to him, 'I'm glad you didn't go to the Chinese
camp.'

He replied, 'It was the Tibetans who stopped me. I only hope
they won't suffer for it.'

The time came for his prayers, and even though they were alone,
even though she was his mother, she performed the ritual of
bowing three times and asking for his blessing.

Every evening after that they walked together.

A mile to the east in Lhasa city, ten-year-old Genyen was playing
with her closest friend, a Chinese girl of the same age, daughter
of one of the first Chinese colonizers to arrive in Tibet. Tan Kwee,
however, had fallen in love with Tibet. He wore Tibetan clothes,
and kept a small general store near Genyen's house—a cubby-hole
of a building crammed with cigarettes, sugar, tea, packets of
aspirin, chewing-gum, balloons, and jars of sweets into which
Genyen and his daughter would dip when the old man was not
looking.

As they played, Tan Kwee strode into the courtyard. Ignoring
the Khambas cleaning their horses near the stables, the old Chinese
asked if Genyen's father was in and when Genyen said he was not
due to return until the late evening, Tan Kwee asked if she could
give her father an important message. It was very short: 'The
Chinese are coming to say hello tomorrow.'

'That's all,' said Tan Kwee. 'Your father will understand.'

The meeting had an immediate and dramatic sequel. That night the Khambas in the stables moved out with their horses. Genyen never saw them again. The next day a Chinese officer interviewed her father, who escorted him on a tour of the stables. When she asked her father what had been happening, he replied cryptically, 'Somebody told the Chinese. But they seem satisfied—for the moment, anyway.'

The next few days dragged on, heavy with tension. And yet there seemed a hope, however faint, that given time, bloodshed could still be averted, for the leaders of the Freedom Committee were on the point of ordering the crowds to disperse when General Tan sent a letter to the Kashag which 'completely defeated our efforts'. Scornfully he commanded the Kashag to demolish a few barricades which civilians had erected. Otherwise there would be 'serious consequences'. Surkhang tried to persuade the Freedom Committee to take them down 'so the Chinese could not find an excuse for more repression', but the leaders refused. They had put up the barricades, they explained, to prevent the Chinese reaching the Summer Palace and (as an intriguing additional reason) in answer to barricades erected by the Chinese 'to protect their Tibetan supporters, such as Ngabo'. The open threat of force infuriated the crowd's leaders, who told the Kashag that they would never leave the palace unguarded, and from now on even ministers would not be allowed to leave the grounds without their permission.

The matter at issue was not very important—the few paltry barricades outside the palace grounds could never have stopped the Chinese—but it does seem that, with the sagacity of 'ordinary people' in a crisis, the Freedom Committee felt that if they gave way on this point it would only lead to further demands, and so when the Dalai Lama took the unprecedented step of calling in sixty leaders of the Freedom Committee and begged them to help him, his appeal had little effect.

The meeting took place in the Dalai Lama's reception room, a long chamber with his throne standing nearly six feet higher than the polished floor, and flanked by pillars covered with heavy silk curtains, and backed by a row of painted thankas. We have a picture of this meeting from Gyamtso, who was again in the presence of the Dalai Lama, and his version is gloomy in the extreme. The Dalai Lama, he says, was seated on his high throne, his head bowed, one hand on his forehead. Still very worried, 'his face had become darker and some of those at the meeting, seeing the Dalai Lama in such sorrow and poor health, feared he might die.' They cried (according to Gyamtso) that at all costs the Dalai Lama must live, though there were doubts as to whether he should be obeyed in the present crisis, one lama called Yishsi Dongchu saying, 'It is right for him to live, but not exactly right to obey him.' Another lama, wearing a pistol in the belt of his yellow robe, cried, 'This time we want to use the flesh and blood of our bodies.' The Dalai Lama, said Gyamtso, waited patiently as the others clamoured, and then finally waved his hand and said, 'Enough! Enough!'

Certainly the Dalai Lama's pleas had little effect. The crowds remained camping in the Vale, while several demonstrations sprang up in other areas as more and more people took matters into their own hands. Five hundred members of Mary Taring's Women's Association marched through the streets before presenting a petition to the Indian Consulate demanding (in vain) that the Consul should accompany them to the Chinese Foreign Bureau as a witness while they lodged an appeal there. The five thousand or so Tibetan troops now encamped by the River Kyichu followed the example of the Dalai Lama's bodyguard and discarded their Chinese-supplied uniforms. Even in the Summer Palace itself there were more signs of war as twice a day an ancient, wheezing truck coughed its way from the Potala to the palace, loaded with guns and ammunition hidden under tarpaulins. No wonder the Chinese diarist Shan Chao commented, 'From my window with the help of binoculars I had a clear view of the Potala and the Iron Mountain. The sills of the innumerable windows of the Potala are usually the favourite playground of doves. Now rifle barrels glint from them. Half-way up the Iron Mountain, Tibetan troops have taken up positions. At its summit in the Medical College there are more signs of military activities. Men are hauling up ammunition and other supplies.'

There was much truth in this. The palace volunteers had started practising with sub-machine-guns. Outside the walls the Khambas had 'over a dozen mortars' in addition to Sten guns. More barricades were being hastily erected as Tibetan spies reported increasing Chinese military activity. Eight miles east of Lhasa four Chinese cannon and twenty-eight heavy machine-guns were secretly moved from a construction project to Lhasa. Another Tibetan spy reported that twenty heavy guns had reached Lhasa from Bomtue, a town fifteen miles east of the capital. Two enormous Chinese military vehicles were discovered within a mile of the Summer Palace, with three soldiers in each taking instrument measurements, presumably for range-bearing. That night a hundred trucks were discovered moving towards the Potala and later making their way to the Chinese camp south-west of the Summer Palace; and the next morning, Chinese 'civilians' were to be seen perched on telegraph-poles which curiously enough did not seem to be in need of repair. Rightly or wrongly, people jumped to the conclusion that the Chinese were making artillery readings.

By March 16 every sign pointed to bloodshed, and Lhasa was quivering with a sort of corporate tension when at last any hopes that violence might be avoided were brutally squashed in an extraordinary letter from Ngabo to the Dalai Lama. It was enclosed in the same envelope as the third of General Tan's letters to the Dalai Lama.* In it Ngabo, who still refused to leave the Chinese camp, wrote that there was little hope of peace, and urged the Dalai Lama to send a sketch-map showing exactly which building he was living in. 'If Your Holiness with a few trusted officers,' he wrote, 'can stay within the Inner Wall and inform General Tan exactly which building you will occupy, they certainly intend that this building will not be damaged.'

* Though the Chinese used Tan's letters and the Dalai Lama's replies for propaganda purposes, they never mentioned the letter from Ngabo enclosed with the General's third letter.

No warning could have been more explicit, and the Dalai Lama's immediate reaction was, 'So Ngabo knew what we had only guessed: that the Chinese did intend to destroy the palace and the crowd, but still wanted to do it, if they could, without also killing me.'

Ngabo made one other interesting point in his letter. Obviously knowing the pressure which had been put on the Dalai Lama to flee, he warned him not to try, as 'the Chinese have taken the strictest measures to prevent your escape.'

The Dalai Lama did not deign to reply to Ngabo, for he felt that as long as the Chinese could not be sure exactly where he was, there was still a hope they would not open up with their heavy guns. He did, however, write to General Tan. It was to say the least a strange letter, for it said, 'A few days from now, when there are enough forces that I can trust, I shall make my way to the Military Area Command secretly. When that time comes I shall first send you a letter.' He ended on the naïve note, 'Please write to me often.'

This letter, like the others, has been used repeatedly by the Communists for propaganda purposes, and one can understand why. Taken by itself, it is a heart-cry from a lonely and desperate man who could no longer trust his people. But the Dalai Lama insists that 'I had no intention of going' and that the whole of this curious correspondence was in fact a ruse to hoodwink the Chinese and, as the Dalai Lama sees it, to persuade the General 'to delay his order to attack so that we could get the people away in time'.

It may well have also been written to allay Ngabo's suspicions that the Dalai Lama contemplated flight, for a plan of escape had already been put to the Dalai Lama who had so far refused to consider it. All the same, Phala—on whom the final arrangements would rest—was under no illusions, and on the evening of the sixteenth, he issued an edict which mystified everybody (and incidentally made him highly unpopular). He banned the use of electric torches, which had become highly popular since China had started importing them. If the worst came to the worst, Phala was not going to have some curious citizen flashing a light by chance into the face of the Dalai Lama as he escaped in a soldier's uniform.

So the evening of March 16 ended, and on this evening the peace and tranquillity of the Dalai Lama's private gardens were in startling contrast to the suspense and anxiety outside. In this garden the Dalai Lama had spent some of the happiest hours of what must have been a very lonely life, and there is something infinitely pathetic in the way in which this gentle, God-fearing man, who was trying so hard and in vain to prevent bloodshed, remembers the scene. 'The garden was quiet as usual. The peacocks strutted about with their plumes held high, unconcerned with the human turmoil; singing birds were flying from tree to tree, mixing their music with that of the fountains near the rock gardens; the tame deer, and the fish and the Brahmini ducks and white cranes were as placid as ever. A contingent of my bodyguard, out of uniform, was even watering the lawns and flower-beds.'

It was the last night the Dalai Lama ever spent in his beloved Summer Palace.

5

Tuesday, March 17

It would be hard for a writer of fiction to imagine a more tangled and implausible sequence of events than those enacted during these days of crisis, now rapidly drawing to a climax. Who would dare to invent a story of spies coming and going freely into the very palace of the ruler, of letters, almost chatty, between enemy potentates, of citizens taking over guard duties as the soldiers inside watered the lawns? And what about the cabinet ministers being searched by the populace who had camped for nearly two weeks outside the gates, while within a stone's throw Chinese soldiers were calmly taking artillery bearings? However grim the battle of wits may have been, the more one examines the official papers or re-reads the testimony of the characters who were on stage at the time, the more incredible it all seems to have been, even taking into account the Oriental nature of the drama, the great difference in manners, cultures and religion, the remote mountain-locked terrain. One has the feeling that to the Tibetans the momentous events were in themselves so unusual that they created a false and artificial excitement; it was all so new to the unwarlike Tibetan government leaders, who, compared to the ruthless Chinese generals, were like children plunged for the first time in the big international stakes of war and diplomacy. Indeed the patchwork quilt of this week of crisis becomes understandable only when one remembers the dominant role played by religion in the country. It was as though the Pope, surrounded by enthusiastic friends and a handful of guards, had elected to take on Hitler when the German dictator occupied Italy.

It was this unreal atmosphere which even made it possible for the Chinese diarist to take a joy-ride in an armoured car almost up to the Summer Palace gates. Shan Chao had got up bright and early on the seventeenth, finding Lhasa 'already too warm to wear a fur coat'. From dawn there was an air of extreme tension. 'Usually we hear temple bells and horns resounding from the Potala calling the lamas to the morning scriptures, but things are different today,' he noted, 'The bandits are showing their real face more and more clearly.' Later in the morning, 'we decided to take a look round the Norbulingka area. We set out in a big armoured car, with two smaller ones accompanying us. The rebels were building fortifications and it looks as if there is going to be fighting soon. The rebels have been busy day and night deploying troops and bringing up ammunition. We cannot just sit by and wait.'

The Chinese were certainly not waiting, for Shan Chao's was not the first armed enemy vehicle to appear in the streets, though to the world Peking Radio still blandly kept up the pretence that nothing was amiss. In this they were assisted by Nehru, the Indian Prime Minister (who must surely have received accurate reports over the Indian Consulate radio), who blithely announced to the Indian Parliament on this very day that reports of trouble in Lhasa were 'bazaar rumours', adding that the situation in Tibet was 'a clash of minds rather than a clash of arms'. There was not, he insisted, 'any large-scale violence there'.*

As Nehru was speaking, Kunchok and the Khambas were busily erecting the barricades that Shan Chao had possibly seen outside the Summer Palace, while in the Potala hundreds of monks were bringing out caches of arms, long stored in secret hiding places, for distribution to the monasteries. In Lhasa itself, Thondup, of the City Council, was issuing arms and ammunition to the police and trying to clear people away from the Cathedral area as women volunteers carried stores of tsampa and butter tea inside in case of siege. Others were filling bottles to make petrol bombs.

Inside the Summer Palace, the position of the Dalai Lama had by now become almost untenable. The Freedom Committee may

* Ironically, Nehru had to admit two days later that the Indian Consulate had been hit by shellfire.

still have recognized him as both God and King, but now they not only insisted on controlling the guards, but had actually started to censor all letters leaving the palace. Despite the censorship, the Dalai Lama decided on one last desperate effort, and asked the Kashag to write to Ngabo suggesting, incredibly, that the Tibetan traitor should help to get the Dalai Lama into the Chinese camp. The Dalai Lama had decided that 'I would have been willing to go there and throw myself on the mercy of the Chinese if that would have prevented the massacre of my people.' The Kashag sent a special code with the letter, asking Ngabo to use it in his reply because of the newly-imposed censorship. The letter was smuggled out by a servant, ostensibly despatched on a shopping expedition. He delivered the letter to Ngabo and returned with a brief acknowledgement, promising a detailed reply later. That letter never arrived.

Mary Taring was playing with her grandchildren just before lunch when the emissary from the Summer Palace arrived at the Taring home on the other side of Lhasa, and Mary's first fear was that something had happened to her husband Jigme. Ever since the crowds had gathered outside the palace she had been worried. The Dalai Lama was in trouble—which meant that Jigme was in equal danger. For three days she had heard no word from him. Mary was a gentle, sensitive woman, deeply in love not only with her husband, but with her three daughters and seven grandchildren, all living under her roof until the troubles were over. And Mary remembers that she could sense the storm of oppression now gathering momentum. Indeed, that was why she had insisted on her daughters and their children sharing her large, beautiful house.

The message was from the Dalai Lama's sister in the Summer Palace. Would Mary go to see her, and give her the latest report on the activities of the Women's Association? Arrangements had been made for her to enter the palace gates the moment she arrived.

The Dalai Lama's sister was subject to none of the restrictions which hemmed in the life of her illustrious brother, and lived the normal life of a Lhasa lady. She had worked extremely hard for the Women's Association, and Mary welcomed the opportunity to give her details of the protest marches which had already taken place, and to tell her of the deputation which had been to see Major Chiba, the Indian Consul, begging him to ask for Indian aid. Chiba had promised 'to send the most favourable report I can'.

Accompanied by an unarmed manservant, she walked in silence to the Summer Palace. It never entered Mary's head that she might have difficulty in returning. Indeed, she had hardly troubled to say good-bye. She did notice now that hundreds of people were moving in her direction; there seemed to be many more Chinese troops about than previously. They were also armed—and that was something new. But if she had any fears, they were quickly allayed when she met the Dalai Lama's sister,* for over tea her husband, General Kusung, told Mary cheerfully, 'There's nothing to worry about. We've lots of troops and Khambas here.' They talked for a while and Mary gave the latest reports of the Women's Association activities, after which she went to see her husband before returning home.

Jigme—who like many officials had private apartments in the park—was grave and preoccupied. Things were not going well with the Chinese, he admitted, though the Dalai Lama still hoped the crisis could be resolved. Mary thought he looked 'very tired and worried', so she did not press him with questions as they shared a late lunch, but instead talked of the children. When the time came to go, Mary rather relished the prospect of the walk. Guards helped her through the crowds at the gates and she set off without any thought of trouble ahead.

She had walked perhaps a quarter of a mile in the direction of the river when the slam of an artillery gun close at hand nearly burst her eardrums. It was followed almost immediately by the echoing roar of another gun. Then silence.

Until now, as with every moment of real drama, there had been

* She died in 1962.

a vague feeling of blind hope in the air, a sense that despite all the portents 'it could not happen to us.' But now Mary knew the moment of actual impact had arrived. The storm she had feared had broken. She quickened her footsteps and hurried towards home.

At this very moment the Dalai Lama was talking with Surkhang, Phala and several other officials in the 'Consuls' Room' which was normally used by the Dalai Lama for receiving the few foreign diplomats in Lhasa. (The Chinese always refused to meet the Dalai Lama in this room, asserting that it was for foreign consuls and they were not foreigners.) It was a beautiful, simple rectangular chamber. The throne consisted of a carved, gilded wooden divan covered with rugs. A small altar with butter lamps and prayer wheels, a few chairs and tables, completed the furnishings.

The last official had hardly been served with tea when the boom of the two shells brought the startled politicians to their feet. The guns were obviously close at hand, and those in the room could clearly hear the splash of water as one shell fell into an ornamental pond inside the palace grounds. (The other landed on marshy ground outside the gates.) Everyone—even the Dalai Lama—felt convinced that the long awaited attack had begun. Yet though they waited apprehensively nothing more happened. Nothing but silence, broken by the rising clamour outside as 'consternation and anger reached a final climax in the crowd.'

Every man in the room must have had different thoughts at this explosive moment of history, but it was left to Surkhang to realize instinctively that the most pressing danger lay not in the room where they were assembled, but outside the palace walls. If the shouting crowds got out of hand, anything could happen. Running into the gardens (and puffing slightly), he reached the main gates— just in time. Several Tibetan soldiers armed with sub-machine-guns were trying to pass the sentries. They made no bones about their objective. They wanted to lead the crowds in an attack on the Chinese. 'It would have been suicidal,' Surkhang realized. Sternly he ordered the troops to return to their barracks; and not until he was convinced that they had abandoned their plan did he return to the palace.

Phala had reacted in a different way. He was the first to realize that these must have been warning shots—and now he knew that only one thing mattered: to get the Dalai Lama away to safety. 'Within the palace everyone felt the end had come,' says the Dalai Lama, remembering that afternoon, 'and the first thought in the minds of every official within the palace was that I must leave the city at once.'

This was the moment of decision the Dalai Lama had been dreading. For days, pressure had been brought to bear on him to escape, but he had always refused, and even now, as the decision was being forced on him, he was so torn that he hardly heard the ministers begging him to flee. Once again—as in 1950—what tormented him was the fact that he knew—and knew for certain—that if he fled it would not help matters, and yet he had to flee if that was what the people demanded. For they could not realize—not even his ministers—that he and his people had been facing this, the greatest crisis in the history of Tibet, from utterly opposing points of view. The ministers, the monks, the teeming crowds outside, all of whom loved Tibet, were, as the Dalai Lama argued with himself, 'convinced that if my body perished at the hands of the Chinese, the life of Tibet would also come to an end'. Yet all his years of training and learning had made him realize that this was a false premise, that since he was the reincarnated instrument of a master who could never die, 'the end of one mortal frame is not of any great consequence.' Still a prey to all the anguish and doubts he had harboured since first the crisis broke, he accepted that the two points of view were irreconcilable: he believed he was right in not wanting to flee, but 'I knew my people and the officials of my government could not share my feelings.' Perhaps Phala may have helped the Dalai Lama to make his decision less agonizing by pointing out that if he did insist on remaining, the crowds would also remain and might be massacred, whereas when they learned of his escape they would certainly disperse, and many lives would be saved.

The only stipulation the Dalai Lama still made was that he would not make for India unless it became imperative. He still had hopes that he might be able to set up his government in Khamba-controlled territory south of the River Tsangpo.

There was one curious incident which was later used by the Chinese as propaganda. The Dalai Lama had already agreed to escape, but according to protocol, this had to be announced formally to the Kashag ministers. There was no question really of the Dalai Lama changing his mind, but what happened was highly unfortunate. At the last moment—before he replied to Surkhang's formal question—the Dalai Lama felt he had to make it clear (if only for historic reasons) that he still entertained doubts about the wisdom of leaving Lhasa. And though he made it clear that he was not being coerced, he wondered whether all who now listened to him were, in fact, making the right decision.

When Surkhang, speaking for the cabinet, said that he was convinced there was no alternative, the Dalai Lama agreed without further demur. The Chinese were later to make great play of the Dalai Lama's first 'refusal' when the Peking propaganda machine ground out the inevitable story that he had only fled under duress.

There are naturally many inconsistencies in all that happened, loose ends that would never be permitted in a work of fiction, questions which until this day remain unanswered. If a servant could reach the Chinese camp to deliver a message to Ngabo, why could not the Dalai Lama have sent the traitorous Gyamtso in disguise with a direct message to General Tan? For that matter, if the Tibetan ministers were convinced they could smuggle the Dalai Lama out of the palace, why could they not earlier have smuggled him to the Chinese camp, since the Dalai Lama had admitted that he was willing to throw himself on the mercy of the Chinese if it would save the people of Lhasa? But the most puzzling

question of all that will never be answered is: why did the Chinese
lob the two warning shells at the Summer Palace?* Possibly
General Tan felt it might help to disperse the crowds, or even
frighten the Kashag. Maybe Tan—known to be a heavy drinker—
became impatient and (not for the first time) issued an impulsive
order he was later to regret. Whatever the reason, it was a fatal
error for, as Heinrich Harrer put it at the time, 'within a few hours
of those shells dropping, the prize the Chinese commander was
playing for—the God-King whose help he needed to quell the
Tibetans—had slipped through his fingers.'

Within half an hour of the two shells falling, the Dalai Lama's
sister and her husband, General Kusung, were talking to the Dalai
Lama's mother in her small house inside the Yellow Wall. The
General came straight to the point.

'You must have a good meal!' she remembers him telling her.
'We're going to make a journey tonight, and food might be
scarce.'

She asked where they were going. Deliberately vague, he said
they would make for a small village in the mountains. She would
need warm clothes, but he would see to that. She realized perfectly
well what lay behind this sudden decision. The shelling of the
Summer Palace had been a clear enough warning of bloodshed to
come, and naturally her first thought was of her family. What
about her daughter and Choegyal—and what about the Dalai
Lama? Kusung was able to assure her that the first two would leave
with her. As for the Dalai Lama, all he said was, 'You will see him
later, so it's better to ask no questions.' Then he swore her to

* Though scores of independent witnesses interviewed by the author
saw this first shelling, the Chinese strenuously denied they had fired
on the Summer Palace. On April 20, 1959, Peking Radio described it
as 'a brazen, outright fabrication. If we really wanted to attack, why
was it that we fired only two or three mortar shells and did not return to fire even one more shell after the first had fallen in a near-by
pond?'

secrecy 'and when he did that it made me feel that somehow my son would be involved with us.'

An hour or two later—just as it was beginning to get dark—this feeling became even stronger when she saw the Dalai Lama. His private apartments were crowded—a most unusual occurrence. The Dalai Lama was standing outside his front door talking earnestly to some politicians. Two of his tutors were eagerly awaiting a few words with him, but as soon as the Dalai Lama caught sight of his mother he walked down the steps and guided her into a stroll by the lake. The first thing he asked her was, 'Is everything all right?'

'I'm confused,' she admitted. 'I'm told I have to make a journey, but nobody will tell me where or why.'

The Dalai Lama smiled at her and said three words, accenting the last one. 'Just go ahead,' he insisted, 'and the way he stressed the word ahead made me feel sure that he was going to follow.'

She was so excited—and aware of others seeking to talk to him—that at the entrance to her house she forgot the customary three bows, or even to ask for his blessing, for her daughter, youngest son and Kusung were standing on the steps waiting for her.

The General had brought an enormous pile of clothing—and some rifles. They started sorting them out—and suddenly the old lady realized that she was going to be disguised as a soldier.

'But I can't walk far with my bad knee!' she told him.

'It's only a short walk,' her son-in-law promised her, 'then there'll be horses.'

By half past eight they were dressed, for at this time, as Kusung well knew, the guard would be changed. This nightly procedure had none of the stiff formality of Western armies, but consisted merely of the old guard returning to their barracks and the new members taking over without any drill. The two women and the small boy slung their rifles over their shoulders and quietly left the inner gardens for the outer park where the motley trio, their faces half covered against the wind and the first signs of a sand-storm, tagged behind other soldiers under the watchful eye of the commander of the guard.

The Dalai Lama's mother has no detailed memory of what happened then, for she was wholly preoccupied with trying to walk. All she remembers is passing through the main gate and hobbling in the direction of the river, with her knee hurting and the rifle cutting into her shoulder. Then, when the crowds were behind her, strong arms gripped her, took her rifle and (in what was probably the Tibetan equivalent of the fireman's lift) carried her towards the Ramagan ferry.

This was the van of the escape party, which would be a cumbersome one. Not only were the Dalai Lama's mother, sister* and brother included; so were the four cabinet ministers, the Chief Abbot, several tutors and officials, plus twenty-five members of the personal bodyguard under General Kusung. On the other hand, one or two men of importance—officials known to be close to the Dalai Lama—would have to remain behind for a day or two and show themselves to the people in order both to bluff the Chinese into believing the Dalai Lama was still in the Summer Palace, and to keep the secret from the crowds outside, for if they discovered the truth, spies would pass the information to the Chinese in a matter of minutes.

But who should be the decoys? General Kusangtse was an obvious choice, for the Commander-in-Chief had been unwell and might not be fit anyway for the arduous journey. And one other man of importance remained behind—Jigme Taring. All Lhasa knew that Jigme and the Dalai Lama shared a mutual passion for photography, that he was a man of wealth and distinction—in short, the sort of man who would automatically head the list of a party escaping with the Dalai Lama. Jigme was not asked to be a decoy. He was merely not included in the escape party— and thus did not even know that the Dalai Lama was fleeing.

Phala now decided that a small group of Khambas should stay outside the gates, not only to give the impression that the Dalai Lama was inside the palace, but to confront any suspicious Chinese

* The rest of the Dalai Lama's family were abroad. Two brothers were in the US, another was in India and his youngest sister was at school in Darjeeling.

who might try to enter. They would follow the main party forty-eight hours later. Twenty 'blooded' Khambas—including Kunchok—were told that other Khambas were being transferred, leaving them on guard duties outside the walls. Some may well have wondered what was afoot. 'I knew something special was happening,' Kunchok remembers, 'but the truth never entered my head—not at first, anyway, though after twenty-four hours the rumours became fairly persistent.'

Phala now despatched six Khambas forty miles to the River Tsangpo, to warn guerrillas in the area to expect 'something unusual'. Another party crossed the River Kyichu to arrange for horses to be waiting on the south bank. A hundred troops of the second battalion of the Tibet army moved off at dusk in a south-easterly direction, to occupy a point on the river bank where the ancient Ramagan ferry—a hundred-year-old rectangular 'boat' which could carry up to fifty people—crossed the wide glacial waters of the Kyichu.

This party ran into trouble right away, when it stumbled on a Chinese patrol which had quietly occupied the Shukti Lingka at the foot of the Iron Mountain, a park and palace which ironically the Chinese had built as a gift for the Dalai Lama. The quick-witted Tibetans fired warning bursts of machine-gun fire. The Chinese, knowing there were usually armed Khambas near the river, withdrew to the Lingka.

Phala now turned his attention to the problem of how to get the actual escapers out of the palace in small groups. Twenty-five men of the personal bodyguard, including Jamyang, would be posted inside the Yellow Wall surrounding the Dalai Lama's private gardens. The men were merely warned to be ready to move at a moment's notice. All other guards were confined to areas near their barracks at the far end of the park. Jamyang, as it happens, was stationed inside the Yellow Wall near the main gate, within thirty yards of the front door of the Dalai Lama's apartments. The gate was lit by a single naked electric bulb, and he had barely reached his post, with his Sten gun crooked in his arm, when an officer thrust a rifle into his hand and told him tersely,

'Carry it as well as your Sten.' As a baffled Jamyang opened his mouth, the officer barked, 'Don't ask questions. You'll understand soon enough.'

Now Phala arranged for the escape of the cabinet ministers and tutors—men like Surkhang and Luishar whose faces were well known. Since the Freedom Committee had warned Phala that no members of the Kashag could leave the palace gardens without their permission, there would be an uproar if Surkhang and the others tried to step out and were recognized, so Phala decided that such a course was out of the question. Then he hit on an idea. He would smuggle them out, hidden under tarpaulins, in the truck which had been arriving daily with arms from the Potala, returning empty to load up again. This would also give Phala the opportunity to smuggle out the few official State papers in the palace, some personal baggage for the Dalai Lama, and the gold Seal of Office and the Seal of the Cabinet*. Only one danger remained. How would the 'empty' truck pass the vigilant eyes of the Freedom Committee, bent on searching everybody and everything leaving the palace? Phala decided to take three leaders, known to him personally, into his confidence. Then, as the truck left, these three would ride in the back, wave to the crowds, and shout that they were off to get more arms. As a precaution against gossip, the men escaped with the Dalai Lama.

Among the personal attendants who were to make the trip was sixty-five-year-old Lobsang Gampa, food server to the Dalai Lama, who was living in the palace grounds with his nephew Lobsang, a government clerk. The first Gampa knew of the escape was when he arrived at the Dalai Lama's apartments around seven o'clock for his normal evening call. Gampa was not, of course, a butler, but more of a manager, responsible for all the food arrangements. (He did, after all, merit a four-roomed house in the grounds.) Without an inkling of what was in store for him, Gampa entered the small sitting-room with its ornate carved table and three

* Most State papers were in the Potala together with 'the immeasurable wealth of jewels and treasures which I had inherited'. All had to be left behind.

chairs and bowed. The Dalai Lama said simply, 'We are escaping tonight—and I want you to come with us. My chamberlain will tell you of the arrangements.'

Gampa was as close to the Dalai Lama as an old family valet is to his master, or a nanny to the children; sometimes, in fact, people like Gampa are closer than families and officials; and the old man must have looked astonished, for the Dalai Lama added gently, 'It is a sad journey and no one knows where it will end. But it would be unthinkable for me to go without you.'

Still stunned at the news, Gampa made his way first to Phala, who provided him with a bundle of servants' clothes (and remembers, incidentally, that 'I laid in quite a stock of spare chubas, for I knew the party would grow.') Then the old man, clutching the parcel, returned to his house, battling against a high wind which was freshening every moment. Lobsang, his nephew, was waiting impatiently for there were strong rumours in his government office that the Dalai Lama was contemplating escape. Had his uncle heard anything? And then the quick-witted Lobsang—an intelligent youth of twenty-one—saw the bundle of clothes his uncle was carrying and asked suspiciously, 'What are you doing with those?'

We do not know much about the old man except from his nephew, but it seems that he was more of a devoted father to Lobsang than an uncle, and doted on the boy. 'He sat down on the divan next to our little altar,' Lobsang remembers. 'He looked very tired and very sad and he said nothing until I had heated the tea, and poured some into his bowl.' Then the old man, with tears in his eyes, said simply, 'Ask no questions, my son.'

'But those clothes?' Lobsang persisted.

Finally, with a sigh, his uncle slowly told his nephew enough of the truth to make him realize that the rumours were based on fact. 'You may not see me again,' he said, 'but try to make your escape.' And then he added, 'Promise me you'll say no word of this to anyone.'

'I promised, of course,' Lobsang remembers, 'and I prepared to spend the last hours with my uncle and console him, but just then a messenger arrived. All government clerks had to report immediately for military duty. I embraced my uncle and left.'

One can imagine the scene when Lobsang reached his office, which was buzzing with rumours. The couple of dozen young clerks were mystified and excited. One had been told to arrange extra food supplies, but did not know why. Another had heard that Surkhang was leaving the palace secretly. A third 'knew' that the Dalai Lama's mother had suddenly cancelled a tea party. A fourth had a friend in the Dalai Lama's bodyguard—who now, for no apparent reason, had been told not to wear his uniform. What was it all about? To these youngsters there was nothing wrong in exchanging the snippets of gossip they had picked up in the government office, but they knew that Lobsang's position was different. His uncle must be 'in the know'—and his colleagues expected him to share his inside information. Fortunately for Lobsang, who was bursting with his secret, he was spared the ordeal of having to keep the news to himself, for at that moment a Khamba officer arrived. All the boys—who as members of the Volunteer Guards had already been issued with arms—were ordered to report for duty immediately. It was windy and there was dust in the air, but they would remain on rotation guard duty for forty-eight hours.

Two miles away, across the Vale and in the city, Genyen was waiting for her father who had joined the crowds outside the Summer Palace. Though he returned each evening, she could not sleep until she knew he was home. She was too young to sense the air of desperate anxiety, the feeling of being helpless and cut off from the world in a moment of crisis, but she knew something was amiss because school had been cancelled for three days, and she remembers hearing the guns firing the two shells.

Her father arrived home about nine o'clock. Carrying a pressure-lamp, he burst the door open and cried, 'Genyen! Genyen! Get up.' Eyes blinking, she tried to focus on her father's young face in the pool of light.

'We haven't a moment to lose,' he said. 'We're going to escape.'

As he spoke, Ma bustled into the room with some clothes and boots, and announced that food supplies were ready and the ponies had been saddled.

Genyen remembers Ma giving her clothes and her father deliberately turning his back as she slipped them on, and then without turning his head asking urgently, 'Ready?' Only when she asked where they were going did he take her in his arms for a moment. It would be a journey of many days, even weeks, he told her, to a foreign country.

'India?' she asked excitedly.

Well yes, it probably would be India, said her father, and then asked why she had thought of India instead of Bhutan or Sikkim?

'Because then I can get another Indian doll!' Genyen replied.

At ten years old, Genyen was too young to be astonished at the prospect of escape, nor did she bother to ask why they were going; and it was not until later that Passang, her personal servant, told her the reason: the Chinese were still suspicious that her father had hidden some Khambas and wanted to question him. But that was later. Now her father only begged her to hurry, and they were almost ready when a thunderous knocking shook the compound gate. The chained mastiffs started to snarl. She could hear shouts, more banging. Lights appeared in the courtyard. Her father cried to Passang, 'Run downstairs, unsaddle the ponies and hide the food.' And then, as she heard the jarring screech of the big bolts being drawn back, her father, quite composed, stroked her hair and his mind must have flashed back to a time when Genyen had been very ill, for he uttered one sentence she would never forget: 'Unlucky child! It would have been better if you'd died then.'

She screamed 'Ma!' as the first Chinese kicked open the door of her room. He pointed his sub-machine-gun at her father, who stood upright by the bed, and then the soldier barked an order. Two men thrust past her, knocking the Buddha off her altar. As she stood petrified with fear, they grabbed her father and tied his wrists behind his back. She tried to reach him but a soldier held her back. She has a vague recollection of her father asking the Chinese some questions. He did not struggle, but as the soldiers pushed him from the room, he cried, 'Look after her, Passang!'

That last cry of despair made her realize more than the sight of the Chinese that something terrible had happened. Weeping, she ran to the door and tried to follow, but a Chinese with a gun barred the way. Fighting off the restraining arms of Passang, she tried to push her way past, but with a sudden gentleness the soldier put down his gun, lifted her up, carried her to her bed, and by sign language told her to stay there.

She could not. The courtyard, with its pump in the centre and the stables around, was filled with noise and light as she reached the window and peered out. A dozen Chinese were grouped around the pump. Her father's servants were shouting, as soldiers, using their guns as staves, held them away from her father who stood alone, silent and dignified. Almost laconically a Chinese soldier hit him behind the knees with his rifle-butt, so that her father's legs buckled and he flopped forward. When he managed to get on to his knees, she watched horrified as his tied wrists were looped behind his ankles, trussing him. A jeep trundled into the courtyard, and her father was thrown in as unceremoniously as if he had been a sack of tsampa.

Genyen never saw him again.

All was now ready for the escape. Spies had brought back word to Phala that the Dalai Lama's family had reached the river safely. The politicians had left without incident in their 'empty' truck. Watches had been synchronized, and the last small party prepared to leave at precisely ten p.m. The Dalai Lama spent the last moments in prayer. His simple soldier's uniform was laid out in his bedroom, ready for him to don at the last moment.

Now only three men, apart from the guard, remained to escape with the Dalai Lama—Phala, the Chief Abbot, and General Kusung, commander of the personal bodyguard. To Phala, 'it was the waiting that got on our nerves. We kept on looking at our watches, but the hands never seemed to move.' It is hard for us to realize what must have passed through the minds of these four men as they waited to leave the mountain kingdom for the outside world—the world which, ironically, they had always refused to admit. What lay ahead was not simply the crossing of a frontier—they would be leaving one world for another, their own lofty private world which had somehow epitomized peace and to which they would probably never be able to return.

Perhaps the tension, which Phala remembers was almost unbearable, gave them little chance to think of the great issues and changes at stake, for all of them knew that the slightest slip could wreck the carefully contrived plans, especially the obvious danger that the Dalai Lama might be recognized. To make matters worse, Chinese searchlights suddenly stabbed the sky from a dozen points.

It was at this moment, with an hour or so still to go, that something very close to a miracle occurred. Almost as though ordained by divine providence, one of the worst sandstorms Lhasa had ever known wrapped the city, the Vale and the Summer Palace in a swirling brown veil. Sandstorms were common in Lhasa at this time of year, and the high winds all day had made Phala hopeful, but according to those who escaped, there had never been a sandstorm like this.*

With the force of a storm at sea, the dust and grains of fine sand tore into the waiting crowds. Men closed their eyes, held their mouths tightly shut—yet, even so, the sand almost blinded them and made them choke. The multitude of loyal Tibetans outside the palace walls could do only one thing—wrap their chubas round their faces and wait until the storm passed. It had a physical force that was frightening. Lobsang remembers how the eddies 'almost

---

* Though to the Tibetans spring sandstorms are commonplace (Phala merely described it as 'There was a lot of sand about') Heinrich Harrer, in his admirable account of the Dalai Lama's escape, says, 'As I see it, their miraculous escape could not have been achieved without the astonishing and timely intervention of this sandstorm. I have myself experienced them. They obliterate everything.'

seemed to turn corners', for as he made his way round the edge of one building, a wall of sand hit him on the body with such force that it almost knocked him down.

After half an hour the first full fury of the storm was spent, but still the noise of the swirling sand deadened all other sounds; and among other things, the moving, twisting brown curtain obliterated even the Chinese searchlights.

At nine-forty-five p.m. Jamyang stood by the gate of the Yellow Wall, eyes screwed tightly against the sand, mouth clamped tight, though nothing could stop the sand gritting into his teeth. As a hand slapped his shoulder, he turned his face to the wall, shielding his eyes with one hand. It was General Kusung. The Commander spared him only a few words. 'His Holiness is going to escape in ten minutes,' he said. 'We are going with him. When he comes out of his quarters, you will hand him your rifle. Tell the others to be ready.'

With the sand biting into his face Jamyang darted along the inside of the wall to the nearest guard, warned him, warned him to pass the news along—and so, in the manner of a relay race, every man was quickly told. Back at the gate Jamyang waited—and tried to keep his eyes open.

Thirty yards away in his bedroom the Dalai Lama was taking off his monk's habit and dressing in the unfamiliar uniform. He went to his prayer-room for the last time, sat down on his throne and read the Scriptures until he reached a passage in which the Buddha was telling a disciple to be of good courage. Then he closed the book quietly, blessed the room and turned down the lights. 'As I went out, my mind was drained of all emotion. I was aware of my own sharp footfalls on the floor of beaten earth, and the ticking of the clock.'

Phala was waiting for him on the steps, watching as the Dalai Lama stood in silence for a few seconds, 'the saddest sight, the most awful moment,' Phala remembers, 'I have ever known in my life.' At the gate, under the glare of the solitary electric bulb,

Jamyang stood rigidly to attention. The Dalai Lama had taken off his glasses and so at first Jamyang did not recognize the man in the simple maroon-coloured chuba, the cap pulled down over his eyes, the lower half of his face shielded with a scarf. The figure stood on top of the steps in front of the heavy golden-coloured doors, the sand swirling around him, and looked back only once. He was holding something in one hand as he walked towards Jamyang. When he reached the gate the Dalai Lama stopped and Jamyang handed him the rifle. The Dalai Lama slung it over his shoulder to complete the disguise. As Jamyang returned to attention, the Dalai Lama handed him a jagged piece of stone. It was the fragment of a sacred charm which the Dalai Lama had broken into tiny pieces. Then he was gone through the gate, with Jamyang and one other soldier following, the others having been told to scatter as the Dalai Lama 'walked through the dark garden which contained so many of the happiest memories of my life.'

They made their way across the park to the main gate, heads bowed against the whistling sand; Phala, Kusung and the Chief Abbot were in front, with the Dalai Lama, flanked by Jamyang and the other soldier, following closely on their heels. The gate was barred. Phala went on ahead and told the guards he was making a tour of inspection—for which an escort of soldiers would be normal. The members of the Freedom Committee saluted him, and opened the massive, old-fashioned complicated lock.

As Phala walked through, someone in the crowd yelled, 'Who are those people?' and a wag with a sense of humour cried above the wind, 'It's Phala! Better not light your torches!' No one took any notice of the three humble soldiers walking side by side, the sound of the sand deadening their footsteps as they passed unchallenged into the dark and towards the river beyond.

6

When men have succeeded in a dramatic and successful bid to escape, it must be hard for them to realize that for those left behind —particularly those unaware of what has happened—there is no lessening of the tension that hangs in the air. To the citizens of Lhasa, still clamouring round the Summer Palace, nothing had changed since the sound of the two shells, and 'there was still,' as Kunchok observed, 'a grim determination to prevent the Dalai Lama going to the Chinese camp.' Inside the palace grounds, where hundreds of employees lived and worked, the daily chores proceeded as usual. The horses were exercised the next morning, the mastiffs in their concrete kennels at intervals along the wall were fed at dawn. General Kusangtse made regular appearances before the crowds. Jigme Taring was busy dealing with deputations during the two-day hiatus between escape and bloodshed.

Despite the increasing sense of frustration, the impotent anger against the Chinese during these two days of stalemate, Jigme Taring found an extraordinary cheerfulness among the crowd 'and it would be wrong to picture the people as being unremittingly grim.' Here they were, away from their homes, eating nothing but tsampa, drinking nothing but butter tea for days on end, living with the prospect of an instant crisis which would tear their lives apart—and still they laughed and joked, fathers flew kites with their children, women cooked endlessly to slake the communal thirst for tea, and there was hilarity whenever (as often happened) a kettle of chang—a Tibetan barley beer—appeared. It was cold in the mornings, but the spring flowers, the trees in bud, must have helped to keep morale high.

It is difficult to estimate the size of the crowd, for it had by now been swollen by hundreds, if not thousands, of Khambas and nomads who cheerfully camped in the Vale merely for want of something better to do. The Tibetans are great campers and picnicking is in the nature of a national sport, so all and sundry joined in. Jigme Taring talked to one group of nomads who frankly admitted that they had no idea why the people had gathered round the palace. They had come from far away, seen the great crowds—and camped there. Others may have wanted to return to their homes, but this was becoming increasingly difficult, for the Chinese were quietly disposing troops in a north-south line, virtually cutting off Lhasa city from the area west of the Vale— this latter area including the Potala, the Summer Palace, the Iron Mountain and the Indian Consulate. At Sho, below the Potala, Chinese troops were preparing to dig trenches across the main road, and their patrols were ranging as far south as the river bank. The Shukti Lingka—which covered several acres—had been transformed into an armed camp.

This we know from hindsight, but to the ordinary people, nothing had changed. Mary Taring still faced the problem of reaching her children. Genyen was trying to discover news of her father. Lobsang was dutifully keeping the secret of the Dalai Lama's escape from his fellow workers, though rumours were multiplying. Kunchok, still on guard outside the gates, was beginning to feel certain that the Dalai Lama had escaped and was wondering how he could sneak an hour or two off to meet Tsering Dolma—for he was astute enough to realize that if the Dalai Lama had gone, the Khambas would probably be ordered south soon, and he had to see her before he left. Shan Chao noted in his diary, 'You don't have to ask what's going to happen. Those who have their eyes and ears open are polishing their rifles and bullets. I have taken out my hand grenades and will put them by the side of my pillow.'

Shan Chao had cause to be worried for, though the crowds

outside the palace could not realize it, there was feverish Tibetan activity. More and more Tibetan troops, equipped with machine-guns, mortars and a few pieces of artillery, were lining up for battle, though they must have known that their ancient cannon, which had to be wheeled into position by mules, could never be a match for the modern swivelling Chinese howitzers which by now stood at almost every exit from the city.

And most significant of all, a thriving black market had sprung up in bullets—Chinese bullets, which the soldiers were selling through Chinese traders for the equivalent of two shillings each.

On the Tuesday, the Women's Association marched in the biggest demonstration so far, and though it can hardly claim to have changed the course of events, it did have one happy result: it was the means of bringing Kunchok and Tsering Dolma together.

For day after day Kunchok had been itching to see her, for he wanted to put one question to her: if, as he felt certain, he was ordered south, would she come with him and later try to reach India? Finally he implored his group commander to give him a few hours off. (One must remember that the guerrillas were unused to the stiff formality and discipline of army life. 'Our discipline,' as Kunchok put it, 'is reserved for fighting.') And so, as Kunchok tells the incident, he and his 'commanding officer' sat down together with two bowls of tea to see what could be done. The first thing Kunchok learned was that his worst fears had materialized. The unit was moving south the following evening.

That left Kunchok with little more than twenty-four hours in Lhasa. Why the rush? he asked. It appears that the Chinese were becoming increasingly suspicious that the Dalai Lama had fled. General Tan had demanded that he should make a 'personal appearance to prove he was well'. Reports said that if he did not, Tan was considering shelling the Summer Palace. In other words, the magnificent bluff had succeeded for two days, but soon the bluff might be called. And when that moment came—indeed before that moment came—every Khamba would be needed south of the river for massive delaying operations once the Chinese set off in pursuit.

Kunchok was granted his few hours of freedom, though he had no idea how he would get through to the city until his officer casually let fall a piece of news which delighted him. He advised Kunchok to take the lower road, as it might be difficult to get through the northern road by the Potala because the Women's Association was staging a mammoth demonstration at Sho. But that was wonderful! 'I nearly jumped for joy.' For if the women were demonstrating, then he could be certain that Tsering Dolma, one of its most active members, would be there.

Once Kunchok had reached Sho, all he had to do was wait until the solid phalanx of women came into view, marching along the Yutok Road towards him, singing, carrying banners ('Tibet for Tibetans')—so many women that as the first ranks reached Kunchok he was almost driven off the dusty road by their mere number. He plucked up courage and quickly persuaded Tsering Dolma to leave the procession (which was to end at Sho, anyway) and they started walking back to Lhasa, taking the roundabout northern route. This looked like being Kunchok's last day in Lhasa and he wanted to visit once again the Chai Tsonkang café in Shagyari Street where they had spent so many happy hours together. When they reached the restaurant, however, it was boarded up, and notices—significantly in Chinese as well as Tibetan—announced that it was closed until further notice. Even more ominous, Chinese sentries were mounting guard at its entrance.

Eventually they found another restaurant that was open, and it was here, sheltered from the dust, that Kunchok begged Tsering Dolma to flee with him. It would mean leaving an old mother. But he was offering her a new life in a new country. After an hour of coaxing and argument he could not make her promise, but she did agree that she wanted to come, and she would let her mother make the decision that same evening. If her mother gave her consent, then Tsering Dolma would meet Kunchok in the square at Sho the following afternoon. If she didn't turn up, then he would know that her mother wanted her to stay. At the last moment she shyly gave him a keepsake—a charm box in silver and gold and begged him to wear it on a sash under his chuba.

By now the Dalai Lama was well south of the city, Once through the palace gates, the small party had trudged along the dried-up bed of a tributary of the River Kyichu, at one time within two hundred yards of a Chinese patrol, though again the Dalai Lama's luck held, and the sandstorm hid the royal party. Now and again they met knots of anxious people demanding the latest news. Phala would have to stop and talk to the leaders while, as the Dalai Lama remembers, 'I stood and waited, trying to look like a soldier.' Finally, after walking through a willow grove which had been planted by the Dalai Lama's old friend Heinrich Harrer and which helped to shelter them from the sand, the party reached the river bank and barely half a mile of white sand-dunes dotted with the dark clumps of bushes separated them from the ferry. A touch of unconscious humour lights this scene, for the Chief Abbot was a giant of a man who insisted on carrying what the Dalai Lama remembers was 'a perfectly enormous sword', with which 'he adopted a very threatening attitude at every bush.'

Finally they reached the ancient Ramagan ferry with its ferocious horse's head on its prow. Several coracles—each one of yakskin and easily carried by one man—had also been collected. Thirty picked Khambas were waiting, and despite the need for urgency, the Dalai Lama had to waste precious time ceremoniously exchanging scarves with the guerrilla leaders.

There seems to have been a slight change of plan at this juncture, the ferry being discarded in favour of coracles—possibly because the sandstorm was abating and the smaller craft would be more difficult for the Chinese to spot. On the far bank of the river ponies were waiting (though without any good saddles, the Dalai Lama remembers wryly) and the party moved off without further delay.

They were still within range of the Chinese camp—indeed, the Dalai Lama could occasionally see its winking lights across the river—as the Khambas led the way over stony tracks hardly visible in the dark. Several of the party soon lost their way, and only joined the others because they could hear the clink of flinty stones. Once the Dalai Lama himself missed the track and had to turn his pony round when he found himself on his own, with the party plodding into the grim, barren wilderness ahead.

Their first objective was to put the wide Tsangpo river,* about forty miles south of Lhasa, behind them, but they did not dare to follow the main tracks leading south from Lhasa in case of meeting Chinese patrols. Instead they made for a lesser-known ferry crossing at a small village called Kyishong, or 'Happy Valley', for once they crossed the river there, they would be lost in the vast ranges of snowtipped mountains which no enemy—particularly a mechanized one—could penetrate in strength. The entire area was a major Khamba stronghold with scores of tracks, used for centuries by Tibetan mule and yak trains, leading to Bhutan or India. The Dalai Lama was still hoping to remain in Tibet, but was shrewd enough to realize that 'if the worst came to the worst we would always have a line of retreat behind us.'

The eighteen-hour journey to Happy Valley was in its way as difficult as anything the Dalai Lama was to face on the later stages of his escape. Not only was there no time for rest, but between Lhasa and the Tsangpo lay the 17,000-foot Che-la pass. By travelling through the night, they reached the foot of the pass at eight on the morning of the eighteenth just as the sun was rising over the peaks. In a stupor of fatigue the column struggled on and up the long steep climb that would take them above the snowline.

In this machine age, it is growing increasingly difficult to imagine what it must have been like on this wild journey across virtually unmapped terrain, especially as most Tibetans took it for granted, so that men like Jamyang—and even the Dalai Lama himself— give one only a hazy picture of the monotonous, grinding climb

* In fact the River Kyichu flows into the River Tsangpo, which in turn becomes the mighty Brahmaputra river.

over the loose flinty 'steps', the uneventful hours, broken here and there by the flash of a cataract or waterfall to change the scene; the absence of people, and above all the sense of utter loss as they left their Holy City behind, perhaps never to be regained. They were half-way up the Che-la when an old man—doubtless more used to mountain climbing than the party or their lagging ponies—caught up with them and offered the Dalai Lama 'a graceful pure white horse'. More than that: the old man accompanied them to the top, and made so light of the journey that the party quickened its pace.

By mid-morning they were there, and Jamyang remembers the thrill of excitement that ran through the party as they reached the summit, marked with wands of prayer flags and a cairn of stones. The Dalai Lama dutifully placed another stone on the pile and looked ahead to the valley spread like a carpet below, with the ribbon of the river which would be their natural barrier of defence glinting in the distance.

Che-la means 'Sandy Pass' and, once over it, the Dalai Lama was faced with slopes of sand; and the excitement of reaching the summit was such that Jamyang suddenly saw the Dalai Lama (surely, despite everything, revelling in the sudden freedom from protocol) almost slide down in his haste. The Dalai Lama himself remembers how 'we could run down leaving our ponies to follow,'* after which the long winding column struck a swifter pace and soon reached the ferry at Happy Valley on the Tsangpo.

A large crowd had assembled on the far river bank. Khamba soldiers mingled with village headmen dressed in white with yellow badges. This was the first village the party had struck since leaving Lhasa and many of the villagers were openly weeping, so that the Dalai Lama felt 'even sadder. There, I thought, were the people of Tibet who had lived in their Happy Valley for centuries

* It is customary in Tibet to ride uphill but to walk downhill, and there is even an old Tibetan proverb which says,

> If you do not carry him up a hill, you're no horse,
> If you do not walk down the hill, you're no man.

in perfect peace and harmony; and now grim fear stood over them and threatened all they lived for.'

There was only time for a brief rest before the party pushed on to a small monastery where the Dalai Lama rested for the first time in eighteen hours. Behind him at the river, three hundred picked Khambas of the Khelenpa, or Suicide Squad, remained to guard the vital ferry. And it was here at Happy Valley that a ferocious battle was shortly to take place—a battle which could have allowed the Chinese to cross the river and almost certainly cut off the Dalai Lama's escape.

It is difficult to know exactly when the Chinese suspicions that the Dalai Lama had outwitted them crystallized into certainty, but it must have been late in the afternoon of the nineteenth, for Gyamtso, who had complained so bitterly at being 'imprisoned' in the Summer Palace, told the *Peking Review* that 'on March 19 three Tibetans told me I was free to leave, saying that the Dalai Lama had already gone.'

There were other signs. Late that afternoon General Tan sent officers to the Indian, Nepalese and Bhutanese consulates requesting permission to search their premises for the Dalai Lama, which indicates that though the Chinese might have had no idea where the Dalai Lama was, they were fairly certain he was no longer in the Summer Palace. When General Tan's request was rightly refused, he sent another emissary to Major Chiba suggesting that all personnel of the Indian Consulate should be evacuated as quickly as possible—a clear indication of the shelling to come. Again the consul declined.

Lobsang, of the government service, who was still on guard with the volunteers, says he first learned officially about six that evening, after a leader of the Freedom Committee had been summoned to the palace and handed a letter. It was from the Dalai Lama. One of his last acts before leaving had been to write to the Committee thanking them for their loyalty and begging them not to open fire unless they were attacked. In the letter he promised to

send detailed orders as soon as he was freed from 'the immediate
dangers and restrictions of my present situation'.

For forty-eight hours—ever since the moment when she had left
Jigme at the palace and set off for home—Mary Taring's life
had been a jumbled, chaotic nightmare. The trouble had started
almost immediately after those two separate booms of gunfire.
She had hurried through the crowds of men and women, surging,
pushing, yelling, towards the river south of the Vale, skirting the
Iron Mountain. She had walked half a mile when she came to a
small bridge over one of the many streams flowing into the Kyichu.
And there, on the far side, was a Chinese machine-gun post, with
a polite young officer who told her firmly that she could not pass.
She had to reach her children, she explained. With exquisite
politeness the officer said she could not. Finally she prevailed upon
him to take her to his superior officer. 'It won't do you any good,'
he replied courteously, 'but if you insist.'

Accompanied by a soldier, he led her to the Shukti Lingka.
This was the first Mary knew about the Chinese occupation of the
park they had given the Dalai Lama (thus making it holy ground)
and she was horrified. The once-peaceful park bustled with
military activity. Officers barked orders, soldiers scurried everywhere, jeeps roared in and out. Machine-guns and mortars ringed
the park. The snouts of heavier guns peeped from underneath
camouflage netting. Mary was so astonished that she blurted out,
'But this belongs to His Holiness!' The officer assured her that
the Chinese would only remain until order had been restored.

After an hour of waiting, the commander still refused to see Mary
and though it was by now nearly dark, she left and walked back
in the direction of the Summer Palace. Half-way there she called
in at the Indian Consulate, for Major Chiba was an old friend and
she vaguely hoped that he might be able to use his diplomatic
status to get her through the Chinese lines. But Major Chiba was
busy with non-stop radio messages between Lhasa and New Delhi,
and she set off again for the palace—and Jigme. The shellfire,

however, had changed everything. Khambas, police, even some Tibetan troops, ringed the crowds and she could not get near the palace. Finally she had to spend the night in the house belonging to the Dalai Lama's mother, where she had been invited several times for tea.

The next morning she set off again for the palace, but no one except armed soldiers could have forced a passage through the dense, milling throng, some armed with guns, others with staves or picks, with knives or even axes. Still Mary refused to acknowledge defeat. Somehow she would reach the children, though she realized she must first get rid of her clothes and effect some disguise; only then might she be able to slip through the Chinese lines.

Finally she decided to make for Drepung Monastery, four miles or so west of the Potala—which meant that she would not have to pass the Chinese lines. She would try and find some of the young monks who regularly visited the Taring house for meals and to collect food parcels. (It was a normal practice among rich Tibetan families to help feed the poorer young monks and in some cases adopt them.) She would persuade them to accompany her as her monk 'children' after she had disguised herself as a peasant woman, for that too would look natural to the Chinese, as most families offered one or more sons to local monasteries and kept in touch with them afterwards.

Dead tired, she reached Drepung on the Wednesday night, to find this vast, self-contained monastery housing over seven thousand monks in a pandemonium, and though Mary was unable to discover what was happening, we know the reason for the excitement from Chopel Tashi, a young monk of twenty-eight who later escaped to India. Just as Mary arrived, Chopel had finished his evening prayers and was watching a procession of three horse-drawn carts slowly approaching in the sunset, with the Chief Abbot waiting to greet them and their precious cargoes in person. For Drepung, the largest monastery in Tibet, one of the 'three pillars of the state' was being armed for resistance, and though the monks might in theory be forbidden to take life, there can be little doubt that many like Chopel were secretly delighted at the prospect of defending themselves against an enemy which had sworn to exterminate them.

It was also something new, thrilling and unexpected for men whose lives traced a regular, uneventful pattern. With an almost childish excitement, the monks in their maroon robes waited until the carts finally drew up before the gates of the monastery, and then they all—Chopel included—set about helping to unload five hundred government rifles, thousands of rounds of ammunition, together with several mortars, which they carried to a storeroom behind the chapel. The guns had come from the arsenal in the Potala, and were being issued to most monasteries near the capital.

Mary knew nothing of all this, though obviously she was aware of the stir in the normally placid routine of the monastery, with the monks walking briskly, the younger ones excited—and with nobody paying her the slightest attention. It was not until the following evening that she was able to find her two young protégés, for the simple reason that all the younger monks had been taken out for elementary rifle practice.

Quickly she explained that she wanted them to pose as her sons. Both were delighted at the prospect of the adventure, and easily obtained permission to accompany her. Mary agreed to meet them at dawn. She had already decided where she would get her disguise.

In the middle of the night—actually, in the early hours of the twentieth—the sound of heavy, sustained gunfire woke the startled monks of Drepung. As they ran out, Mary looked through the window. Flashes lit the sky to the south-east. The slow, echoing roll of heavy cannon hardly seemed to stop. None knew just what the barrage signified—that the Chinese had started the systematic shelling of the Summer Palace; and that for the people of Lhasa the real killing was now about to begin.

7

Friday, March 20

Long before dawn the Chinese had ringed the city with tanks and every main exit had been blocked. Truckloads of troops roaring through the main streets of Lhasa during the night had established machine-gun posts and barricades at critical points. We do not know what was in the Chinese mind, but they appear to have disposed their forces with two main objects in view: firstly, by establishing several strongpoints in the Cathedral area, they hoped to contain any violent Tibetan reaction to the shelling of the Summer Palace; secondly, by reinforcing their rough north-south line, they planned to prevent the Summer Palace crowds, which were known to contain many armed Khambas, from returning across the Vale to Lhasa. Even though General Tan had wilfully ordered the shelling of the palace, the Chinese troops do not seem to have been disposed with the idea of making unprovoked attacks, but more as a precautionary measure, for General Tan knew the threat of an uprising was too great to be ignored, and it was this factor, more than any other consideration, which determined the positions of his strongpoints.

During the night the Summer Palace had been shelled intermittently for five hours, but though several buildings were hit, Jigme Taring says the damage was not as extensive as the first reports indicated, and there were few casualties. (One stray shell knocked out the ancient plumbing system for the Dalai Lama's English bath, though the bath itself was undamaged.)

According to the Tibetans, the shelling started at two a.m. and was confined to the Summer Palace. According to Shan Chao, it started much later and was more widespread, for he described the

133

scene at length in his diary: 'March 20. It was already long after midnight. The weather had turned cold. I put on my overcoat intending to take a stroll in the courtyard before going on with my editorial work. Just as I stepped out, bursts of flame came from the Norbulingka and the Potala. Instantly the whole city resounded with rifle and artillery shots. I looked at my watch. The time was exactly forty minutes past three. Everyone was up and listening to the guns. The radio announcer Dekyid Drolkar kept on asking "Why don't we attack? Are our artillery asleep?" No one could pacify her. Nobody went to bed. We sat up till daybreak.'

Jigme Taring, on the other hand, says the barrage started at two o'clock. It was intermittent and there was certainly no report of firing in other parts of the city. Shan Chao's impression of heavy firing in 'the whole' city does not tally with that of the Tibetans who were in Lhasa that night. They say that though there were sporadic outbursts of firing, the real fighting did not start until after dawn.

To get a clear picture (all the more difficult because of the awkwardly named streets) it is perhaps worth while dwelling for a moment on the scene as it was at dawn.

In the city, the Chinese had established their strongest fortified post in a big house at the corner where Shagyari Street joined the rear entrance to the Cathedral. They had also occupied three other houses from which they hoped to dominate the cobbled square in front of the Cathedral. Wide and spacious by Tibetan standards (wide enough, anyway, to have a traffic policeman on a dais), Shagyari Street was the Piccadilly or Fifth Avenue of Lhasa and boasted some fine houses, including a four-storey building with a large flat roof at the corner dominating the Cathedral, and which was now bristling with Chinese machine-guns at every window, while mortars on the roof were ready to lob shells into the Cathedral.

Half-way up Shagyari Street, the reason for the sentries which Kunchok had seen outside the Chai Tsonkang was now obvious. The Chinese had occupied Lhasa's most popular restaurant with good reason, for it faced the capital's sprawling fruit and vegetable market—a warren of alleys which could afford shelter to countless guerrillas. The market in fact lay between two roads—Shagyari Street and Thatchen Street which ran parallel to it—and in Thatchen Street the Chinese had occupied another large house facing the Chai Tsonkang in order to dominate the market from two sides.

On the north side of the Park-hor or Sacred Inner Ring* the Chinese had taken over a famous old building known as the Paljor House which overlooked the Cathedral square and the main exit to the Vale, and was guarded by the handsome portico of the Lubok Gate. On the other side of this gate, just outside the city walls, they had occupied the Lhasa cinema.

Against these methodically prepared strongpoints the Tibetans in the Cathedral area were woefully unprepared. Despite the fact that they had two hundred regular troops and a hundred armed police in the area (their headquarters hurriedly established inside the Cathedral) and despite the hundreds of Khambas willing to fight to the death, they had been able to throw up only two barricades. Outside the rear gates of the Cathedral, a timber and sand-bagged machine-gun post had taken shape. In addition, hundreds of men had torn up the old cobblestones in the square for a second makeshift barrier which was reinforced with anything the Tibetans had been able to lay their hands on—old chairs and tables (not that there were many), bales of cloth from the row of Nepalese shops that were a feature of the Park-hor, while hundreds of flower-pots and old tins already filled with earth and with a few early flowers in bloom topped the rough and ready breastwork. Above the Nepalese shops, which were invariably on the ground floor, machine-gun barrels peered out of the small windows.

Inside the Cathedral the night had passed in feverish activity, with Thondup of the City Council co-ordinating the various preparations. At twenty-eight, Thondup was the youngest member of the four-man Council of Lhasa, a post to which he had been

* The Park-hor or Sacred Inner Ring circling the Cathedral is the collective name for a series of differently-named streets which run into each other. For the sake of simplicity these names have been omitted.

elected after joining the government service at eighteen. Tall, thin, with nervous gestures, his handsome aquiline face seemed at first to be almost forbidding. 'He always looked,' one of his colleagues remembers, 'as though you weren't even in the room.' But when he answered a complicated question, 'you knew he had taken in every word.' Thondup was also a man of great courage, of immense drive; nothing dismayed him, nothing exhausted his energy; so that by dawn the once-peaceful mecca of the faithful presented a startling appearance. Women had blocked up all the outside apertures with bales of wool drenched in water to make them bullet-proof, leaving only slits for the dozen or so Lewis machine-guns and about a score of mortars which comprised the main strength of the armoury. Hundreds of men and scores of women were camped in the great central courtyard, with the smoke of dozens of tiny fires drifting upwards to the open sky. Ammunition dumps lined one wall. Provisions were stacked against another—sacks of tsampa, skins of iron-hard butter, bricks of tea, the carcases of dried meat, the last adding what to us would be a ghoulish touch, for the Tibetans freeze their animals whole, with the heads on, so that they look embarrassingly lifelike. Thondup reckoned there was enough food and ammunition—with unlimited water from a well in the courtyard—to withstand a siege of several weeks. Contrasting incongruously with this warlike picture were hundreds of lamas already at their scriptures before some of the Cathedral's two thousand images or statuettes, illuminated by thousands of lamps which required more than fourteen thousand pounds of butter a week to keep them flickering.

So much for the city. In the Vale, the Chinese had concentrated on reinforcing their north-south line, which was not of course a continuous line in the accepted military sense of the word, but consisted more of a series of strongpoints. The Chinese had moved one group of tanks north of the Potala, knowing this building to house the greatest arsenal in Lhasa (but not knowing that thousands of guns had already been distributed to the monasteries). In front of the south face of the Potala, by the hamlet of Sho, the main road had been cut by a wide sandbagged trench. Still farther south,

where the Vale became meadowland studded with poplars, the
Chinese had reinforced the Shukti Lingka with heavy artillery to
be used against the Tibetans on the Iron Mountain.

The Tibetan army still controlled both river banks—or rather
the Chinese had not yet attacked the four thousand men deployed
there by General Kusangtse to cover the Dalai Lama's escape.
Nearly four thousand Tibetan reserves remained in their main
camp north of the city, nestling under the mountains by Sera
Monastery. The Chinese had an unknown number still in their
camp south-west of the Summer Palace.

By dawn, several unrelated incidents were in the making. In
the Shukti Lingka the Chinese had decided to launch an all-out
attack on the Tibetans on the Iron Mountain, from where Tibetan
artillery had caused considerable damage in their camp. General
Tan had also given orders for an attack in strength on the Tibetans
guarding the Ramagan ferry—for this was the only contraption
(one hesitates to call it a boat) large enough to carry armour across
the Kyichu, and Tan expected light tanks to be in full cry after
the Dalai Lama as soon as his whereabouts had been established
by spotter planes already scouring the mountains for signs of the
caravan.

None of this was of course known inside the Summer Palace,
where workers were clearing up the debris following the shelling,
and preparing to withstand a siege. With an irony that can only
occur when opposing sides are in the dark about each other's
intentions, the Tibetans had decided that their attacks from the
Iron Mountain on the Shukti Lingka were so effective that it was
worth while drawing two thousand troops from the river bank to
launch an all-out assault on this sacred park. Thus while General
Tan was planning to attack the troops at the ferry, the Tibetans
were actually weakening their forces there. One hundred members
of the Tibetan Volunteer Guard—including Lobsang—were
detailed to reinforce the regular Tibetan troops in the Medical
College on the summit of the Iron Mountain.

In the city itself there were no plans—only a blind, collective
urge to get to grips with the Chinese. As in East Berlin, as in

Budapest, as in Prague, ordinary simple people who had only asked to be left alone, who had hardly ever raised a finger in anger, had now been pushed so far that reason no longer counted. Lhasa had reached that moment of the spirit when even victory was unimportant, when death and defeat were preferable to inaction.

Shortly after dawn Thondup decided to climb to a vantage point under the gilded roof of the Cathedral, the highest point in Lhasa. From here the city was spread out before him. The desultory firing of the night had given way to an 'edgy stillness' and looking down, he could see Tibetans bringing up ammunition, women lugging sandbags across the square, others carrying jerricans. In fine weather, dawn—with a cold nip in the air—was beautiful in Lhasa. To the east the mountains were pink-tipped, and the altitude made the light so clear that 'it gave you the impression you were looking at a picture.' Everything and everybody seemed too sharp to be real.

Thondup turned his eye to the Chinese stronghold at the corner of Shagyari Street. Behind the lines of flower-pots that looked as though they would fall at any moment from the roof, the Chinese had piled up sandbags with the snouts of machine-guns pointing towards the Cathedral. The Chinese on the roof could not of course be seen from the ground, but from his peephole under the eaves, Thondup was able to watch them unobserved and 'it gave me a curious sense of superiority, for with a machine-gun I could have picked off every man.' In one corner of the roof Chinese troops had a coalpot going, the smoke rising from the charcoal in its funnel as they cheerfully cooked breakfast. Near-by three soldiers were sleeping on their backs, using sandbags for pillows. Another group was cleaning and reassembling a machine-gun. Though Thondup could not make out what they were saying, the sound of their voices floated clearly across the air and 'it was hard as I looked at them to realize that these were our enemies, ready to kill us, and not just ordinary people starting a new peaceful day.'

Thondup was a remarkable man. The youngest Tibetan ever to hold official rank, he had above all an uncanny ability to make other people work as a team. Much of the heroic nature of the fighting was due to this quiet, grave young man, who now decided that it was time for him to return to the ground.

At that moment the silence was shattered by the spatter of Chinese machine-gun fire. Thondup had counselled the Tibetans not to start firing, but now the Chinese had opened fire without warning, and a party of Tibetans with four machine-guns took up positions behind the cobblestone barrier facing the Chinese house in Shagyari Street. His eye was caught by scores of men running across the Cathedral's enormous rectangular courtyard—was it really only a couple of weeks since he had watched the Dalai Lama taking his examination there?—while others spilled out of the dark galleries surrounding it, tumbling down the wooden stairways as everyone made for the main gates.

Before Thondup could make out exactly what was happening, a new and more menacing sound split the air—the heavier thuds of Chinese mortar fire from Shagyari Street. The streets behind the Cathedral were tangled with running figures. As the machine-guns opened up again, several men fell—looking to Thondup just like men slumping on the ground and falling asleep. Then a detachment of Tibetan troops with Lewis guns loped towards the barricade. Shots rapped out from the Chinese-held house. Three men in the van fell as the rest hurled themselves behind the pathetic protection of the cobblestones.

Thondup realized that the Chinese tactics were to remain in their big houses rather than to venture out and engage in hand-to-hand fighting. Nor was there any reason why they should make sorties, for they held a far better defensive position than the Tibetans, who quickly lost more unprotected men. The trouble with the Tibetans was that 'they were too eager'—and this meant that they frequently forgot to keep their heads down. Their barricade had no proper gunslits and so, somewhat in the manner of a

Western film, men peeped over or round a makeshift rampart and fired a few bursts. It was an expensive way of fighting, but it was nothing to what happened next.

About twenty soldiers scrambled over the parapet and darted forward, Sten guns blazing. None could have hoped to live. Racing under the lee of the buildings, they reached the corner of Shagyari Street and then, without a second's hesitation, every man charged for the Chinese-held house. They were running straight into intensive machine-gun fire which turned the wide road into a pattern of spurting, dancing lines of bullets. All but two of the soldiers fell, though not before some had got near enough to hurl grenades into the house. Miraculously, two soldiers actually managed to evade the attacking fire and disappeared inside. Two flashing explosions showed that they had not thrown their lives away in vain.

Without warning the battle spread, though at first a puzzled Thondup, looking down on the scene, did not realize what had happened. One thing, however, was certain—the new burst of firing did not come from the Chinese for, as Thondup watched, running puffs of dust or smoke shot off the façade of the Chinese-held house in Shagyari Street as bullets tore into the plaster. The Chinese gun crews on the roof scuttled to their posts. Thondup had no idea where the burst of firing had originated as he watched 'almost as impersonally as if I were looking at a war film'. Only when he saw the Chinese machine-guns swing round did he realize what had happened.

Between Thatchen and Shagyari Streets, and almost hugging the Cathedral, was a conglomeration of houses, mostly belonging to the five hundred Moslems who traded in the city. During the night (as Thondup later discovered) a group of Tibetans—soldiers and civilians—had crept up to one house and gained the roof under cover of dark. Now he could see them clearly. They had dragged sandbags up to protect four machine-guns and a mortar. Even as he watched he saw the puff of smoke from the roof, followed a second or so later by the dull thud of the mortar. The shell landed in the centre of the group of Chinese he had watched cooking breakfast.

One minute they were there, the next they were obliterated in smoke and screams. As though stung to fury (though they could hardly have known what had happened), Chinese machine-guns from the Chai Tsonkang restaurant opened fire on the Moslem house, and then Chinese troops with sub-machine-guns spilled out of both the restaurant and the corner house and poured across Shagyari Street.

This was, in fact, just what the Tibetans wanted—they had opened fire in the hope of stinging the Chinese into direct action, for it was only when they fought at close quarters that the Tibetans had a decided advantage. One Chinese soldier hurled a grenade into the Moslem house. Others fired mortars. Covering fire from the two Chinese strongpoints sent a stream of bullets towards the house. But then an astonishing thing happened.

Out of the tiny alleys—some barely three feet wide—which separated the Moslem houses, came the Tibetans. Some had Stens, others rifles, others brandished swords as though they were extensions to their arms. Yelling ferociously, they went straight into the attack, and in a matter of seconds the empty Shagyari Street had become a battlefield with hundreds of men fighting to the death. From his eyrie, Thondup found it impossible to sort out the sides in the melée. There must have been up to five hundred men, each one (or so it seemed) engaged in a personal duel. Soon the numbers dwindled as the street became littered with dead and wounded. It was evident that the Tibetans were winning, for the Chinese were being pushed nearer and nearer to their two houses.

Due to the tangled nature of the fighting, the Chinese did not dare to open machine-gun fire on the street, yet they had to keep their guns at the ready in case the Khambas burst into the houses. This gave another group of Tibetans in the Cathedral an opportunity to act, and now Thondup saw scores of Tibetan women stumble across the street below him and dump sandbags and bales of wool at the corner of the Cathedral square directly opposite another Chinese strongpoint. Taking advantage of the lull in enemy firing, a party of Khambas raced up and, under cover of Sten gun-fire, built some sort of barricade while more women lugged up more sandbags. Before the last Chinese and Khambas in Shagyari Street had returned to their strongpoints, the Tibetans in the square had brought up five Lewis guns and two mortars, and were manning a rough and ready machine-gun post.

Now the Tibetans had three barricades, all of which could be supplied with comparative safety from the Cathedral arsenal.

In this first pitched battle, it was the Khambas who surged into the attack after deliberately drawing the Chinese out of their defensive posts, though Shan Chao's diary version is, perhaps understandably, somewhat different. 'At ten o'clock sharp,' he noted, 'our troops launched their counter operation. It was a stirring moment for the people of Lhasa and Dekyid Drolkar was elated, her voice on the loudspeaker came over strongly, excited and full of spirit. From our watch-tower we could see the rebel positions in utter confusion as soldiers ran for cover.'

The worst tragedy on this first morning of bitter fighting took place outside the Chinese Transport Centre which was besieged by a peaceful crowd of some hundreds of unarmed demonstrators, including many women and children. It appears that a vast concourse marched on the Transport Centre—an ugly, sprawling building which the Chinese had built near Yutok—waving banners with the inevitable slogans. On their way others had joined in, including more children. Still singing lustily, they reached the patch of green in front of the building. Machine-gun barrels jutted out of the windows but the crowd felt no alarm for these popular manifestations had long been a normal part of 'occupation life' and had always been tolerated by the Chinese.

According to Peking Radio* the crowd sang patriotic songs, then started tearing down Chinese posters and pictures of Mao Tsetung, replacing them with posters 'Go Home Chinese'. No one has ever been able to explain just how the crowd was able to produce posters of this sort out of thin air, and one might be tempted to regard this minor expression of Tibetan solidarity as

* April 4, 1959.

exaggerated had not Peking Radio specifically complained of the crowd 'tearing down posters near the Transport Centre and substituting inflammatory slogans against the state'.

The Chinese, however, have never made any mention of the tragedy which followed—one which duplicated to a remarkable degree a similar tragedy in Magyarovar during the Hungarian uprising in 1956 when eighty-four young unarmed demonstrators were killed by Communist machine-guns.

According to the Lhasa survivors, the few troops inside the Chinese Transport Centre building tolerated the crowds. The demonstration, however, was also seen by the Chinese occupying the cinema. Whether or not they panicked we do not know, but four Chinese machine-gun teams were sent out. They crossed the Turquoise Bridge and deliberately fired into the unsuspecting crowd with casualties that have never been determined to this day.

All over the city pitched battles were springing up on this bloody Friday, on which (at a fair estimate) between two and three thousand Tibetan civilians died. In some cases the people of Lhasa achieved miraculous successes, though they must have known that the ultimate result could never be in doubt. One large crowd, led by Khambas, even managed to attack the sentry-boxes and walls of the main Chinese camp south-west of the Summer Palace. From somewhere they had obtained an ancient field gun and a team of mules to haul it within range of the camp. They fired six rounds, causing extensive damage before the Chinese had time to bring out their modern swivelling cannon and blast the gun and its crew.

There is no doubt that the Khambas scored their biggest victories when they could tempt the Chinese out of their strongpoints, or if they came across a patrol by chance. At the far end of That-chen Street, near the Lhasa meat market, a party of guerrillas on the prowl came across a Chinese patrol. The Chinese bolted—but not quickly enough. The Khambas chased them, killing every man.

This sort of minor skirmish (perhaps of no military importance but of immense moral value) was duplicated all over the city, often with civilians taking part, and inevitably ending with a Tibetan victory, for every single account stresses the genuine Chinese fear of the Khamba sword—something quite understandable, for one must remember that the Khambas, in much the same way as the Mamelukes fighting Napoleon in Egypt, had been brought up from birth as an élite cadre of supermen who regarded fighting with the sword as their natural destiny. Not for them the traditional Tibetan and Buddhist doctrine of non-violence, and the Chinese knew it.

Women frequently took part in the attacks. Many carried home-made petrol bombs to hurl against Chinese outposts. Casualties among the women were high on the first day—including twenty who were trapped in the Women's Association building and refused to surrender to a Chinese patrol. Like the demonstrators at the Transport Centre, they were machine-gunned.

By the afternoon, scores of fires had sprung up in the tinder-dry wooden houses, and yet the Tibetans could make no real dent in the Chinese strongpoints. Paljor House, which dominated the Lubok Gate, resisted several attempts by suicide squads of armed civilians.

Even the Potala came under artillery fire, according to Shan Chao, who remarked in his diary that 'our artillery now turned to the Potala,' though he hastened to add, 'however, we saw shells exploding only on the concealed pill-boxes at the foot of the palace, we found later that our artillery had been given orders that no shells should fall on the Potala.'

His version hardly tallies with that of a twenty-year-old Tibetan regular soldier, Gyantsen Chopel* who was in the Potala at the time. 'Our job was to prevent the Potala with its priceless treasure from being invaded,' he remembers. 'When the Chinese tanks appeared north of the Potala, they deliberately fired on the building, causing a great deal of damage. Even men on guard on the south face of the Potala could feel the vibrations of the direct hits

* Now a schoolteacher in Mussoorie, India.

on the other side. After shelling us, a small party of Chinese tried to get into the Potala by the north gate. We drove them off with machine-guns and grenades.'

Much of the heroic fighting on this and subsequent days was due not only to the natural bravery of the Tibetans, but to one other cause which deepened its significance. The flight of the Dalai Lama was by now common gossip in the capital, but no one knew where he had gone. All they did know was that, wherever their spiritual leader was hiding or travelling in the mountains, the Chinese troops would do everything in their power to ferret him out. Any thoughts of compromise with General Tan were forgotten. The people of Lhasa, knowing only that their God was being hunted like an animal, were seized with a fury that made them utterly indifferent to the overpowering odds against them. All they blindly realized was that every hour, every minute, in which they could kill or contain Chinese troops in Lhasa must help the Dalai Lama, wherever he was by now.

All over the city men, women and children were caught up in the wake of revolution. By the evening of the first day, thousands— especially those with families—were trying to escape; not necessarily on the long road to India and freedom, but more often to relatives outside the city. Most were turned back, though some were luckier. Yet even when they did escape, they sometimes faced agonizing decisions.

Dolma Lhaki, the beautiful twenty-two-year-old wife of Gormo Rimpoche, an incarnate lama,* had just given birth to a son when the opportunity came to escape. Dolma, however, had not enough milk in her breasts to feed the baby, and she knew there would be no hope of finding milk on the journey. Yet would it be fair to her other children if she insisted on remaining? Dolma was given an hour to make up her mind. In the end she gave her newborn child

* Normally it is impossible for an incarnate lama to marry. Dolma Lhaki says vaguely that she was 'given as a bride to the lamas'. Gormo says 'I know that no incarnate lama should live with women. I have broken the rules and I am sorry, but I cannot deny that I am happy.' They both live now in India.

away to friends who she knew could feed it, and left, never to see it again.

Genyen was not thinking of escaping—not on the first day. After her father's arrest, Genyen had gone to Tan Kwee's sweet shop round the corner and changed a pretty dress for servants' clothes. Then she set off to try and find news of her father. The search was hopeless, of course, for long before the end of the first day the forlorn streets, lit by occasional fires, bore the stark imprint of war: smashed houses, uprooted trees, electric light and telephone poles wrenched down by the Khambas, leaving a curtain of trailing wires like grotesque weeds. Here and there the skeletons of burned-out carts and the occasional jeep littered the dusty roadways. Genyen came across one jeep lurching at a drunken angle with its front axle in a hole dug by Tibetans. Two dead Chinese in the front seats looked as though they had fallen asleep. North of the city she came across four burned-out trucks, now rolled over on to their sides to form a barricade behind which crouched a score of Khambas—including three or four who had been dipping into a kettle of chang. Farther on she met a party of civilians armed with rough crowbars and axes; they were tearing up the shining steel bars of a miniature railway which the Chinese had installed between two camps—and which they presumably did not dare to come out and defend.

Oddly enough, there were two oases of comparative calm untouched by Friday's fighting. The Tibetans did not attack Yutok, where Ngabo was already drafting the proclamation which would herald a Chinese victory. And the Summer Palace was also left alone after its night of shelling, though it is hard to understand why General Tan refrained from attacking it after meting out such punishment before dawn.

Inside the Summer Palace the defenders were taking no chances. The huge grounds—no longer sacred—bristled with guns as more than a thousand Khambas and troops prepared for a fight to the death. Walls were unceremoniously pierced to make gun-slits. The ornate houses of high government officials became armoured strongpoints. Several cannon appeared, together with mortars and machine-guns. All were old by our standards, but all were serviceable.

Jigme Taring was undecided about his future. He had been unable to get word from his family; yet he knew that if he were caught he would face the prospect of immediate execution. For the first time he had to consider escaping without them, now that his role of decoy was ended. Yet what had happened to his children? And what had happened to his wife?

Mary was almost at the end of her tether. After the night of gunfire she realized that she could not, for the time being anyway, hope to reach her home. She would lie low for a few days, then perhaps try again. And so Mary decided to make for a small farm a few miles north of Lhasa, which belonged to relatives.

The simplest way to get there from Drepung was to strike north from the Potala, though she realized that Chinese troops must be encircling it. Shortly before midday she and her two 'sons' left Drepung with its layers of buildings reminding her of a vast, fortified city. She knew where she would obtain her disguise. At the foot of the monastery was an outcast butchers' village which catered to the monks and also acted as slaughterers (receiving the feet, head and intestines in payment). There she exchanged her beautiful clothes for a greasy chuba and an equally dirty striped apron. She was just about to take off her scarlet boots (which she particularly liked) when she said to herself, 'No! I'm going to keep them!' And she did keep them—though as she set off on the road to Lhasa she found it extremely difficult to make them look old and dirty. She took them off, she rubbed them first in sand, later in marsh water, yet they still looked new.

In order to be every inch a scrofulous peasant, Mary pretended to be lame and walked with a stoop, dragging her feet. To add to the impression of an old hag, she resorted to one more device: she took out her dentures and thrust them in the pouch of her chuba. Somehow she and her 'sons' reached the Potala and made for the barricade at Sho. A Chinese dug the barrel of a gun into her ribs and demanded her business—giving Mary just the chance for which she had hoped. Opening her toothless mouth, the bent old crone grinned and cackled while her two 'sons' explained that they were taking their mother back to her village.

'Well, walk faster!' cried the sentry.

Mary had hoped that at Sho she could strike northwards, but once at the hamlet she was caught in a dense mass of people, and the Chinese flatly refused to allow any to pass the trench which they had dug right across the main road. Directly facing them, on the other side of the trench, another mass of Tibetans was trying to cross in the opposite direction. Mary felt the crowd behind her pressing. Though she was actually within a couple of feet of the trench, an officer waved her back as Chinese troops fired a few volleys over the heads of the crowd. Any attempt to cross the trench would fail, so Mary decided to retrace her steps and try and walk northwards from a point outside the city.

Just as she was about to turn back a curious, if unimportant, thing happened. In the jumbled faces on the other side of the trench she saw a beautiful girl whom she immediately recognized as a regular attender at the Women's Association meetings. She was in tears, begging the Chinese to let her cross to Mary's side, while the Chinese troops, holding their rifles horizontally, started to push the crowd back. Mary saw the girl hold up her hand and wave.

As Mary trudged back in the direction of Drepung, she could not get the girl's beautiful face out of her mind, perhaps because of a vague irritation at not being able to place her. It was not until she had left the Potala far behind that Mary remembered who she was—Tsering Dolma, the daughter of a widow who lived near the Association building.

Though we shall never know what happened, Tsering Dolma and her mother must have talked far into the night, for hers was a problem as old as history—having to choose between a mother and a lover; and right up to the last minute when Kunchok set

148

off to meet her, he had felt certain she would not keep their tryst. He had barely two hours before his rendezvous with the Khambas when he set off to cross the marshy land of the Vale towards Sho. In the distance he could hear firing in the city. He managed to scramble over a low wall flanking the main road only a few yards from Sho. Seething crowds jammed the road where he had arranged to meet her, and not until he reached it did Kunchok realize that two files of armed Chinese were guarding the trench with its breastworks on either side.

And then his heart leapt. Tsering Dolma was there! She was waving violently from the other side of the trench. And that meant that she had chosen to come with him. Excitedly he waved back, unable to believe she was so close, even if still separated by the strip of no-man's-land. Of course there would be delays, arguments, but she was there. Kunchok could speak no Chinese, but using sign language he pointed out his girl to a sentry. The Chinese pushed him roughly back together with the rest of the crowd.

Until this moment it had never occurred to Kunchok that they would not join each other *somehow*. The biggest battle—to persuade her to come with him—had been won. Nothing else seemed difficult. But now he began to panic. Time was running out. Obviously the Chinese were not going to let anybody across the trench, and soon he would have to rejoin the Khambas. There was only one thing to do. Pushing his way to the edge of the road, Kunchok scrambled over the wall and jumped into the soft grass, below the height of the road. Crouching, he ran under the lee of the wall until he judged that he had passed the trench and was behind the crowd on the other side.

He started to scramble up the stone wall, which was higher at this point. Kunchok was a big, tough man and it presented no problem. Gripping the top of the wall with his fingertips, he started to hoist himself up. It was at this moment that the most agonizing pain he had ever experienced shot through his whole body as a rifle-butt smashed down on his fingers. Writhing with pain, he fell in the grass as a Chinese face appeared over the wall. Kunchok had a blurred impression of a soldier taking aim as he ran. He heard the sounds of shots as he skirted the wall back to where he had started, and where he could clamber up into the crowd.

His hands were bleeding, but though the pain was intense, he could move his fingers for the soldier had only hit the fleshy tips. He managed to push his way to the front. At first he could not see her, but then suddenly she appeared. He shouted, but cannot remember if his voice made any sound. Then came the angry, irregular rhythm of light tanks. Sporadic machine-gun fire mingled with the slap of rifle bullets. The tanks came tearing down the road behind the crowd on the other side of the trench. Dully, Kunchok watched the guards line up, holding their rifles with both hands crossways like bars in a gymnasium, to form a fence so they could push the crowd back. The tanks came rumbling round the edge with jerky movements, then twisted in front of them, by the side of the trench. Kunchok had one last glimpse of Tsering Dolma waving to him and then she cried out some words he could not understand. Again she shouted, and he caught one word— 'Tsona!' He remembered she had relations in the small town of that name.

Then she was lost to sight behind the brutal outline of a tank; but at least Kunchok knew where he would eventually make for when the business of fighting was over—Tsona, not far from the Indian border.

That evening Kunchok and his colleagues prepared to cross the river by coracle. Their destination was a small village on the Tsangpo which he had never heard of. Its name was Happy Valley.

By nightfall a hundred Volunteer Guards had climbed the five-hundred-foot Iron Mountain and reached the Medical College. It was the first time Lobsang had been to the summit, from which one could see Lhasa, the Vale, and directly below, the Shukti Lingka—from which shells were whistling into the ancient, four-storey Medical College where from time immemorial would-be monk doctors had taken an eight-year course in mumbo-jumbo. The garden outside was littered with bodies, already freezing. The rooms were crowded with untended wounded; the Volunteer Guards settled in and prepared for a last-ditch stand.

Far to the south, the Dalai Lama's party had, after leaving Happy Valley, swollen to a hundred, escorted now by more than three hundred troops of the regular Tibetan army, plus nearly a hundred guerrillas. The unwieldy party made such slow progress along the narrow tracks that it was decided to split up during the day into small groups, a move that would also lessen the chance of detection from the air. From time to time they heard the drone of enemy aircraft, when all would scatter and take shelter, though fortunately the weather remained overcast.

One curious phenomenon attended these small groups, numbering perhaps fifty people each, and perhaps wondering what would happen if the Chinese suddenly appeared in the lonely mountains —as they might have done at any moment. They were meticulously guarded—by men they could never see. Each mountain, each pass, each thick forest of rhododendrons, hid hundreds of invisible Khamba warriors, silently following the Dalai Lama, keeping out of sight yet in some strange manner acting like a huge protective cloak, passing the word along from one mountain peak to another that the God-King was approaching.

Even the Dalai Lama found the atmosphere almost uncanny as he plodded on, to all intents virtually unescorted, yet despite the silence, despite the apparent absence of armed might, knowing that 'we were surrounded by faithful determined men whom we never saw.'

Until now the Dalai Lama knew nothing of the uprising in Lhasa. He had a small battery radio, but Lhasa Radio was off the air, and only once did he catch a brief mention of the capital when the Voice of America reported 'unrest in the city'. Because he was unaware of what had happened, the Dalai Lama still hoped to remain in Southern Tibet and was making for the fortified town of Lhuntse Dzong, within striking distance of the Indian frontier.

So, with an irony hard to match, the Dalai Lama, still knowing nothing of the savage fighting in Lhasa, pushed slowly southwards, in the belief that the misery of his flight—made against his own innermost convictions—had at least saved the people of Lhasa from massacre.

Nothing mattered except for the straggling party to put as many miles as possible between them and Lhasa, for every day, every hour, increased the risk of Chinese pursuit. Once at Lhuntse Dzong, the Dalai Lama planned to try to reopen peaceful negotiations with the Chinese, for he still hoped that 'while I remained in Tibet, the Chinese might see some advantage in coming to terms.'

In the heart of Lhasa the street fighting died down by sunset and an uneasy calm wrapped the city, broken only by the occasional shot. One has the impression that the Chinese were anxious to keep the revolt as local as possible, and doubtless this is why they did not bring in tanks on the first day; perhaps General Tan hoped that after a night's sleep, the Tibetans would think twice before returning to the attack.

Thondup, however, was wondering whether there were more sinister reasons for the lull in the Chinese attacks. Like everyone else, he had no idea of the whereabouts of the Dalai Lama, but it seemed to him inconceivable that the Chinese, with all the armour and modern aircraft at their command, were not by now on the trail of the escaping party. If the Chinese felt that the capture of the Dalai Lama was imminent—if, for instance, they had spotted him and were closing in—might that not be a good reason for General Tan to call off the attack in Lhasa? The thought, he remembers, passed swiftly. Since he knew nothing, he had to act on the assumption that the Dalai Lama was still free—and fight with every weapon the people of Lhasa could muster.

So far the Chinese had not opened fire on the Cathedral, and now Thondup—who could hardly remember the last time he had slept—was trying to organize some order out of chaos. Though nobody had counted the number of civilian dead, the Tibetans in the Cathedral area had lost two hundred or more Khambas and soldiers. Still, every position had been held, even the isolated Moslem house. And the Tibetans had certainly killed five Chinese for every Tibetan lost. Now Thondup wanted to plan tomorrow's attacks—including one on the cinema, not as revenge for the outrage on unarmed demonstrators, but because if the cinema were in Tibetan hands, the way would be open for reinforcements from the Vale.

All around this severely handsome man, the new 'inhabitants' of the Cathedral were preparing for their first night of siege. The cooking-pots glowed, strangers pressed bowls of tea on him, dimly seen forms slouched asleep on every spare inch of the courtyard. In the alcoves and the chapels the monks prayed as though nothing untoward was happening. Thondup knew they were not concerned with success in battle or freedom from the Chinese. They were praying for mankind, for the future, for eternity. All the same Thondup felt a sudden compelling urge to join them.

He stayed praying for nearly half an hour and then, feeling strangely refreshed and almost light-headed, he called the leaders to his office in the Kashag to put in train the plans for tomorrow's battles.

8

Saturday, March 21

A bizarre character now makes a brief appearance in this chronicle. Rupon Gurgur was an ageing policeman whose duties consisted of helping to guard the Cathedral. He was a hunchback,* as well known to the people of Lhasa as the hunchback of Notre Dame is known to readers of Victor Hugo. His duties were negligible, for some years previously he had been given a sinecure post after the Chinese had broken his back during a brutal beating. Though nearly seventy—a ripe old age in Tibet—he was remarkably agile. Now his moment for revenge had come.

The most serious problem facing the Tibetans, now virtually isolated in the Cathedral area, was the fact that Chinese troops in the cinema just outside the city effectively prevented any reinforcements reaching the Cathedral, which already had the air of a besieged fortress. Any civilians trying to return to their homes by way of the cinema, which lay near the main raid, would be mown down, as the attack on the unarmed demonstrators outside the Transport Centre had proved.

Thondup realized that the cinema—which bore the romantic name of Dhekyi-Wonang, meaning 'Happy Light'—would have to be stormed, whatever the cost, for only then could the road from the Turquoise Bridge and the Vale be opened. And so, in the early hours of Saturday, he summoned police chiefs, army officers and civilians to a conference in the Kashag council chambers on the south face of the Cathedral. There is no doubt that Thondup's natural qualities of vigorous leadership, backed up by his official

* Gurgur is the Tibetan word for hunchback.

status as a council member, made him an ideal planner of aggressive action. Now he discussed ways and means of driving the Chinese out of the cinema.

There was no shortage of arms. Machine-guns, mortars, grenades, automatic rifles, together with ammunition, had been stored for years in the Cathedral arsenal (as in most Tibetan monasteries). Nor was there a shortage of volunteers. Thondup's plan for the attack—which would have to start under cover of dark—was very simple, and took into account the fact that at the south-west corner of the Cathedral, south of the Lubok Gate, the street outside—part of the Inner Ring, of course—was skirted by a low wall, in front of which fields with clumps of trees stretched towards the cinema. The long grass and trees would offer excellent cover, always providing the attackers were backed by heavy covering fire. And this could be done, for the mortars would be directed from behind the wall, hidden by a curve in the road from the Chinese in the Paljor House.

Thondup planned to let seventy volunteers creep through the fields and woods to the very walls of the Happy Light cinema—just the sort of exercise in which the Tibetans revelled. There they would wait for a signal—the mortar fire. At the same moment, the Tibetan machine-gun posts in the square and at the rear of the Cathedral would open intense fire as a feint. A messenger was also dispatched to the Tibetan-held Moslem house, and the occupants warned to open fire the moment they heard the sound of machine-guns.

During the night, women from the square were brought into the Cathedral and started to carry mortar shells up from the cellars below. It must have been a fascinating scene—the disorder of a besieged arsenal, the stir of military preparations, yet with a curious calm as monks prayed by the rows of butter lamps. 'There was an air of safety inside,' for no Tibetan even remotely imagined that the Chinese would dare to shell the holiest place in all Tibet. So the lamps were burning in the two courtyards as the files of women emerged from the cellars below and walked past the praying lamas, each woman clutching her apron, filled with grenades, as nonchalantly as a farmer's wife bringing in the eggs.

Long before first light the Tibetan volunteers crept out in twos and threes, scrambled over the wall, and were lost in the fields, while Gurgur, who had some knowledge of mortars, was placed in charge of the battery of five mortars, together with a sixth hidden behind the Lubok Gate (so that it could not be fired on from the Paljor House). This would provide intense covering fire, but there was one problem: 'We suddenly realized we didn't have six men who knew how to fire a mortar.' Thondup himself was going to lead one of the machine-gun crews operating the feint manœuvre, yet it was essential for the Chinese in the cinema to believe that this was an attack in force. A few sporadic shots would be of no value to the Tibetans waiting to charge into the building.

It was then that Gurgur spoke up. Thondup cannot recall his exact words, but in effect the hunchback pleaded, 'I can handle five or six mortars easily. The women can have the shells ready for me, and I'll run from one to another firing them.' And that is just what the old man did.

Shortly after four a.m. Thondup in the Cathedral square fired the first bursts into the Chinese strongpoint. Almost simultaneously, the Tibetans in the Moslem house opened fire, and within a few seconds came the duller thud of the first mortar. It was not the first mortar, however, which Thondup was anxiously waiting to hear. It was the second, the third, the fourth. Incredibly they came—one boom after another in quick succession. As Thondup raced back through the Cathedral, he almost knocked Gurgur down, for the old man was not darting from barrel to barrel, he was actually carrying one on his (literally) broad shoulders. Thondup realized immediately that most of the ancient mortars must have been defective, and as he ran out to help, Gurgur lowered the mortar. A woman with her apron full of shells handed him another. Gurgur fired—and almost before the smoke had cleared, the hunchback was half-running, half-hopping, to the other end of the street. Only a few seconds seemed to elapse before the mortar roared again, and Thondup, who had seen his quota of American films on his travels, was irresistibly reminded of the old-fashioned Western with one lone survivor manning a dozen slits in a fort.

'I wouldn't have believed it possible if I hadn't seen it with my own eyes,' Thondup recalls. 'Naturally I wanted to help by carrying the mortar and giving the old man a rest. But you know, Gurgur pushed me away—and I realized that the old hunchback was actually enjoying every second of it.'

So Thondup left him and ran under the shelter of the wall to the Lubok Gate—the one place which Gurgur had not been able to reach. The sixth mortar was there. So was a woman, patiently waiting with an apron full of shells. Thondup lobbed half a dozen shells into the cinema, now glowing with the dull red of several small fires. Then on an impulse he crept round the corner of the big stone arch framing the gate, and before the Chinese had time to spot him, lobbed a shell into the Paljor House.

How long the battle for the cinema lasted it is hard to say, for the Tibetans have little sense of time. There was confusion, too, when the Chinese in Shagyari Street attacked in force and Thondup had to leave Gurgur and race back. Until this moment the Chinese had used only machine-guns, but now they opened with mortar fire, lobbing shells across the street and into the midst of the pitifully unprotected crew manning the barricade. Four people—including two monks—were killed with the first shell, and now in the grey light of dawn, Chinese troops started cautiously appearing in the street, obviously preparing for a frontal attack. Though they were mown down, it did not seem to matter. More appeared. It seemed that nothing could stop the Chinese from overrunning the post until Thondup saw half a dozen women creeping from the shadow of the Cathedral up Shagyari Street. When they were within a few yards of the enemy-occupied house they ran forward and hurled bottles of petrol into the house. Five women were shot down and left in the street.

At the same moment Gurgur came charging across the square behind Thondup's post—charging being a comparative term, for he was carrying a mortar. Two women carrying grenades followed him. Oblivious of the moans of the wounded in the post, Gurgur yelled 'We've taken the cinema!' Then he got his mortar into position and lobbed shell after shell into the Chinese house. The roadway in front was littered with Chinese dead, and for the moment the Chinese called off the attack. 'If only we had had more men,' Thondup remembers thinking, 'we could have taken the house.' But there were no men to spare—not for the moment, anyway. The pick of the fighters were in the cinema, clearing out the dead Chinese who had been wiped out almost to a man, though (as it transpired later) the Tibetans had lost forty out of seventy men.

Yet it had been a vital victory and, according to the reports reaching Thondup later, it had been a classic Tibetan attack in which, as the mortars rained down a massive dawn bombardment, demanding the total attention of the defenders, the Tibetans stormed in. The concrete building, which normally held an audience of a thousand, had a balcony, and a score or so of Tibetans managed to reach the projection room at the rear, from where they fanned out, firing down from the empty balcony into the main auditorium below, where half the Chinese had been sleeping. Others forced an entry behind the proscenium and attacked from the other end. 'It's always easier to win a battle when your life isn't important,' was Thondup's modest way of summing it up.

Once the Tibetans had control of the cinema, they quickly liquidated the barricade which the Chinese had thrown up across the road near the Turquoise Bridge. Now the besieged men in the heart of the capital could expect reinforcements.

No official word of the vicious fighting had so far been permitted to reach the outside world. Lhasa Radio had gone off the air on the first morning, and remained silent for four days.* Peking Radio's only mention of Tibet during this time was an occasional account

* Foreign Office Monitoring Service.

of construction projects on the Sino-Tibet frontier. Nehru must have known, of course, but he professed ignorance. Without doubt the Chinese were hoping the revolt would be stamped out in a matter of hours, in which case they would be in a position to insist blithely that it had never happened.

Yet, astonishingly, fragmentary news did quickly leak out of a country not only isolated from the world, but occupied by a ruthless enemy. By Saturday the London *Daily Mail* was printing a big page one story based on reports from Delhi that serious fighting had broken out in Tibet. There seems little doubt that in Delhi the news had been put about by a remarkable Tibetan-speaking Scot called George Patterson, who had insisted for weeks that Tibet was on the verge of revolt, and had so embarrassed the Indian government that Nehru had threatened to ban him from the border areas; indeed, Nehru had told the Indian Parliament that Patterson's reports had been so full of exaggeration that he had been compelled to warn him. (Patterson, of course, was extraordinarily accurate in his remarkable despatches. It was Nehru who was afraid of antagonizing the Chinese.)

The Sino-Indian conspiracy of silence, however, did have the effect of minimizing the news, simply because no factual material was available. And one must remember, too, that the rest of the world was busy with its own affairs. Details of a meeting between President Eisenhower and Harold Macmillan to plan a summit meeting with Krushchev had just filled the pages; Klaus Fuchs, the arch-spy, had been seen in East Germany; fighting in Cyprus was flaring up again; and the Easter holidays were barely a week away. In the absence of any official news, the fighting in Tibet must to the people of the West have seemed not only insignificant, but very remote.

On this Saturday—a day of savage killing—the Tibetans in Lhasa would have been dumbfounded had they known that stories of their heroism were already appearing in worldwide newspapers. Indeed, one of the factors that distressed them most—as Thondup discovered time and again—was the feeling that all this blood-letting would be in vain if the sacrifice remained hidden from the outside world. There was no Lhasa radio station any more, 'and it was terrible to think,' Thondup says, 'that perhaps nobody would ever know the way in which Tibet had staged a revolt against Communism.'

No doubt this was why several abortive attempts were made by Khambas to seize the radio station, the first target in all classical modern revolutions. One attempt nearly succeeded, though the radio station was one point where the Chinese, knowing the value of propaganda, were taking no chances. Situated near the conference room in the gardens of Yutok, it consisted—despite its grandiose title—of little more than an army hut, but it was guarded by a troop of crack Chinese. Some Khambas from the cinema actually penetrated the building, but every man was lined up and shot. The Chinese (like the Tibetans for that matter) did not approve of taking prisoners.

Though the Chinese were determined at the time to minimize the magnitude of the revolt (and thus make some people wonder if Nehru had been right in referring to 'bazaar rumours') it was the Chinese themselves who ultimately admitted—indeed confirmed—the ferocity of Saturday's fighting. This they did when they had to explain why they had taken over the country completely. Then Peking Radio—which had insisted there was no revolution—announced* that 'troops of the Chinese People's Liberation Area were ordered to take *punitive action* [author's italics] against the clique of traitors who had committed monstrous crimes,' while in another long domestic broadcast,† Peking Radio admitted that the Tibetans had 'destroyed highways of importance to national defence, bridges, dams, pulled down poles and cut electric wires and set fire to the premises of the organizations of the Central Peoples' Government in Lhasa.'

This was the scene by mid-morning on Saturday, when the battle for Lhasa—both military and civilian—was raging in a dozen

* On March 30, 1959.
† On April 10, 1959.

different places, with the Chinese by no means having it all their own way. Almost as soon as the Tibetans had captured the cinema, Khamba patrols were crossing the Turquoise Bridge towards the Chinese headquarters, looking for trouble. One band of Khambas seized a military lorry which had been left in a compound, drove to the Transport Centre, and while Khambas kept the guards at bay, loaded it up with petrol and oil before driving back in triumph through the Lubok Gate to the Cathedral square. (The petrol was needed for Molotov cocktails.)

The heady, intoxicating atmosphere of victory—even temporary victory—swept the city. As in Budapest three years previously, people realized that in the last resort the Chinese could, at the time of their choosing, crush the revolt. But this did not seem to matter. It was the moment that counted, for 'the future,' as Thondup argued, 'could be no worse than the past.' And so the very recklessness and bravado of the Tibetan attacks was if any-thing intensified by the knowledge that 'we had nothing to lose anyway.' Lives did not count—so long as you could take at least two Chinese with you. And so we have instance after instance of suicidal attacks by small groups determined to wipe out pockets of Chinese even if they presented no threat, and even if it meant certain death to the attackers.

Some people threw their lives away—others died in strange ways, as though picked out by fate. Thondup saw a woman standing behind the main barricade in the square sheltered by a burly man. She was shot dead when a bullet passed underneath the man's upraised arm as he waved to somebody.

Ingenuity knew no bounds. One party of Tibetans actually succeeded in penetrating the most important Chinese strongpoint —the house in Shagyari Street. Knowing that a frontal attack would have been impossible, they crept into a house farther up the street, bored holes through the plaster walls until they were one house closer, and repeated the operation until they were in the next house to the Chinese. From there they climbed to the roof, leapt across and killed several of the gunners before Chinese reinforcements arrived and overpowered them.

The scattered nature of the fighting must have produced a curious pattern, for merciless hand-to-hand fighting would flare up in one street, yet the next would be deserted. An hour later, maybe, the first street would be empty except for corpses, but a new and unrelated struggle would be taking place in the second street.

Thondup remembers one moment on the Saturday when the Tibetans launched yet another bloody and unsuccessful attack on the Paljor House. Helped by Gurgur and his mortars, this was the biggest assault so far—and yet, even though the Paljor House was only a stone's throw from the Cathedral gates, civilians were walking about the square, apparently unconcerned with the fight to the death around the corner. But then any Tibetan attempt at cohesive action was impossible. Nobody in one street or square knew what was happening round the corner. 'We only knew what we could see.' Indeed, in a curious way, some Tibetans hardly seemed to take the uprising seriously. In a situation not dissimilar to that of the civilians in Saigon, the menace of the fighting did not necessarily involve everyone—but that did not prevent everyone from being fascinated by what was happening. Men, women and children would actually stand and watch (from a safe distance) an engagement, as though taking advantage of some theatrical distraction in their normally drab lives. Thondup actually heard one mother threaten a child that unless he behaved he would be sent home.

Life for many went on surprisingly as usual. Despite the sandbagged posts around the Cathedral and the sudden violent battles that flared up, thousands of people were untouched by the series of localized struggles. The few cafés might have been closed, but they had never catered to more than a handful of people and so were hardly missed; food being a simple matter, entire families which had a modest stock of tsampa and butter tea merely stayed in their homes. They did not even barricade the doors. 'There was no panic,' Thondup remembers, and when he toured the outskirts he saw several families quietly eating in front of their doors as though nothing had happened, while small boys quickly became immersed in a new and fascinating game—seeing who could collect the most spent bullets.

The first Chinese attack on the Summer Palace came during the late morning. It was prefaced by an artillery bombardment, though Shan Chao in his diary insisted that 'our men did not destroy a thing in the Norbulingka, as they had been told they could fire only on places of secondary importance so that no buildings should be destroyed.' By all accounts the battle was short, fierce and indecisive, for the trimly-kept gardens of the Summer Palace had by now been turned into a vast armed park, while the empty galleries of the holy temples had become arsenals. In the absence of yaks, the blood horses from the Dalai Lama's stables had been hurriedly formed into teams to haul the cannon. The Tibetans fought ferociously, and Jigme Taring saw scores of dead inside the park, as well as hundreds outside. The temples were hastily converted into hospitals of a sort, though more than once Jigme 'saw Tibetans shoot their wounded comrades to put them out of their agony.' After the barrage had (in theory) softened up the defence, the Chinese attacked from the Shukti Lingka, but they were totally unprepared for the reception that awaited them. 'When the rebel bandits in the Norbulingka were cornered,' Shan Chao admitted, 'they put up a desperate fight, knocked out corners of houses, broke down walls, dug holes and put their rifles through.'

Survivors later said that Chinese troops tried to storm the main gates, but were driven back with heavy losses, and though one might wonder how the Chinese, with their overwhelming superiority in men and arms, could fail, one must remember that several hundred picked Khambas were inside the Summer Palace with mortars as well as machine-guns, and that the walls—'built of huge blocks of granite laid in lines' as Spencer Chapman had seen them —were more than ten feet high. Then too, the heavy civilian losses indicate that the remnants of the crowd must still have been milling around. Short of using tanks or bulldozers, the Chinese could not have launched a close-range attack, or attempted to scale the walls.

What undoubtedly happened is that the Chinese in the Shukti Lingka kept up a sustained machine-gun and mortar fire from the comparative safety of their heavily armed park, while infantry attempted to attack the gates. Whatever the tactics, the damage inside the Summer Palace was appalling. Figures vary so much—and tend to become so magnified—that it is impossible to give any accurate appraisal, and George Patterson, a man of impeccable honesty, may well have been misinformed in arriving at the conclusion that 'eight hundred shells were poured on to the Norbulingka, destroying about three hundred houses belonging to leading officials.'

Had the Chinese attack been continued, the Summer Palace, which was in a chaotic state, might have fallen later in the day, but now an event occurred which caused the Chinese hastily to call off the assault. The Shukti Lingka was falling to Tibetan regular troops.

To see how this victory came about we must go back a few hours in time, and follow the events on the neighbouring Iron Mountain which dominated the Chinese encampment, but where the Tibetan garrison in the Medical College was in its death throes.

This heroic force of fifty artillerymen had somehow managed to haul five ancient cannon up the hill, and almost as soon as the fighting had started, they had cheerfully started blasting the Chinese in the Shukti Lingka below with every shell they could lay their hands on. At first all had gone well, and they had inflicted serious damage on the Chinese. But their ammunition was limited, their guns so old that they heated up; nor was there sufficient water in the crumbling building to cool the guns. Before long the Chinese, stung by the first Tibetan onslaught, were starting to wreak a terrible revenge. With the most modern cannon at their command, the Chinese trained every gun on the summit of the Iron Mountain—and for ten hours maintained an almost unceasing barrage. It was then that the hundred government clerks including Lobsang —members of the volunteers—were detailed to climb the mountain. By the time they had reached the summit, the rain of shells was so fierce that Lobsang could barely see the shell-lashed skeletons of walls enveloped in smoke. It was no longer a college, not even a building, and certainly not a fortified position. Barely a dozen out of the original fifty men were still alive, and Lobsang almost vomited as 'I tried to avoid treading on the bodies,' for these were not men killed neatly by the small round hole of a bullet, but men 'slaughtered by heavy lumps of metal, mangled and torn, shattered into fragments so that no one could ever hope to recognize the human ruins.'

Four out of the five cannon had been smashed by direct hits. The meagre food supplies had literally gone up in smoke. There was virtually no water—and still the searing bombardment continued. Untrained in artillery, the volunteers were of no value to the remnants of the garrison. Shells were whistling down at the rate of one every two minutes. And since there was virtually no cover, many volunteers were killed almost as soon as they reached the top.

Then the commander of the artillery hit on what he considered a brilliant idea. Since he had no intention of abandoning the position, he sent the volunteer guards in Jack-and-Jill fashion all the way down the hill again—a matter of minutes when running—to collect two shells each. In this way about eighty shells were carried from the Summer Palace to the Medical College, thus affording fresh employment to the sole remaining gun.

With fanatical zeal the commander now used all the available manpower to haul the old gun from one part of the ruins to another, crunching over stones, over corpses, to give the Chinese the impression there were several guns, and to prevent the Chinese from getting its range. For two hours the bluff worked magnificently—until the Tibetan gun received a direct hit.

At this point the commander,* surrounded by dead and wounded, decided that—with or without his beloved gun—he was going to stay. 'If the Chinese want me,' Lobsang heard him say, 'they will have to climb the Iron Mountain.' He ordered the Volunteer

*We do not know his name, but Lobsang not only took part in this action; General Kusangtse had a record of the engagement and described it to the author.

Guards to return to the Summer Palace after making one last request. 'They were preparing to fight to the last bullet,' Lobsang remembers, 'so even the wounded asked us to leave all our arms. We left every Sten gun. To the best of my knowledge not one of the men survived.'

If at first this heroic action seems to have nothing to do with the Chinese attack on the Summer Palace, the truth is that, though the dwindling garrison on the Iron Mountain could hardly have realized it, their final artillery attack played a decisive part in the one major Tibetan military victory; for while the men on the hill were hauling their gun from one part of the college to another, nearly two thousand Tibetan troops from the river were marching to storm the Shukti Lingka, and it seems they arrived just when the Chinese were fully occupied with the shelling.

Easily outnumbering the Chinese garrison, the Khambas in the regular army swirled in with drawn swords, overpowering the sentries who were totally unprepared for a frontal assault. Within a matter of minutes, the Tibetan army was inside the large compound, and the Chinese commander was ordering back the troops who had been attacking the Summer Palace. It was a total victory for Tibet, and even Peking Radio* had to admit that 'rebel bandits launched a direct armed attack on one of our military commands,' while Shan Chao rather theatrically noted that 'the bandits are showing their real face more and more clearly. They are raising such havoc all through the city that it is as if some imperialist marauder had entered our land.'

Though the victory at Shukti Lingka probably averted a Chinese victory at the Summer Palace, tragically it came too late to aid the troops on the Iron Mountain. It had one other consequence. By the afternoon of Saturday, General Tan was attacking the weakened Tibetan forces on the river—and was slowly gaining the upper hand in his bid to gain control of the vital ferry.

The news from the Cathedral area was equally bad, for despite the

* May 6, 1959.

magnificent manner in which the first Chinese attacks had been repulsed, the defensive Tibetan line was now cracking badly; and though the Cathedral was still untouched, the Chinese, in a suicidal attack, overran the two barricades nearest their strongpoint in Shagyari Street. Nothing could have stopped them. Though the Tibetans still held the Moslem House—from where they poured intense fire on the enemy position—the Chinese after an hour-long mortar bombardment attacked the first barricade in force during the afternoon, killing every man defending it. Once the Tibetans had lost the barricade, they found it difficult to train their guns on Shagyari Street and the Chinese—helped by reinforcements from the Chai Tsonkang café—used the first captured barricade as a strongpoint from which to storm the second. Losses did not seem to matter. By four in the afternoon only the cobblestone barricade across the square remained in Tibetan hands. Behind that was the Cathedral, now filled with even more refugees than ever.

It was a disaster of the first magnitude, but not, after all, unexpected, for Thondup knew only too well that the Chinese could draw on unlimited reserves of men whenever they wanted to. It was only a question of time.

Genyen had combed Lhasa for news of her father, but with the revolt now flaring up in almost every street it had been impossible to discover even the smallest clue. It was not until the Saturday, however, that Ma was able to persuade the distraught child that she must get out of Lhasa, pointing out that the Chinese had in the past thrown out several suggestions that Genyen should go to school in Peking. Now they were quite capable of sending her to an indoctrination school by force.

Genyen had an uncle living near a village called Medo-Gongkar, half a day's ride north-east of Lhasa, but she knew that she could not possibly ride. Many districts of Lhasa were in flames by now, and Chinese tanks surrounded the city. Anybody, even a child, riding out of Lhasa on horseback would be arrested—whereas a beggar girl might pass almost unnoticed. But who should escort her? Ma was too old, and Genyen—who had remarkable courage and spirit for a girl of ten—insisted that Passang, her personal servant, should remain behind for a few days more to search for her father. So it was agreed that Tan Kwee would take her; after all, when Tan Kwee was dressed in his Tibetan chuba no one would ever guess that he was a Chinese who had been sent out six years previously to 'colonize' Tibet. 'Passang didn't really like the idea,' Genyen says, 'but he agreed when I promised faithfully to wait for him at my uncle's.'

For the last time in her life Genyen went up to her room to prepare to flee—the room with its Goddess of Love, its butter lamp, and the Buddha which the Chinese had knocked down when they came to take her father away. Quickly she dressed as a village girl in the old stained chuba, a white towel with blue stripes on her head, and a basket for collecting dung strapped on her back. Passang had half filled it from the stables. On a last impulse, she hid her Indian doll under the flat rock-like cakes of dung. Then she walked out of her house for the last time to meet Tan Kwee, who was waiting for her. It was nearly midnight.

Genyen's house lay north of the city, outside the perimeter of the heaviest fighting, and though she could clearly hear the occasional bursts of machine-guns and see the fires, at least she would not have to cross Lhasa, for her route lay to the north-east, on the road to Ganden Monastery—a road starting only a few hundred yards from her home.

There was only one danger point—the bridge crossing the River Kyichu (much narrower at this point) on the north-east city limits, for this would surely be guarded by Chinese sentries, and she was afraid that if Tan Kwee spoke they would quickly realize he was not Tibetan. So they agreed that he would be her deaf and dumb father whom she was taking back to their village.

The ruse all but succeeded. The Chinese at the bridge were so kind that Genyen felt they were genuinely sorry for the little girl setting off into the night with a helpless old man. After a few desultory questions they were waved past the sentry post, and she took Tan Kwee's hand, as she thought a dutiful daughter would have done, and started to cross the bridge.

It was a longish bridge and they were almost at the other end when a sentry with a torch who was guiding them across— in fact trying to help them—yelled as Genyen felt him grab the basket on her back, obviously trying to pull something out. She could not see his face, but he was holding up her Indian doll and when, without thinking, she tried to grab it back, he pushed her so that she fell down. Then he beckoned both of them to return.

What happened after that is only a hazy nightmare. She remembers seeing the glint of a knife—Tan Kwee's knife—as he pulled it from his chuba and sprang on the sentry. She remembers the torch clattering to the ground. She remembers picking up the doll which had fallen. She remembers Tan Kwee screaming, 'Run! Run!' She remembers the sound of commotion in the sentry's hut, a vague impression of Tan Kwee's arm moving up and down as he stabbed at the man—one Chinese fighting another to save her—and then she ran, ran away from the bridge into the darkness beyond.

Time and time again one is puzzled by one question: why did General Tan not use the tanks already deployed at the city's exits? And for that matter, why did he not call on more troops who were still garrisoned in the main camp? (The Tibetans also refrained from using their reserves.)

Several theories spring to mind. One (supported by several Tibetan politicians) is that since the revolt was basically a civilian uprising in which no serious attacks were ever launched on Chinese official posts such as Yutok, the Chinese were determined to try and control the revolt without repressive measures for as long as possible.

Secondly, there is no doubt that General Tan's predecessor had fallen from grace because he had allowed the Khamba uprising to become a national movement which had received worldwide publicity harmful to the Communist cause. General Tan was therefore most anxious to play down the uprising—not only in Lhasa, but probably also in his despatches to Peking.

There is still one more theory that bears examination. There is no doubt that Ngabo and his Tibetan colleagues were whole-hearted supporters of the Chinese Communists; they were not betraying their country merely for money—or at least not for money alone; and traitors of this sort are nearly always marked by one flaw: they believe so passionately in their own convictions that they cannot imagine others not sharing their views. Several Tibetans feel that Ngabo—who had a great influence with General Tan —urged him not to take even more brutal or punitive measures to quell the uprising because he was convinced that when the uprising had been crushed tens of thousands of Tibetans would joyfully thank their Chinese liberators.

Whatever the reason, by the end of the second day there were still no Chinese tanks in the streets, though the city—if not slowly running down—must have been a shambles.

On the outskirts, Khambas had cut down hundreds of poplars and willows for barricades. Looking across the Vale one could see scores of trees lying on their sides with machine-guns poking out. But the price had been high. The streets were littered with empty mortar shells and spent bullets. In some of the wealthier houses, such as Surkhang's, the Chinese had broken in and wrecked all the costly furniture, smashed mirrors, the gramophone and the radio, bedding, piling up the debris into barricades before siting guns in the beautiful gardens. In any of the houses which had shown resistance the dead had been left where they had fallen. (We know this because in several cases the Chinese changed their minds and did not remain in the looted houses which were afterwards visited by Khambas.)

Fires had sprung up all over the city—though fortunately for the Tibetans they did not seem to spread. One would have thought that when the women, with their home-made petrol bombs, set fire to a house, the fair weather, assisted by the winds blowing from the mountains encircling the city and the plateau would have fanned the flames. It was not so—possibly because the bombs were small, possibly because the Chinese were more efficient that the Tibetans would have been in dealing with scores of minor outbreaks. Certainly, it seems that it was the women who specialized in ferreting out houses containing Chinese and then hurling in their home-made petrol bombs, and there were several more instances of women being caught in the act by Chinese and shot on the spot. (On the other hand, the legend of the women arsonists of Lhasa may have become embellished with the years. Certainly, several genuine cases of women fire-raisers, such as those seen by Thondup, did occur—but then, in the feverish desperation that gripped Lhasa, it is possible that any hurrying woman carrying anything was destined to become a legendary heroine.)

Fires were not the only hazard. To Thondup, there was an even more serious problem—that of the useless mouths. After the liberation of the cinema, Thondup had hoped for reinforcements. Instead the road had remained empty. But after the defeat of the Chinese in the Shukti Lingka it had become jammed—not with troops, but with endless columns of families, the women trailing behind the men with whimpering children tugging at their aprons. Most of the dense crowds—who had been encamped outside the Summer Palace for over two weeks—were hungry, thirsty, and had been sealed off from all news of the desperate fighting in the Cathedral.

Now, however, the Cathedral, together with the ritual clockwise walk round the Park-hor, had become their first objective. And of course, nothing could be done about it, though the useless mouths were to prove one of the Cathedral's most terrible encumbrances. One can hardly call the presence of these enormous crowds a miscalculation, for there was nothing Thondup could have done about it in such an undisciplined city. But it made him angry that so many people seemed to think that the Cathedral was the safest sanctuary in all Tibet. No doubt this belief was intensified by the almost superstitious feeling that the Chinese would never dare to attack it.

Thondup was more realistic, and under no delusions. He knew the Chinese would attack the Cathedral with brutal force if they

171

decided it was in their best interests to do so. And if that happened, the slaughter would be terrible. Something—he knew not what—would have to be done about the useless mouths. They would have to be cleared away, forced to seek refuge in the outskirts of the city. If necessary, he would call in regular troops tomorrow to escort them away; the crowds which, as he walked to the Kashag council chamber, were so dense that he could hardly force a passage. Not only the courtyard, but every sacred chapel was crammed with sleeping figures, while from the Kashag he could see vast crowds of men, women and children lying huddled together on the cobblestones, blissfully certain that here, on holy ground, they would be safe.

On a sudden impulse—perhaps following a sudden premonition—Thondup held a midnight conference with senior army officers billeted in the Kashag and asked their help in getting the crowds out of the Cathedral area. The regular officers were glum. They would do their best, they promised, but with the Chinese dominating the square, the only exit for the crowds would be through the Lubok Gate and back into the Vale from where they had streamed in, and as one officer remarked dryly, 'They won't like *that*.'

There must have been ten thousand people cramming the Cathedral and square. The army estimated that even if there were no fighting it would take at least two days to escort them outside the city. But they would make a start in the morning. With that Thondup had to be content, and the meeting broke up.

Thondup was almost ready to snatch an hour or two of sleep when a Tibetan soldier arrived with a message from the Summer Palace—a message which instantly banished all thoughts of rest.

Spies had brought in reports that the Chinese planned to use their tanks on the morrow. And their first target would be the Cathedral.

9

Sunday, March 22

It was a perfect spring morning. Not even a breeze ruffled the normally wind-bitten plateau. To the east a diffused aura, like concealed electric lighting, shone from a sun still hidden below the rim of white peaks, as the first Chinese mortar shell tore into the golden roof of the Cathedral, which had stood unmolested for thirteen hundred years. It landed in the inner courtyard. Screams and near-panic gripped the hundreds of refugees lighting their small fires, believing themselves to be immune and safe. Then the rolling boom of heavier gunfire, mingling with the stutter of machine-guns, echoed from outside. The Chinese had launched their final assault to bring the city to its knees, and it took the form of a three-pronged attack.

While mortar fire was rained on the Cathedral, Chinese machine-gun fire was tearing into the crowds in the Cathedral square. For the moment, however, this was in the nature of a softening-up process, for the first main attack of the day was concentrated on the heroic Tibetans still entrenched in the Moslem House.

For two days this outpost had held out against all odds, and yet, paradoxically, nothing is known of the men who first barricaded the house. A succession of men and women had crept there with food, water and ammunition, but in the confusion none seemed able to give any concrete information about them. 'There were two machine-guns.' 'I think there were about twelve men.' 'I saw three bodies on the roof.' Yet these unknown men had inflicted heavy punishment on enemy strongpoints, for the Chinese did not relish attacking them in the only way possible—by entering the labyrinth

173

of dirty, smelly alleys separating the Moslem houses, where scores
of Khambas were hiding—and waiting.

Now, however, three Chinese tanks appeared at the far end of
Shagyari Street and trundled in file until they reached the Chai
Tsonkang café. Almost lazily they swivelled round, straddling the
street, facing the Moslem houses. Their guns were elevated, and
then they fired as one. Before the acid smell of explosives had
drifted away, they had re-loaded and fired again into the white
cloud of smoke, plaster and debris. In all they fired nine shells,
and when the dust had settled, huge gaps showed where Moslem houses had vanished. And in place of the Tibetan outpost,
there remained only a gaping ruin, jutting upwards like a rotten
tooth.

Inside the Cathedral, Thondup was marshalling the innumerable civilian refugees in an attempt at orderly evacuation. Despite
the fighting in Shagyari Street, the ground between the west wall
of the Cathedral and the cinema was still dominated by the Tibetan
machine-guns in the cinema, and all that Thondup wanted was to
get rid of the refugees before the guns were turned on the
Cathedral. True, they had to run the gauntlet of the Chinese in the
Paljor House, and many might be gunned down, but once over the
wall and in the fields, they would be comparatively safe. Hundreds
escaped this way, for the Chinese were not yet ready to attack the
Cathedral itself. First, the defenders of the square had to be
liquidated.

In Shagyari Street the tanks twisted round, then lumbered
towards the Cathedral. Thousands of the civilians outside the
Cathedral were pouring towards the Lubok Gate and the Vale,
leaving those who remained behind to stage a last-ditch stand in
front of the Cathedral gates which had been closed during the
night. None could have failed to see the signs of imminent defeat,
yet it did not seem to make any difference. At first Thondup
imagined the attack on the Cathedral would come in a matter of
minutes when the tanks rammed the gates, but for the moment
the tanks held their fire, and the first attack came from Chinese
troops surging out of their strongpoints to the sound of machine-

guns. Nor had Thondup reckoned with the almost terrifying frenzy of the Tibetans in the square—hundreds of men (and many women) who, almost in an ecstasy of fury, were pulling, grabbing, tearing at the advancing Chinese.

They were so densely packed, and the confusion was so complete, that when a detachment of Tibetan troops arrived—galloping past the cinema, through the Lubok Gate and surviving the fire from the Paljor House—they were at first of no value, simply because they could not penetrate the undisciplined Tibetan crowds from the rear. Even without their help the Khambas and civilians mowed down the first rush of Chinese, and before long the crowds were attacking the tanks with any weapon they had been able to lay their hands on.

For three hours the Tibetans managed to prevent the Chinese tanks from reaching the Cathedral gates. One tank was burned out, and not even the Chinese machine-gunners could subdue the Tibetans, despite the casualties inflicted. The Chinese, too, suffered high casualties—particularly after those Tibetan troops who had been unable to cross the square galloped round the Parkhor and attacked the Chinese from the rear. While this battle was raging in the square, more Tibetans with machine-guns drove the Chinese out of the Chai Tsonkang café—a magnificent victory.

The fighting that morning—swaying from one street to another—must have had a bizarre touch about it, for in the wake of the Tibetan troops and Khambas there always seemed to be hundreds of civilians. Some had guns, others petrol bombs, still others staves or knives; and the grotesque effect of the picture was heightened when the outcast butchers, who had their meat market at the end of Thatchen Street, came storming towards the Chai Tsonkang armed with their huge carving knives and deadly hooks.

When the Chai Tsonkang had been cleared, the mob rushed forward to help their comrades in the Cathedral square, but here they met stern resistance from the well-organized Chinese at the corner of Shagyari Street. The more disciplined troops, however, by-passed this dangerous corner, and filtered through the smoking, burned-out alleys in the Moslem area, leading into the Cathedral square, where the two remaining Chinese tanks were battling for survival. The entire square, according to one survivor, was one chaotic battlefield. Chairs, tables, beams, bricks, cobbles had been torn from the houses or road to make barricades. Khambas had chopped down the few wooden lamp-posts and electric pylons whose wires now draped the square. The plant pots (or to be more accurate, old tins) which were such a feature of the flat roofs of Lhasa were being hurled about without (as even the Tibetans admit) any discrimination. Bullets flew everywhere. Even the first yellow blossoms on the two old and sacred weeping willows in front of the Cathedral (believed to have sprung from the hair of the Buddha) were falling as stray bullets clipped them. At one time Thondup climbed up again to the eaves of the Cathedral—this time to put out a small fire. From his vantage point he could see the terrible punishment the Chinese were inflicting on the Tibetans. Yet nothing seemed to daunt them. Utterly fearless, they charged time and again into ranks of Chinese soldiers. Women hurled 'Molotov cocktails'. As he watched, a stray shell exploded at the end of Shagyari Street and the policeman's dais—that ridiculous and unnecessary symbol of 'civilization'—vanished in a puff of smoke.

Once again Thondup could see the entire battlefield in the heart of the city spread out before him like a relief map. Every street, every square, every major building stood clearly defined in intimate detail in the sharp, pale mountain air, so that it reminded him of a model town fashioned in clay, with the moving figures below like dolls. And when they moved into battle, he could from his height see so much more than they could. 'If only I could have told them what to do', he felt, battle after battle could have been won. If some of the fighting Khambas had only turned up this or that street, had only done this or that, they could have attacked the Chinese from the rear and saved the day. But the one last move—just the one simple move Thondup could see should and could be made—was rarely attempted, simply because there was no possibility of organized action.

Even the Chinese admitted the ferocity—and the success—of the Tibetan attacks. According to the New China News Agency,* 'The rebel bandits caused the greatest damage to the buildings of the Lhasa town centre, the Lhasa Civic Construction Department, and some other Government organizations. Using machine-guns and mortars, they launched attacks on the Lhasa Transportation Centre. Even the Tibet offices of the New China News Agency were attacked. The editors and reporters defended their positions in the editorial department for more than an hour. Bullets flew into the rooms and the rebels dug holes in the walls to shoot into the courtyard. A whole building was burned by the rebel bandits.' The Chinese did not, however, admit that among the 'casualties' was the Nepalese Consulate in the Inner City which was damaged by Chinese shellfire.†

It is, however, virtually impossible to analyse this last morning's fighting, in which even unarmed Tibetans were seized with such madness or religious fervour that their lives were of no account. For since there was no overall plan, the confused engagements often degenerated into a series of decisions made on the spur of the moment; each group of fighters did not seem to know or care what anyone else was doing, and though the fighting took place in a relatively confined area, none of the attacks seemed to bear the slightest relationship to one another, so that on this last crucial day, the overall scene takes on a strange nightmarish quality. Without warning, a raging mob which had seemed to be on the point of driving the Chinese back—with victory a hairsbreadth away—would evaporate into thin air, as though suddenly exhausted. Men like Thondup literally could not see where they went; only a few puzzled Chinese soldiers and a few corpses remained. And then it would all start again two blocks away, as an empty street would unaccountably erupt with shouting men, the Khambas in the forefront. The Chinese would rush in from the

* May 5, 1959.
† Announced by Nepalese Foreign Ministry, April 14, 1959.

near-by alleys—and then the issue would be brutally simple as the mob charged and died; yet, there was no apparent reason why the battle and the fearful carnage should have moved from one street to another.

Nobody could predict what would happen in the next half hour, in the next street, or even in the next house. Only one thing *could* be predicted—and that was the outcome, and no one is quite certain what happened to bring this about. Towards the end of the morning the Chinese rushed in armoured cars to rescue the two surviving tanks and finally started firing blindly into the crowd.

Other reports say that Tibetan troops were cut off, whereupon the civilians fled to the comparative safety of the nearest buildings. Shan Chao, the Chinese, was probably near the mark when he entered in his diary, 'From our watch-tower we could see the whole city. The rebel positions were in utter confusion.'

Inside the Cathedral Thondup realized that the end must come soon. For three hours the Chinese had poured mortar shells on to the building in batches of three or nine. The firing had hardly ceased, and Thondup alone counted seventy-two shells before he tired of making a tally. The roof was pock-marked with holes and though casualties were lower than expected, several praying monks were among the killed.

The interior of the Cathedral was a shambles. Thondup himself had narrowly escaped death when Gurgur the hunchback had pulled him out of the path of falling beams. Though the main shrine appeared to be undamaged, many of the lesser ones had been smashed. It seemed a miracle that those inside had been able to withstand the constant shelling, yet now there came a brutal realization: Chinese tanks, aided by armoured cars, must shortly storm the front gates. It was this which made Thondup decide to evacuate the last defenders of the Cathedral. For despite the impressive bulk of the gates, they were old, partially eaten away, and would be blown off their ancient hinges by the first shell.

Escape from the Cathedral was not difficult, for the same route used earlier was still open, though Thondup and Gurgur elected to remain behind for a short while to burn the official government papers. Thondup knew just where they were—in the 'office' near his own room. He had no keys, but he and Gurgur smashed open the unwieldy Tibetan locks and ransacked the chests. Gurgur started a fire in the main courtyard; Thondup found it simpler to destroy papers in some of the larger incense burners. If it seemed almost an act of desecration, 'I was sure His Holiness would understand.'

They were still burning papers—and the mortar shells were still raining down—when Thondup heard the scraping, rasping sound of tearing, breaking wood for which he had been waiting. The tanks were battering down the front gates. Leaving the rest of the papers, he told Gurgur to run for it, and together they darted into the Kashag building, along a dark corridor leading to the south-west corner of the Cathedral, where there was a door used only by the Kashag staff. It was locked. Thondup led the way up rickety stairs to a balcony, with Gurgur following, until they reached a large, paper-covered window. Thondup dragged up a form, stood on it and thrust his fist through the flimsy material. There was a twelve-foot drop, but it was the only way—that is, if the hunchback could make it, for by now the old man was beginning to show signs of strain. Balancing precariously on the form, Thondup managed to give him the one shove he needed to scramble through. Then Thondup heaved himself up, gripped the cornice and scrambled astride it. Gurgur had already vanished. Thondup did not hesitate, for he knew what he wanted to do—carry on the fight. Jumping the twelve feet, he landed with nothing worse than grazed knees, and darted for the cover of the open fields. Crouching low, he ran through the grass in the direction of the cinema.

Even to this day no Tibetans have been able to produce an accurate computation of the number of civilian deaths in Lhasa during the three days of the uprising.

In Budapest during the period of heavy fighting it had been a very different story; most of the population had been provided with Communist documents. The uprising had been staged by the genuine inhabitants of the city. Identity cards had made it comparatively simple to trace those who vanished, and to arrive eventually at a fairly accurate estimate of twenty-five thousand killed. No such aids to identification existed in Lhasa, however—and the problem was even further complicated by the influx of Khambas from the east who week by week had increased the city's normal population. After many attacks (particularly on this last day) it was discovered that scores of men, women and children had simply vanished—and more often than not the officials had little or no idea as to their identity.

Estimates of the killed vary enormously from the wildly exaggerated report in New Delhi that '50,000 Chinese Communists and 15,000 rebels were killed in the fighting since the revolt broke out,'* to the more reasonable figure of George Patterson that 'more than 10,000 Lhasa Tibetans are known to have disappeared, either killed or sent into forced labour.' The Dalai Lama puts the number at 'some thousands'. The most interesting gauge, however, comes from the Chinese themselves. While refusing to admit that a single Tibetan had been killed (and conveniently ignoring the fact that neither side took prisoners during the struggle) the official New China News Agency was, within the week,† claiming that 'a rough count shows that by the twenty-third more than four thousand rebel troops were taken prisoner, and eight thousand small arms of different kinds, eighty light and heavy machine-guns, twenty-seven 81-mm mortars, six mountain guns and ten million bullets were captured.'

If the Chinese did take four thousand prisoners—and it is a big if—it is not unrealistic to assume that in three days of ferocious fighting, between ten and fifteen thousand Tibetans were killed in or near the city. And it is probable that at least half of them died on the Sunday, the most terrible day of all, when, as the city ground to a halt, passions on both sides increased to a dangerous

* US Joint Publications Research Service.
† March 28, 1959.

pitch as more and more Tibetans refused to believe themselves sufficiently revenged.

Mary Taring escaped on this last day. She had finally reached the small farm north of Lhasa and was still hoping to return to her family. Back in the Summer Palace, Jigme, her husband, with a heavy heart, was preparing to flee. He had had no word from the Dalai Lama, so still hoped that his master was setting up his government south of the Tsangpo, within reasonable reach of Lhasa. He would have to join him, and wait until later to arrange for Mary and the children to journey south.

The chaos in the Happy Light cinema was complete. The original attacking force of around fifty had trebled. Hundreds of smashed-up chairs and forms were stacked up against one wall, and on the large sloping floor Tibetans had formed separate groups, so the auditorium presented an astonishing appearance, with a dozen small fires burning, on which the invariable butter tea was being brewed. To increase the appearance of disorder, the Khambas had torn down every poster, picture, slogan, effacing every scrap of evidence of the Communist régime. In their places Tibetan slogans now decorated the walls. Two stone pillars with Chinese emblems had been smashed. The swaggering Khambas, often with two or three guns and a sword, exuded confidence. They transmitted an intangible feeling that from now on everything was going to be all right. As one man explained earnestly, if they could do this to the Chinese once, they could do it a thousand, ten thousand, times— until the last member of the Han Dynasty was back on Chinese soil.

Of course they were unaware of what had been happening else-where. One of the perilous aspects of an uprising is the undue optimism which comes from not knowing what is going on just around the corner. Though they had heard the sounds of battle, the Tibetans were horrified to hear the Cathedral had been attacked with tanks and evacuated.

Thondup was in no doubt that 'the end was very near,' though he was as astonished as any one at the manner in which it came. By two o'clock the firing seemed to have stopped, giving way to a curious, uncanny silence. Even the fires had been doused. And if any stray pockets of resistance were still spoiling for a fight, there was in fact no one to fight, for the Chinese had evaporated from the streets.

In the cinema there was jubilation. The Khambas had won! Why otherwise would the Chinese run away? It never seemed to occur to anybody that General Tan had realized that if he withdrew his troops the few Tibetans still roaming the streets would quieten down, while he and Ngabo prepared to broadcast a 'message of peace'.

Around two o'clock loud-speakers started blaring all over Lhasa. Those in the cinema heard one from Yutok. General Tan told everyone to lay down their arms. All would be forgiven. His speech was received in the cinema with jeers and catcalls and several pistols were fired into the air by the more bloodthirsty Khambas. Then the voice changed. The Chinese general had ended his speech, and now a Tibetan spoke into the microphone. 'My name is Ngabo,' he began slowly, 'and you know I am a member of the Kashag.'

Immediately the buzz in the cinema stopped. Every ear was listening now to a recording being played simultaneously from a score of points in the city. Slowly, carefully, the modulated voice continued. All fighting must stop. That was an order from the Tibetan government—not the Chinese, he emphasized, for the government had agreed terms with the Chinese to end the revolt. The Dalai Lama had not, he assured his fellow citizens, been killed (as some said) but had been abducted against his will by 'the reactionaries'. There were a few more homely phrases—'Go back to your work', 'Lay down your arms and you will remain free'— and then with a scraping sound the recording abruptly ended.

The immediate reaction of the Tibetans in the cinema was one of stupor, followed by unbounded rage. Perhaps none realized that Ngabo was a traitor, and that no Tibetan government had given any order for a cease-fire, but after the first astonishment had passed, every man in the cinema—almost as though obeying words of command—reacted in the same way. In grim silence they packed their few belongings, stuck their revolvers in the sashes of their chubas, slung their swords in their colourful scabbards across their shoulders, tied the coloured woollen laces up the backs of their boots. They were off—off as one man—to the mountains to carry on the struggle.

To Shan Chao, this was the moment of victory, and he noted that 'Some time after three o'clock in the afternoon our national flag was hoisted high on Yo Wang Hill and our troops dominated the Potala, the Norbulingka and the Chokhang.' In fact Shan Chao went in the afternoon to the Summer Palace where Chinese troops were carefully examining the corpses in case the Dalai Lama had been killed. 'The call came to us to fall in,' Shan Chao noted. 'It turned out we were to go and help take prisoners. The remaining rebels had been captured. They filed past us.' The rest of his entry deals with the kindly way the Chinese treated the prisoners, particularly one old man who had been pressed into service 'by the rebels' and who was weeping as the Chinese gave him some steamed bread.

Shan Chao omitted, however, to mention that the cinema was still in rebel hands, and as the last of the Khambas left to take to the hills, Thondup prepared to leave Lhasa. He felt certain in his own mind that the Dalai Lama would have to make for India, and he decided to travel south and continue the fight next to the man he had served all his life.

There were no Chinese around, for General Tan was obviously keeping them off the streets until tempers cooled. Thondup walked swiftly towards Shagyari Street, the scene of so much desperate fighting, the buildings pock-marked by shell-fire, with the occasional blackened, charred beams marking the site where a house had once stood. Torn or broken sandbags spilled out on pavements. Bodies and carcases lay everywhere. Here and there dejected civilians were returning to their homes through the streets, normally throbbing with life and colour, but now reminding Thondup of 'the emptiness of a city struck by plague'.

Thondup was looking for Gurgur, and he found him near the Chai Tsonkang from where the Chinese had launched their bitter assault on the Moslem House. The two men hardly exchanged a word as the hunchback hopped after Thondup, who was thrusting his way through the market, past knots of silent people wondering how best to gather up the threads of life. No one seemed to be talking as they poked among the spilled mounds of fruit. No children shrilled, no dogs barked; even the beggars importuned them with gestures rather than cries.

It was a kind of corporate emotion, beyond words, and Thondup knew only too well what it signified. It was the silence that heralded the death of a great and noble city.

Up to March 25, 1959

Not until the Dalai Lama was five days' ride south of Lhasa did the news of the fall of Lhasa catch up with him. He was riding across a plain towards a monastery called Chongay Ruidechen—known to be a major Khamba centre—when one of the army horsemen reined to a halt. Far, far behind, a group of horsemen—little more than a cloud on the horizon—was galloping at speed, obviously in a desperate attempt to catch up with them. The Dalai Lama's party halted, while a detachment of troops rode back to investigate the strangers. When they finally arrived, the Dalai Lama immediately recognized Tsepon Namseling, one of the five government officials he had sent to persuade the Khambas to stop fighting and who had never returned. Tsepon had news which hit the party with the force of a bombshell. Grimly he told the Dalai Lama that Lhasa had been shelled, and though he knew no details, accounts had reached him of heavy street fighting.

Within a few hours—that same evening in the monastery at Chongay—Tsepon's vague news was confirmed in detail when the Dalai Lama received a letter from Tara, his private secretary, who had remained behind. Tara had been wounded by a shell splinter in the Summer Palace but had managed to escape and hoped soon to follow his master. His letter was a bald recital, making no attempt to spare the Dalai Lama's feelings. He described detail after detail of the fighting, even the moment when the Summer Palace was a deserted, smoking ruin filled with dead, and 'the Chinese were seen going from corpse to corpse, examining the dead faces, especially of the monks', in case the Dalai Lama had, after all, been there and had been killed.

To the Dalai Lama, alone in his monk's cell that evening, the dreadful news provided at long last the answer—or at least the partial answer—to an agonizing question which had haunted him for eight years, for it was on this night—though perhaps the Dalai Lama did not realize it at the time—that he finally came to terms with his conscience and his country. He had chosen to stay the night at Chongay because it was a big Khamba centre, and he wanted to thank those protecting him. Now, with the news of what had happened in Lhasa still fresh in his mind, the Dalai Lama left his small cell for the main courtyard of the monastery to meet and talk to some of the leaders. And it was on this night—perhaps for the first time in a life dedicated to non-violence—that the Dalai Lama realized that 'I could not in honesty advise them to avoid violence.' As he spoke to them—man after man who had sacrificed everything for the love of the country he ruled—this young man of humility and intelligence realized in a blinding flash that 'Now they could see no alternative but to go on fighting, and I had none to offer.'

It did not mean that the Dalai Lama had suddenly changed his entire philosophy on the use of violence. It did not mean that he now begged his subjects to fight where before he had unavailingly begged them not to. But some of those who were with the Dalai Lama remember that after Chongay he always seemed more reposed, more calm than ever before. Perhaps in some strange way the totally different ideologies of the man born a Khamba and yet trained as a God had at last been fused, not only by the fall of his capital and his country, but by seeing, by talking to the men he had rarely been permitted to meet before—the men who were fighting for freedom and to whom, when they humbly asked his advice, he found that he had none to give.

Late that night the Dalai Lama's military leaders impressed upon him the urgent need to sacrifice sleep and press on as quickly as possible. Now that Lhasa had fallen, the Chinese would, without doubt, be surging southwards. In addition to this, there was another threat. Lhasa had radio communication with the many Chinese outposts ranged along Tibet's southern borders and the possibility of being cut off was very real. The Khambas guarding the Dalai Lama may not have had accurate knowledge, but their instinct was right, for the faithful Tara had not told the Dalai Lama one vital detail in his message, doubtless because he had escaped before the action happened.

Within a few hours of the end of the fighting in Lhasa, Chinese forces had gained control of the Ramagan ferry. Already crack troops, with supporting armour, had swarmed across the River Kyichu and would already have reached Happy Valley on the Tsangpo—one of the few places which had an ancient raft capable of carrying armour across the river.

Before dawn the next morning the soldiers were loading the pack-horses with tsampa and dried meat and the Khambas were cleaning their rifles. As first light came over the mountains, the Dalai Lama mounted the white horse which the old man had given him on the Che-la, and the long, straggling line of men and beasts set off in the cold mountain air towards Lhuntse Dzong, 'still with the hope, which only slowly died', that he could establish his government there.

The fall of Lhasa, coupled with the news—which spread like wildfire—that the Dalai Lama was heading for India, was the signal for a mass exodus to the south. Overnight, families rich and poor—but all sharing the common fear of increasing Chinese oppression—uprooted themselves, packed what they could of their meagre belongings and took to the lonely mountain tracks south of Lhasa's River Kyichu. To all it was a gamble and not all could win, for the odds were high; but the prize made the hazards of the journey insignificant, for the prize was freedom. Lhasa had gone; the Dalai Lama had gone, and most of the simple God-fearing Tibetans knew what that signified—the start of a reign of Chinese terror far worse than anything that had happened before.

The chances against reaching India were enormous, for none dared to take the normal trading routes between Lhasa and the south. The Chinese would show no mercy to those they caught. Yet the smaller routes were uncharted. None of those leaving their homes forever could be certain that if they gained the pass of one mountain, they would be able to find a way over the next. And too, as with all refugees the world over, horses and yaks were cumbersomely laden with food, clothes, tents, even precious pots and pans which tearful wives had hated to leave behind. Chime Youngdong came across one family trudging on foot carrying two babies, while their single horse was burdened with the only precious item they owned, and which must have been handed down from generation to generation—an elaborately carved altar, complete with a statue of the Buddha.

No one will ever know how many perished on the long trek south. Some were caught by the Chinese and promptly executed, while their children were packed off to Peking. Some starved to death, or died on the snowcapped peaks when their mounts were trapped in deep rifts and could go neither backwards nor forwards.* Others lived but never reached India. Once in Khamba-controlled territory, they found a small village to their liking, and settled down to live there, hoping for the best.

Many reached foreign soil thanks to the unstinted help they received from the monasteries. In the mountain wilderness south of the Tsangpo tiny lamaseries had often been deliberately built by monks in incredibly inaccessible places, clinging to spectacular narrow mountain ledges, their white front walls flush with cliff-faces sometimes dropping five thousand feet or more to the narrow gorge below. They could be reached only by the most hazardous trails, and certainly few of the lamas ever expected to be disturbed. Yet it was these very tracks which the refugees, in their efforts to avoid encountering the Chinese, were taking, and many families on the point of starvation or death from exposure owed their lives

* Many who reached freedom in later years said they owed their liberty to the piles of bones on lonely tracks which warned them to search for an alternative route.

to monks who took them in, fed and housed them until they were able to continue their journey.

To many escaping along the mountainous southern trails the journey was surprisingly unadventurous. Others quite unaccountably, as though it were a question of chance, suffered terribly.

When Chime Youngdong set off from Lhasa, with a party of nearly ninety, all went well for a time though his seven-year-old brother, who had been hit in the knee by a stray bullet during the battle with the Chinese on the plateau, was in great pain. Worse was to come, however. After a week or so on the march, Chime's old mother became very ill. Her legs started swelling. She tried not to complain but she was obviously also suffering from exhaustion, 'and we had no medicine of any sort and in the mountains there were no such people as doctors.' Soon she could not remain on her horse without support. Finally, in an isolated village, Chime was able to change two horses for a placid, broad-backed dzo—a cross between a yak and a cow—on which the old lady was a little more comfortable.

Few can have had such a terrifying start to their journey as ten-year-old Genyen who had run along the bridge out of Lhasa as Tan Kwee stabbed the Chinese sentry. After reaching a belt of woods she hid there the first night, sleeping fitfully. A nightmare journey of four days lay ahead. She was only ten, she was all alone. She did not dare to travel during the day in case the Chinese were following her, for she felt certain that Tan Kwee had killed the sentry and Chinese troops were bound to search for her, if only to find out who he was.

She lived on berries, ferns and brackish water, sleeping by day, walking by night. Because of the danger of meeting Chinese troops, she did not dare to throw away the basket of dung which was soon cutting into her shoulders. And by the end of the second night, her feet had become a mass of blisters so that she had to walk barefoot.

By the time she reached the village of Medo-Gongkar and

stumbled into the courtyard of her uncle's house three days later, she had lost all sense of time. She vaguely remembers servants bathing her feet and shoulders before she fell asleep across the big kitchen table. She was still clutching her Indian doll.

How long she slept, she does not know. She has an indistinct recollection of being wakened and fed, of seeing Passang, her servant, whom she had left behind in Lhasa, leaning over her. It was night when she really woke up properly—though at first this seemed to be another nightmare, for there was noise and music everywhere, voices laughing, and when she peered out of the window, the courtyard was a blaze of lamps. She could even see someone talking affably to Chinese officers. The music seemed to get louder and louder. She could hear the stomp of ceremonial dancers, usually hired for parties. Bewildered, Genyen tiptoed out of her room, along the corridor towards the large reception room on the first floor. It had a small gallery at one end, reached by dark, twisting stairs. From here she looked down on a staggering scene. There must have been more than a hundred people in the room, watching the dancing, eating Chinese food, or just talking or drinking. All wore their finest clothes. She could see her uncle, dressed in a yellow silk robe over which he wore a bright blue loose gown. Beautiful 'chang girls'—paid to encourage drinking—were coercing guests to imbibe more. They would fill a glass with chang from an enamel teapot, hand it to a guest, and even nudge him gently if he were slow to drink, for their task was to make the party a success.

Suddenly someone spotted the little girl crouching in the gallery. Heads were turned upwards, and then Passang was next to her, whispering that her uncle wanted her to come down and meet his guests. Her uncle patted her head and introduced her to a smiling Chinese officer who said how pretty she was. Then Passang took her back to her room—and there, to her astonishment, the bed was littered with heavy travelling clothes, blankets, a sheepskin chuba, woollen Balaclava-type hats, thick boots. Passang let her into the secret. In less than an hour they were going to escape. Everything was planned. All through the evening, with the party in full swing, trusted servants had been making preparations behind the closed doors of the stables lining the courtyard. Mounds of luggage were being sorted out and loaded on to twenty horses or mules—striped saddle-bags of tsampa, bricks of tea, sacks of dried peas for the mules, skins of hard butter, frozen haunches of meat and (though she could not know it at the time)—caskets of jewels, gold dust, bars of silver and her uncle's most precious religious objects.

The party now in progress had been deliberately arranged by her uncle to put the Chinese off the scent. There was only a small Chinese post in Medo-Gongkar, and her uncle had invited all the Chinese officers, while the soldiers were feasting and drinking chang with the servants in the back wing of the rambling building, safely away from the stables.

Late that night, Genyen and Passang made their way down to the stables. Ten members of the family planned to escape, together with ten trusted servants. They would leave one by one, at intervals of a few minutes, and meet when they reached the open country. The servants, already wrapped in thick clothing, were busy strapping the last loads on the pack-horses.

Finally she was hoisted on to a pony in front of Passang, who, as soon as he was mounted, was issued with a revolver. Then, for no reason, a thought struck her. She was escaping, but her uncle was going to stay behind. She burst into tears and refused to be consoled until Passang promised that her uncle would follow within the hour. He would make an excuse to leave the party for a few moments once all the Chinese were drunk. Passang even pointed out the heavy chuba which her uncle would put over his silk clothes at the last moment. With that she had to be satisfied, and she and Passang rode off into the night.

As the Dalai Lama approached the region of Lhuntse Dzong—the township which he still hoped would afford him refuge on Tibetan soil—the Chinese were intensifying their search. Spotter planes like those which had discovered Chime's whereabouts on the plateau wheeled and dipped above the bleak mountains, looking for the snakelike caravan. Without doubt, the thick grey clouds, hanging low like a blanket over their heads, saved the Dalai Lama's party from detection. Time after time the planes could be heard above them, but in an uncharted area of savage peaks, Chinese pilots doubtless did not dare to pierce the cloud layer and dive low.

Yet there was fresh evidence that the Chinese were on their trail. Just before the Dalai Lama reached Lhuntse Dzong, Khambas from a near-by guerrilla centre arrived with the grim news that the Chinese had crossed the Kyichu in force by the Ramagan ferry. And that could mean only one thing—General Tan was sparing no efforts to hunt down the Dalai Lama.

The Khambas bearing this information had—as so often happened—overwhelmed a lonely Chinese barracks in a night attack and had seized copies of radio messages from Lhasa warning Chinese in the south that light tanks and trucks had been ferried across the river and were now moving in a massive convoy along the main Chinese north–south military highway. No one could tell just where they would be by now—nor did their presence in the south necessarily mean that they would be able to penetrate the wild country which the Dalai Lama was crossing—but obviously the Chinese were closing in.

The Khambas had other fragments of news, including one which confirmed the worst fears of the Dalai Lama's military officers. Captured radio messages made it clear that Chinese troops, ranged in strongpoints along the Tibet–Bhutan frontier, had been ordered to try and move eastwards to cut off any possible escape route into India. If these orders were being carried out, the danger could rapidly become acute.

Then came the blackest news of all. One evening, as the party rested briefly, the Dalai Lama turned on his radio. He heard the announcement that Chou-en-lai had signed an Order of the State Council in Peking dissolving the Tibetan government and replacing it with the Preparatory Committee for the Tibet Autonomous Region. The announcement also named the Secretary-General and Vice-Chairman of the Committee. This signal honour had fallen to none other than Ngabo.

The Dalai Lama had barely time to digest this shattering information before another shock followed—one that carried him back in his mind nine years to the moment when, alone in a small cell, he had listened to the distant, crackling voice of a man he trusted who betrayed him.

As in 1950, when Ngabo had betrayed the Dalai Lama in Peking, as on the last fateful Sunday in Lhasa when he had broadcast the deceitful summons to surrender, Ngabo lost no time in going to the microphone. 'We have deep affection for the People's Liberation Army and oppose the imperialists and traitors,' he declared. 'The rebellion of reactionary forces of Tibet and its fiasco is opening a new page in the history of Tibet. The rebellion has not led to a split of the motherland. On the contrary it has promoted the national unity of the country, thus bringing limitless light and happiness to the broad masses of the Tibetan people.'

Bitter pills like this had to be sweetened, and so from time to time Peking Radio broadcast sickly recitals of the way the capital was returning to normal. 'The ancient city of Lhasa', said Peking Radio,* 'is bustling with life again. As Tibetan peasants drive their donkeys loaded with fuel and cereals into the city, students with satchels hanging from their shoulders walk to school, the postman on a bicycle begins distributing the day's newspapers, and gradually more and more vehicles of all descriptions come on the streets. In the centre of the city, the shops which had to close in the rebellion stand open, their shelves once more stocked with merchandise. The reek of leather curing comes from the tannery, and the din of metal sounds from the coppersmiths and silversmiths. The vegetable market is crowded every day.'

Listeners in flight might have taken this idyllic picture with a grain of salt, especially as the Chinese, with an unexpected naïvety—for, after all, they had been earnestly minimizing the size of the revolt—spoiled the effect by adding in the same broadcast that 'bridges destroyed by the rebels have been repaired. Most of the high tension wires which they damaged have been put up again. Telephone communication inside the city has been

* March 24, 1959.

resumed.' And Peking Radio even appended the ominous remark, 'The most frequented place in the city is the office of the Military Control Committee, where lines of people are registering for relief.'

Peking also admitted, with surprising frankness, that the guerrillas were still fighting. When a reporter of the *Peking Review** glowingly described a visit to Lhasa in late March with the words, 'The Potala which towers above the city now breathes freely again, and the willow groves in the Norbulingka have donned their spring green,' he could not forbear to add that 'There are still some armed rebels committing arson, murder, plunder and rape.'

In fact, as the Dalai Lama was approaching Lhuntse Dzong, guerrillas were still fighting fiercely within a few miles of the capital, particularly near Drepung Monastery, where Mary Taring had 'adopted' two children at the time when the monks received three cartloads of guns from the Potala. The Chinese must have learned about the arms, for shortly after the cease-fire three truckloads of troops and three light tanks crunched their way along the four-mile road running westwards from Lhasa to Tibet's greatest monastery. From inside the monastery Chopel Tashi, the young monk who had helped to unload the arms, saw two tanks fire warning shots, obviously as a signal to the Chief Abbot to offer no resistance when the Chinese demanded entry.

The old Abbot, however, was made of sterner stuff. Calling together five hundred of the youngest and healthiest monks— including Chopel—in the central courtyard, he told them that though in theory they should never take any life, 'You have one other task—and that is to defend the religion of your country.' Within a few minutes Chopel had a rifle and a hundred rounds thrust into his arms and with nearly five hundred others was scrambling up a hill called Gampa Utse behind the monastery. For two days the Chief Abbot somehow prevented the Chinese from entering the sacred precincts of Drepung, until finally he politely allowed a search party into the monastery to look in vain for arms. Before this happened, Chopel and some of his colleagues

* Printed in the issue of April 14, 1959.

had ridden to the near-by village of Gebak, where Chopel had been born, and at his mother's house they changed their monks' robes for old and dirty chubas. Fortified—morally, anyway—by the Chief Abbot's virtual absolution from the sin of taking life— Chopel, like hundreds of monks, had come to an historic decision. They were throwing in their lot with the Khambas.

Now Chopel begged the local group of Khambas to ride immediately to Drepung, and they arrived just as the exasperated Chinese were systematically ransacking and pillaging some of the main chapels in the vast, sprawling monastery. In one chapel Chinese were prising precious jewels out of the statues of the Buddha. In another they were tearing priceless thankas off the walls. A few small fires had been started. At one corner Chopel saw the corpses of three monks in their robes.

Ignoring those pillaging the monastery—a comparatively small party—the Khambas made for the rest of the Chinese who were grouped near the butchers' village where Mary Taring had changed her clothing. Disregarding the tanks, the Khambas charged, and though they suffered heavy losses, they routed the Chinese and even disabled two tanks before the third trundled off. To twenty-eight-year-old Chopel—who had followed the placid routine of life in Drepung since he was eleven—this was his first taste of blood, and his reaction must have been secretly shared by thousands of monks as they saw their beloved monasteries ransacked. 'I had never wanted to fight before,' he remembers, 'but now, after what I had seen, I never wanted to stop fighting until the last Chinese had been driven out of Tibet.'

Happy Valley was a small, walled village facing a rich plain of neat cultivated fields irrigated from the River Tsangpo. Behind the square houses tier after tier of mountains—green in the foreground, brown and blue in the middle distance, with white peaks above them—seemed to fill the sky. It was the sort of place where nothing had ever happened to disturb its rural calm until the Dalai Lama had passed that way. The ancient ferry—with prayer flags on either bank to protect wayfarers—did not bring many travellers, for most caravans of horses or yaks crossed the river by flimsy bridges on more favoured routes, though the ferry was the only contrivance in the area large enough to carry heavy carts across the river—or for that matter light tanks and armoured cars.

To the Westerner the ferry, which would hold up to fifty men, would have looked like a product of Heath Robinson's fertile mind, for it resembled nothing so much as a huge orange box with its long, flimsy planks fastened together so casually that one wondered why the water did not seep in. At the prow a savage horse's head had been fastened as though by an afterthought, together with a prayer lance; at the stern a huge pole with a paddle at the end—attached to the ferry but worked in the manner of a single oar by four men—made the flat-bottomed craft easy to manage.

The village itself lay south of the river, separated by a few fields in which the farmers were busy with the spring sowing. On the north bank five hundred picked Khambas awaited the Chinese onslaught which they knew must come shortly, for, without warning, the box-like ferry at Happy Valley had assumed all the critical importance of a vital bridge in modern war. All knew that as the Chinese were now following the Dalai Lama with vehicles this was the only place where they could cross; so that, as the guerrilla leader told Kunchok and his colleagues, 'Even if it costs the life of every one of you, the Chinese must not get a single armoured car across the river.'

It seemed certain the Chinese would come in from the west, along the north bank of the River Tsangpo. There were several reasons for this assumption. No tanks could cross the seventeen-thousand-foot Che-la (the route chosen by the Dalai Lama) and attack from due north. Nor could the Chinese rush armoured vehicles across country from their strongholds in the south, for the southern bank of the Tsangpo—in contrast to the flat northern bank—rose in great impenetrable cliffs. The only southbound motor road from Lhasa of any consequence went to Shigatse, many miles west of Happy Valley, but it would be pointless crossing the river there for the mountains south of the river were impassable. There remained, therefore, only one alternative: to take the motor road from Lhasa to Shigatse but instead of crossing the river, turn due east and drive along the north bank of the Tsangpo to Happy Valley, several hours' journey to the east.

To the Khambas waiting at Happy Valley one thing was of paramount importance: ample warning of an approaching enemy force, and this had been arranged in an unusual fashion, for among the scores of peasants who joined their ranks as 'auxiliary fighters' —identified by yellow badges on their arms—were several local postmen. These were, in fact, postal runners gathered from many miles around, who could travel faster than any wheeled vehicles. They normally ran with messages from dawn to dusk in relays of eight miles,* and these were now posted along the river bank, stretching as far west of Happy Valley as their numbers would permit.

One morning an exhausted runner loped into the Khamba camp on the north bank of the river and gasped out the news that the Chinese were approaching. He had no idea of their strength, but had been told that their trucks and scout cars were half a day's ride behind him.

The Khambas—armed with Sten sub-machine-guns, and four Lewis machine-guns—lost no time. They had already moored the ferry safely on the south bank of the Tsangpo, which was a quarter of a mile wide at this point. They had also managed—despite the lack of any modern digging implements—to excavate one shallow trench in the hard flinty ground, while as a final precaution, they had hidden half a dozen yakskin coracles† a quarter of a mile down

---

* Relays of good post runners could cover the 330 mountainous miles from Lhasa to Gangtok in Sikkim in eight days.

† Coracles made of yak hide stretched over frames of willow branches are rectangular, normally about eight feet long and six feet wide, and weigh only about 80 lbs, so that they can be carried easily by one man. They tend, however, to be unstable so that frequently two are lashed together.

river. If any Chinese managed to cross the Tsangpo, a few Khambas, at least, could chase them.

The northern bank had a curious configuration, for two or three hundred yards from the river's edge the ground was pimpled with dozens of small hillocks, some barely fifty feet high, which to Kunchok, when asked to describe them, 'looked like extra bits of hills left over from the Che-la behind them'. These hillocks provided the backdrop for a dramatic transformation which now took place. At one moment the Khamba camp, with its fretting horses, was a hive of activity. The next—or so it seemed—there was nothing but a bare stretch of barren land leading to the river. Every man, every gun, every horse had vanished, for the Khambas had swiftly folded their tents and taken shelter behind the foothills. To the Khambas, nothing matched the ambush as the perfect form of fighting.

The battle for the Happy Valley ferry was short and ferocious. Six Chinese trucks, four of them heavy with troops, the other two with supplies, came lumbering in from the west, headed by two scout cars. Each vehicle carried modern mounted machine-guns. The trucks grouped in a rough semi-circle with their backs to the river. Behind the hillocks the Khambas waited until the lead car was stopped by the shallow ditch.

Though the hole in the ground could not have been more than two feet deep, the scout car suddenly lurched. Immediately thirty or forty Chinese leapt out of the nearest truck to help, leaving only the machine-gun crew behind. This was the moment the Khambas had been waiting for. Those on horseback led the charge, indifferent to the spattering fire from eight machine-guns. Before they could be cut down, the Khambas were galloping in, then hacking with their swords at the soldiers clustered round the disabled vehicle. The Chinese were killed to a man before the Khambas turned their attention to the other five truckloads. These, however, proved a tougher proposition. The infantrymen had taken cover behind their trucks, firing from behind them while their machine-guns raked the open ground between the river and the hillocks. When the mounted Khambas tried to charge the nearest truck, their horses were shot from under them. Those who penetrated the semi-circle and reached the rear of the trucks killed many Chinese by riding over them, though at a terrible cost to the Khambas.

Yet the Khambas, by all accounts, refused to give in, even though they faced superior fire-power against which their antiquated Lewis machine-guns stood little chance. The Chinese were also using hand grenades which, when tossed into the midst of charging Khambas, killed scores of men and horses.

Almost as the battle started, Kunchok was hit in the right shoulder by machine-gun fire. He could not use his sword, and though the wound was not dangerous he could not even fire his Sten. Stanching the blood, he lay on the edge of the corpse-littered battlefield. It seemed as though for Kunchok the fighting was over.

Had an impartial military expert watched the battle, he would undoubtedly have decided the Tibetans were losing, yet in a way they were not, for all that mattered was to prevent the Chinese controlling the ferry, and if in dying the Khambas took most of the Chinese with them, then there would be none to cross the ferry and the Dalai Lama would be safe from pursuit. This seems to have been the nub of the Tibetan plan, and they would undoubtedly have chalked an unusual, if negative, victory had not an entirely unexpected development occurred.

After sporadic fighting in which both sides seemed to be reduced to a few score of men, four more truckloads of fresh Chinese troops rounded a bend of the river. To the Khambas—without a reserve to call upon—this must have been a moment of utter despair.

To their amazement, however, the four trucks drew up in a rough square beyond the perimeter of the battlefield, and made no attempt to go to the relief of their hard-pressed comrades. Instead they were busily occupied, and Kunchok, from his position on the hillside, could see quite clearly what they were doing. The Chinese were inflating a number of collapsible rubber boats. And that could mean only one thing: while the remnants of the Chinese contained the remnants of the Khambas, the new arrivals planned to cross the river and seize the ferry.

It was at this moment that Kunchok, the burly one-time ladies' man, faced his finest hour. 'I couldn't use my right shoulder,' he remembers, 'but otherwise I felt fine, and in a flash I realized there was only one thing to do—I must blow up the ferry.'

It never seems to have entered Kunchok's head that anyone else should do it. His legs were strong. Cautiously he crawled behind the hillock then, safe from view, crept down-river towards the hidden coracles. When he reached them 'I saw something that made my heart leap.' A volunteer from the village, proudly displaying his yellow badge, had been left to guard them. Quickly, Kunchok—who had wondered vaguely whether he could manœuvre the flimsy boat with only one arm—ordered the guard to help. The man carried a coracle into the river. The two set off for the opposite bank.

Kunchok has no idea how long the crossing took, but when they jumped ashore on the southern bank they ran as fast as they could to the village and ferry. Almost at the moment they clambered aboard—without the slightest idea how they were going to disable it—the first Chinese rubber boat arrived with two men. Others, like black beetles, were bobbing across the river.

Lying hidden behind the high plank-like sides of the boat, Kunchok and the villager waited until they heard the scraping sounds of boots as the Chinese scrambled on board. The second Chinese boat was still some distance away, and as the first head appeared, followed by the trunk of the man flopping half over the side, Kunchok handed his Sten to the villager. The man hesitated. Kunchok grabbed the gun back, somehow overcame his pain and immobility and shot the Chinese. Then he leaned over and killed the other man in the water before the gun dropped from his hand. As the two Chinese in the second rubber boat opened up with sub-machine-guns, Kunchok knew exactly what he wanted to do. He remembers that 'the first dead Chinese was slouched half in, half out of the ferry. With my good left hand I grabbed at his body, which was bleeding terribly. I was looking for a grenade.'

Ignoring the shooting as the other Chinese boats drew nearer, the two Tibetans scrambled over the side on to dry land. Two enemy boats drew alongside the ferry. Kunchok turned to face them, and at that moment, as he drew the pin out of the grenade and hurled it into the ferry, two things happened. The nearest Chinese fired. Before Kunchok felt any pain the entire front of his chuba was suddenly streaming with blood. Then, as he sank to the ground, the ferry went up with a blinding roar and flash.

Kunchok must have lost consciousness, for the next thing he remembers is waking up in a strange house. The villager had carried Kunchok to his home, stripped off his chuba and his wife was bathing a long gash, bleeding profusely, along one side of his stomach. Kunchok owed his life to one thing—Tsering Dolma's charm box, which had deflected the Chinese bullet so that it had sliced across the flesh rather than penetrated the stomach. The wound was savage, yet Kunchok knew it was not fatal—and he knew, too, that he must get a horse without delay and make for the mountains, 'otherwise I would be dead before nightfall.'

Medical attention was urgent, but Happy Valley did not boast a doctor. And so there was only one thing to do. The volunteer's wife went to fetch her old-fashioned needle and some thick thread, and while Kunchok lay on his back, his colleague pressed the gaping wound together with both hands until he had made lips of flesh, after which his wife calmly began to stitch up the wound with yak-thread. At one moment she hesitated, possibly afraid of the pain she was inflicting. Kunchok grabbed the needle, which was half-way through the flesh, and pulled it out the other side. Then the old lady wrapped Kunchok's stomach in a swathe of rough bandage. Though Kunchok could hardly stagger, the unknown villager found two horses, and with Kunchok draped over one like a sack, the two men set off for the mountains. Kunchok had only one destination in view. He would make for Tsona—and Tsering Dolma.

The Chinese made great play of their victory at Happy Valley and most Chinese newspapers headlined a delayed Lhasa despatch from the Hsinhua News Agency which said in part, 'Troops of the

People's Liberation Army which sped southwards from Lhasa and crossed the Tsangpo at three places—east, west and centre*—and mopped up the hard core of rebel fighters. Pursued by the PLA troops, the rebels broke up and scattered after fierce battles, and in more than ten days of fighting the PLA captured over thirty administrative towns and villages south of the Tsangpo *east of Gyantse* [author's italics], wounding or taking nearly 2000 prisoners.

No doubt there was a hard kernel of truth in this report, and certainly nothing was ever heard again of the Khamba group which had fought so valiantly at Happy Valley. But what the Chinese did not announce was the Pyrrhic nature of their victory at this small and peaceful village. They may have wiped out every single Khamba, but they had lost the coveted prize for which both sides had fought so ferociously—the vital ferry, the only means in that area of transporting trucks across the Tsangpo in a last desperate effort to cut off the Dalai Lama.

For another week the Dalai Lama trekked slowly southwards. It was a miserable saddle-sore journey, in which at times members of the party had to sleep in cowsheds at heights up to nineteen thousand feet. And yet, to the Dalai Lama even the most desolate places had their spiritual rewards. One night the party camped at a village of barely five hundred people boasting the unpronounceable name of E-Chhudhogang, a collection of huts so desolate that Tibetans had long since coined a proverb about it, 'It's better to be born an animal in a place where there's grass and water than to be born in E-Chhudhogang.' There may have been no firewood, for there was no cultivation, but every man and woman, 'destitute but happy, for they knew how to look poverty in the face', offered their homes to the party. In contrast, the arrival of the Dalai Lama at Lhuntse Dzong—a vast, fortified building, built on rock, looking not unlike a miniature Potala—was the signal for hundreds

* This despatch was not printed until April 13 and could only refer to Shigatse, the river north of Gyantse, and Happy Valley.

of people burning incense to line their route while monks on the Fort's terrace played haunting music.

This was the place where the Dalai Lama had hoped against hope to remain, but by now he realized that there was no possibility of tarrying anywhere. Perhaps more than anything else, the Dalai Lama's resolve to remain on Tibetan soil was weakened by the added knowledge that 'My presence there could only lead in the end to more fighting, and more deaths of the brave men who would try to defend me.'

It was at Lhuntse Dzong, before pushing on towards the frontier, that Phala met an old friend at a ceremony attended not only by monks but by hundreds of Khambas, and ending with the Dance of Propitious Fortune. A handsome well-built man, with the sword and gun of a Khamba, stepped out of the throng and greeted Phala with a smile of recognition. At first the Chamberlain could not place him—but then the man's Chinese cast of features brought memories flooding back of a midnight meeting in the Summer Palace. It was Lobsang Tashi, alias the Chinese commander of the artillery, who had defected during a camp cinema show. He had been fighting with the Khambas ever since, and Phala noticed with fascination that even in a few weeks some of the swagger, the braggadocio of the Khambas had rubbed off on him, so that now he actually walked in a typical Khamba way.

Phala asked if he had any regrets. No, replied the Chinese, he had never regretted his decision for an instant, though more than once he had barely escaped death, for Chinese bent on revenge had never ceased searching for the member of their forces who had become a 'reactionary lackey'; even Khamba leaders had warned him that, because he could so easily be recognized, he should leave Tibet before he was killed. He had refused—but now the flight of the Dalai Lama had made him think, he said, that he would try to make a new life in India.

The festivities over, the Dalai Lama had one duty to perform. To a background of music chanted by lamas, monks, lay officials, village headmen bearing the Scriptures, flags and other emblems, stood before the Dalai Lama, together with cabinet ministers and local leaders. An official read out a proclamation announcing the establishment of a temporary government. The Dalai Lama formally signed it, and copies were sent to all the major cities of Tibet.

Only then did the Dalai Lama agree to move on, but even so, and even though he realized that it would be impossible to remain in Tibet, he still hesitated to make the irrevocable move of asking the Indian government for asylum. Perhaps he was praying for a miracle. Some of those close to him felt that he still hoped against hope that Peking would ask him to return, and there is little doubt that had a reasonable request arrived from Mao-tse-tung over the radio, the Dalai Lama would have turned round without hesitation. But though radio reception was good, that request never arrived.

Instead came the final warning of imminent danger. Fifty miles or so from the Indian frontier, Khambas reported that Chinese patrols were swiftly moving eastwards from Tibet's southern border. Already they were only a few days' ride distant, and their objective was obvious: it was to cut the line of retreat.

Many Khambas wanted to stay and fight. They had superiority in numbers and felt confident that they could easily resist any Chinese attacks, but the civilian members of the government were horrified at such a course. Anything that endangered the life of the Dalai Lama was unthinkable. And as they rightly pointed out, the Chinese patrols would certainly be equipped with radio, and once they were able to relay details of the Dalai Lama's position to Lhasa, General Tan would even be able to send bombing planes.

There was another point. Swiftly deteriorating weather in the high passes leading to India was having a marked effect on the Dalai Lama's strength. Unused to the rigours of a journey like this, his health was beginning to fail. He was still able to ride his white horse, but he was far from well—and one of the hardest parts of the journey lay ahead.

And so, fifty miles or so from the frontier, and knowing that Chinese patrols were thrusting closer every hour, the Dalai Lama

finally decided to leave his country. 'Stories were still coming in
of Chinese movements which sounded as though they were preparing to attack us,' he remembers. 'We held a meeting. By then,
all of us admitted the unwelcome truth to ourselves that wherever
we tried to stop in the mountains, the Chinese could hunt us out.'

That night he agreed to send a fast-riding party ahead to ask
the Indians for asylum, for 'we did not want to cross the frontier
before we had permission.' The advance riders would cross the
undefined frontier and press on until they reached the nearest
Indian post. There, a message could be sent to Nehru in Delhi
and the Tibetans would wait for a reply before returning to the
frontier.

The advance party set off at midnight. At five in the morning
the Dalai Lama followed, only to be beset by some of the worst
weather he had encountered. First came the snow. At the summit
of one high pass the Dalai Lama's eyebrows were frozen and, as
he also remembers, his younger brother 'had a very bad time of it'.
None in the party had extra clothes and the only hope of keeping
warm lay in leading their ponies rather than riding them. At eleven
that morning the party stopped for a makeshift meal of bread,
hot water and condensed milk. 'It seemed delicious,' the Dalai
Lama remembers. Then the long winding procession of nearly
three hundred pushed up towards the next pass, where heavy
snow, whipped by a strong wind, bit into their faces. No sooner
had the storm abated than a fierce sun threatened them with snow
blindness. Those without goggles protected their eyes with strips
of coloured cloth or the braids of hair which many wore wound
round their heads. Then came the rain lashing everything—and
that night the Dalai Lama slept in a leaking tent so that he was
awakened by rain dousing him through a hole. He tried in vain
to find a drier spot, but in the end had to sit up all night.

The next morning he felt really ill. He did get up, but when he
tried to mount his white horse he could not remain in the saddle.
During the day the Dalai Lama grew worse. He must have been
almost fainting and, despite new information that Chinese forces
were approaching to within a day's ride, there could be no thought

of the party going on. The rain still pelted down remorselessly, and it was essential to find some sort of shelter. After hours of searching, scouts discovered a peasant's shack, and they carried the Dalai Lama there—to spend his last night in Tibet in a small house, dirty and black with smoke, with cattle lowing on the ground floor and roosters crowing in the rafters above. Early the next morning Khambas brought news that Chinese troops were in the vicinity of a village called Tsona, through which the Dalai Lama had passed after leaving Lhuntse Dzong. This meant that the Chinese were within a few miles of the party, and even though the Dalai Lama was still far too ill to ride a horse, there could be no thought of remaining where they were. Somehow they had to reach the frontier or capture would be inevitable. Luckily, a local farmer offered the Dalai Lama a broad-backed dzo, similar to the one Chime had found for his mother, and he was able to proceed.

That placid dzo almost certainly saved the life of the Dalai Lama, for many lamas, deeply concerned about his health, counselled a longer rest in territory so close to the frontier that they felt no sense of danger, and their advice might well have been taken had the dzo not been forthcoming.

Now, as he approached the frontier, the Dalai Lama had to make yet another agonizing decision: 'Who should come with me into India and who should be left behind.' One can imagine the heartburning among those who had travelled so far and so bravely and who might now be told they had to remain in Tibet—a decision which for the unfortunate could also mean a death warrant.

But why did the Dalai Lama have to leave any of his party behind? Some who later escaped say bluntly that at this juncture the Indians refused many permission to cross the frontier (though they relented later) and that the Dalai Lama's decision was hurriedly made at the last minute.

The Dalai Lama, understandably, is more reticent, and merely says that it was agreed that the religious and political officials should cross the frontier, while most of the soldiers and Khambas should remain behind—some, he admits, because they were

ordered to do so, others because 'most of them wanted to turn
back into Tibet to carry on the fight.'

Among those who did not cross the frontier—not then—was the
faithful Jamyang of the Dalai Lama's personal bodyguard. When
the Dalai Lama reached the frontier Jamyang had to turn back,
so he made for Tsona where, as it happened, Kunchok, Genyen
and Chopel from Sera Monastery were all at that moment converging, unaware of the Chinese patrols in the vicinity.

That evening—the night of March 31—the Dalai Lama left his
country. There was no drama to the crossing. There were no
markings, no boundary fences, no police, no customs posts. One
step was taken in Tibet, the next in India—and each step was
taken in the same wild, uninhabited terrain. Of that moment of
history, as the Dalai Lama left not only his country of serenity, of
peaks and lamas, but was about to be jettisoned into the hurly-
burly of the Western world, the Dalai Lama has little memory.
Astride 'that primeval Tibetan transport' his dzo, the moment
passed swiftly and sadly 'in a daze of sickness and weariness and
unhappiness deeper than I can express.'

Epilogue

So ended, for the present anyway, the story of a man who wanted only peace in a country that asked only to be left alone. Once he was on Indian territory, with the knowledge that, short of invading India, the Chinese could no longer catch him, the Dalai Lama slackened his pace and rested until he had recovered from his illness. What happened later—his reception at Tezpur in Assam, his first temporary home in Mussoorie—is common knowledge. But what happened to the other brave men, women and children who were caught up in events beyond their control?

Some remained in Tibet. Some reached India only after perilous journeys.

Chime Youngdong, who was making for Bhutan, remembers that 'the ride was by no means as difficult as the one from Jyekundo to Lhasa.' Tragedy, however, struck in another way. Three days before Chime reached the frontier, his mother died. She had never had the strength for the journey and had been ailing for weeks. With freedom so close, Chime refused to leave her body, but carried it on his big tan horse which had brought him all the way from Jyekundo. Finally, he even had to part with his horse. As they approached the last barrier of snow mountains before Bhutan, it was so exhausted that it could not go up to the pass. Chime could not kill him, but he turned him loose in the grass-covered foothills, together with the other horses, and the party—with Chime and the Khambas carrying his mother's body in turns—travelled their last stage towards the frontier on foot.

Little Genyen had one of the worst journeys. On one occasion she and Passang were separated in mountain fog from the main party for two days, during which they had no food. Genyen slept in the snow—perhaps only because, when she was fitfully dozing, Passang quietly covered her with his warm, dark, homespun chuba. When they eventually found the others, who were making for Lhuntse Dzong and then Tsona (which lay between Lhuntse and the frontier) they ran into the aftermath of the snowstorm which had so ferociously hit the Dalai Lama's party. It took them three days to reach the pass to Tsona—three days in which they lost four mules, in which all the men had to be roped together, and three nights during which Genyen had to be tied to trees to prevent her falling off the narrow ledges. Finally they made Tsona 'where I remember we changed our frozen clothes and had an enormous meal.' Unknown to Genyen, her distant relative Kunchok had reached the village the same evening. So had Chopel, the monk turned Khamba, all of them, as though drawn by fate, converging on the last friendly village before they left their country for ever.

To all the weary travellers, the villagers threw open the doors of their homes. Chopel found a refuge for the night with four strangers on the floor of a simple two-roomed house owned by an old woman. He had to sleep on the floor in his clothes, though he kicked off his heavy felt boots. Kunchok spent his first hours in Tsona searching in vain for Tsering Dolma, though it required only an hour or two before he realized that she could not have reached Tsona or he would have found her easily in such a small place. Then he too dossed down for the night in a small room. Jamyang and his colleagues who had returned from the Indian frontier slept in a cowshed. Genyen's party spent the night—or rather, part of it—in one room belonging to the equivalent of the village mayor.

No one has to this day been able to explain why no Khambas mounted guard that night. Possibly with the end of a perilous journey in sight caution had given way to exhilaration. And this would be understandable for Tsona was, literally, at the end of their world. It was a sleepy sort of place, cut off from the realities of life, and none could have believed that the Chinese would attack a village so unimportant that it did not have even the usual wall surrounding it. No motorway approached it. The main street was unpaved. There was not even a single café, let alone an hotel. And, of course, no one knew that the Chinese were so near.

The ambush was laid at two in the morning. Genyen was asleep in the Mayor's house. She had kept on her chuba—using it, in the way Tibetans often do, as a nightgown. Cries and shots awoke her. As she jumped off the floor, a Chinese burst into the small dark room brandishing a torch. She could see nothing, and her one instinct was to get out of the house. At that moment a shot filled the room with noise and smoke and the torch of the Chinese clattered to the floor and went out. Cries from the surrounding buildings split the night air. She heard Passang's voice shouting for her, then one of her party must have found a torch, for the smoke in the room was suddenly pierced by a beam. Passang was next to her. He pushed her through the door. Her uncle followed. Running along a corridor, they climbed some steps to the main floor, then found a ladder leading through a trapdoor to the top floor, consisting of the usual granary filled with wheat, barley and peas, together with bales of wool. Before the Chinese searching the house below had reached the last ladder and the trapdoor, over which Passang had placed some sacks, her uncle, shading his torch with his hand, guided her by a pencil of light past a mound of carcases to the hole in the roof through which, as in every large Tibetan house, grain is poured, to be drawn out from the trapdoor below when required.

There was no time to lose. She could hear the Chinese below. Three servants took off their chubas, knotting them to form a rope. The lightest man, standing on Passang's broad shoulders, was pushed through the roof. Once there, he pulled Genyen up, then the others joined her until only Passang remained below. The servants made the improvised rope fast, and hauled Passang up. They clambered along the flat roof, finally huddling behind some ramparts, listening to the Chinese moving around the granary below until apparently they were satisfied no one was there. They crouched hidden until daylight.

Kunchok had also been asleep, but Kunchok was a trained guerrilla, 'and we always slept with one eye open.' Though still suffering from the bullet wounds in his stomach and right shoulder, the shoulder had been tightly bandaged so that he could use his sub-machine-gun. Some instinct—some sound, perhaps—made him instantly awake. He crept to the small hole that served as a window. There was no moon, but he could see half a dozen bobbing pinpoints of light approaching. He slotted the magazine of his Sten into place. As the Chinese apparently moved in for a house-to-house search, Kunchok waited till those approaching his house were almost at the door, then he leaned out of the hole through which he had seen them and fired a burst. Kunchok had no time to listen to the screams and shots. Wrenching open the door with his left hand, he burst out, trampling over three or four groaning men on the ground, and ran, under cover of the houses, for the edge of the town and the hills beyond.

Not far away, Chopel, still in his chuba, heard shots before the Chinese reached him, so never saw one before he bolted, forgetting in his haste to put on his boots. Jamyang also escaped before the Chinese reached him.

It is impossible to estimate the strength of the Chinese attack, nor the number of Tibetans killed, for the only accounts we have come from those who escaped, and each one had only a personal, fragmentary experience. It does seem, however, that the attack was on a small scale, not unlike a commando-style raid, and this tends to support the belief that this small force was not interested in the ordinary inhabitants of Tsona, but had been hoping to find the Dalai Lama.

With varying degrees of slowness, those who escaped reached—and then crossed—the frontier. Jamyang and Kunchok met on the outskirts and made their way together to the border, neither realizing at first how near to each other they had been working in the Summer Palace. Chopel had the worst time of it, for since he had no boots, his feet were badly cut and became infected. No one seemed to have a pair of boots to spare, but finally he persuaded a friendly lama to give him an old butter-stained robe, which he cut in two, wrapping the pieces round his feet. Genyen, of course, had the luckiest escape of all, but after the Chinese had gone—leaving the town after dawn as mysteriously as they had arrived—she set off for the Indian border. There the little girl who had lost everything—her father, Ma, her home—had to face up to one more crisis.

As they reached the first Indian post, and were welcomed with food and drink, Passang—Passang whom she had known for as long as she could remember, who had tied her to the trees, who was the only one left from her beautiful yellow house—broke the news to her. He could go no farther. He knew his duty was to serve her, he said, but now she was in India with her uncle and she would be safe. He was too young to escape. He had to go back to fight.

Dimly she remembers her uncle putting a protective arm round her shoulder as she tried to stop crying. She looked back once, to see Passang's sturdy figure walking in the direction of Tsona; still one more, and this time the last of her childhood friends whom she would never see again.

Others reached sanctuary more easily. Jigme and Mary Taring escaped by different routes, but were reunited after three months. Thondup and Gurgur the hunchback crossed the frontier about the same time.

Today, ten years later, many have settled in India and live on the slopes of the lower Himalaya, some separated by little more than a mountain peak from their own country. In the north-east Indian settlement of Dharamsala, the Dalai Lama has set up his government-in-exile in what has become a little corner of Tibet. Here the high lamas pray; here the Kashag—its members different from the night when Surkhang was smuggled out of the Summer Palace in a truck—watch over the destinies of Tibetans who have settled in a score of countries all over the world, and help those who even now are escaping across the frontier.

Upper Dharamsala—where the Dalai Lama lives three thousand

feet above the township proper—is not unlike Tibet. Occasional jeeps dart past ancient groaning buses twisting round the perilous hairpin bends backed by forests of tall rhododendrons. The wheezing buses, steam spouting from their bonnets, reach a small square, flanked with Tibetan stalls, beyond which they can go no farther.

Here lives the Dalai Lama, still young-looking, still with that same grave serenity, still with no regrets 'that I followed the policy of non-violence till the end,' and still so tolerant of human failings that in spite of all that has happened to his people and his country, he can still say that 'I have absolutely no hatred in my heart for the Chinese people.'

It is curious to reflect that the Dalai Lama's position today—and his ability to send emissaries to many parts of the world—might have been very different had not the boy of sixteen, when he first assumed temporal power, been wise enough to send some of his treasure across the frontier, where it lay for nine years, despite repeated efforts by the Chinese to get it back. The traitor Ngabo had even written to its custodian in Sikkim, giving official instructions 'from the Kashag' for it to be returned, but the Dalai Lama's friend in Sikkim refused; and so when the Dalai Lama finally reached India, it was awaiting him, and he sold the gold dust and silver bars for cash.

Not far from the Dalai Lama's modest bungalow—with electric 'butter lamps' on the altar these days—is a group of offices, and in one of them sits Thondup, who is now the Dalai Lama's Minister of Information. As lithe and lean as when he gave Gurgur a final heave through the Kashag window, Thondup's face is still severe until lit by his sudden smile. Not far from his office are two houses. In one lives the Dalai Lama's mother, still remarkably active at seventy. In the other lives General Kusangtse, now in retirement, but as straight-backed as when he was Commander-in-Chief of the Tibetan army. Among their regular visitors is Jigme Taring, now Director of Education, who lives with Mary four hundred miles to the west at Mussoorie, an old British-built hill station above Dehra Dun.

It would be hard to find a woman with such rare tolerance and understanding as Mary. With virtually no money, she founded the Tibetan Homes Foundation for children in a wild and rocky valley a few miles outside Mussoorie. Perhaps Mary's compassion, her love of children, helps to compensate a little for the loss of her daughters and grandchildren from whom she has never heard a word since the morning when she light-heartedly set off for the Summer Palace. The Tibetan Homes, which started humbly, have grown until now there are houses, dormitories, schools for six hundred Tibetan children who live there and are educated by their elders who have escaped or by those children who have grown up since 1959, such as Genyen, who is now a beautiful dark-haired girl of nearly twenty, studying to take up social work in Mary's homes.

Many others who lived through the grim days of 1959 are there. Kunchok waited seven years for Tsering Dolma to turn up. He wrote in vain to every Tibetan settlement in India for news, but recently he married, and today he is one of the most popular figures in the district—for the very good reason that he runs the best Tibetan restaurant (and makes an excellent kettle of chang). Chopel Tashi, the monk from Sera, cooks too. He is chef for three hundred of Mary's children—except on Holy Days, that is, when he dons his lama's robes and goes to the settlement's colourful monastery.

Jamyang, who by chance became so personally involved in the Dalai Lama's escape, also lives in Mussoorie. He is 'father' of a dozen of Mary's children, who are grouped in scores of houses dotted over the valley, each one with its own house parents. Lobsang, the government clerk who fought on the Iron Mountain, has learned to speak fluent English and has made a fine career for himself as a qualified school-teacher at the Wynberg Allen School at Mussoorie. His father, the food server, has died. So has Gurgur the hunchback.

Others have gone farther afield. Lobsang Tashi—who was once a Chinese general—works happily with one of the hundreds of

Tibetan road gangs earning their own living in different parts of India, though it was only thanks to Phala that he is in India at all, for when he tried to flee from Tibet across the frontier, the Indians—somewhat naturally suspicious of his Chinese countenance—firmly refused him admittance. Once again—in the curious way that people are recurringly linked—Phala came to his rescue. Somehow the Chinese managed to get a message to Dharmasala, where Phala was then living, and once again he was able to vouch for the man he had helped to defect from Communism.

Phala is no longer in India, for he is now the head of the Office of Tibet in Geneva, which looks after the many Tibetan children living in the Swiss Alps. Luishar, Foreign Secretary at the time of the crisis, held a similar post in New York until he retired some years ago to Trenton, New Jersey; whilst Surkhang, the Prime Minister—the one man above all others the Chinese hated and blamed—has carved out a new life for himself as an adviser on Far Eastern Affairs at the American University of Seattle, Washington. He still has his silver snuff-box, though he no longer mixes his own; instead he imports a regular supply from Canada.

Finally, there is Chime Youngdong, who in a way—after the abduction of his father—precipitated the crisis, because it was when he decided to ride to Lhasa for help that thousands of his Khambas followed him. Still slim and startlingly handsome, this young man—who in so many ways resembles the Dalai Lama—has been living in Europe, learning foreign languages and social sciences so that he may return to India, no doubt destined to hold high office and keep the flag of Tibet flying just a few miles from the country which in ten years has been viciously plundered by the Chinese.

Even allowing for any exaggeration by refugees who have escaped, the story of Tibet since 1959—and what is still happening —is a dreadful one, confirmed in the greatest detail by the International Commission of Jurists, an independent legal association from fifty countries, which collected sufficient evidence to consider the Chinese guilty of 'the gravest crime of which any person or nation can be accused', in other words, genocide, 'the intent to destroy, in whole or in part, a national, ethical, racial or religious group as such'.

No one will ever know how many thousands of Tibetans have been rounded up and taken to distant labour camps in the past ten years, nor how many have been murdered. Certainly tens of thousands have been killed without trial on the merest pretexts of 'crimes'.

Thousands of monasteries have been destroyed, and lamas have, if anything, been more severely persecuted than lay officials, largely because in Chinese eyes the lamas are regarded as unproductive. So great is the hatred of the materialistic Chinese for anything spiritual that at times respected and revered lamas have been harnessed to ploughs and used as horses, merely in order to humiliate them.

Much blood has flowed since 1959. How long ago it seems since Phala quietly ordered a uniform as a disguise; since the Dalai Lama and General Tan were exchanging polite letters while the crowd clamoured outside the Summer Palace; since the moment when Phakpala was stoned to death and his body dragged through the streets; since the first two warning shells landed and the Dalai Lama, torn by emotional conflict, knew the time had come to escape. How long ago it seems since he walked for the last time out of his beloved Summer Palace, with Jamyang at his side, to start his march to freedom, while Thondup, the hero of the revolt, was stacking up the sacks of tsampa as the Cathedral prepared for a siege.

Does the brave and resolute Thondup ever think back to the moment when, from his eyrie under the Cathedral eaves, the battlefield below was spread out like a relief model? Does he ever think back to the Khambas hurling themselves on the Chinese gun positions in Shagyari Street, to the women with their petrol bombs? Does he ever think of Gurgur the hunchback, or of the last moments when he destroyed state papers in a holy incense burner and walked out into the deathly hush of a dying city?

It seems even longer since the last days of the uneasy truce, when Genyen was playing with her Indian doll; when Kunchok first took the beautiful Tsering Dolma to the Chai Tsonkang for 'English' tea; when Chime Youngdong first gazed up from the Vale of Lhasa at the awesome beauty of the Potala, white and maroon in the sun, encircled by peaks, on that Friday the thirteenth. And does Surkhang ever think back to the moment he crossed the beautiful Turquoise Bridge to enter Yutok and hear General Tan snarl, 'He's the man behind this plot'?

All so long ago, all so far away. And though, as in Hungary, as in Czechoslovakia, the non-Communist world was impotent, the revolt in Tibet has at least done one thing: it has compelled acknowledgement of the ruthless nature of Communism in one part of the world which had preferred to ignore it. For events in the land of lost content proved at last to Asia and to Africa—to whom imperialism had inevitably been identified with the West—that a new imperialism had risen, that it came from the East, and that imperialism was no longer the prerogative of men with white skins.

One day it will, like other empires, crumble; and meanwhile Lhasa, the distant city unlike any other in the world, still stands, despite the Chinese who strut its streets, a symbol (for those who do not forget) of defiance by the puny against the mighty, of the unquenchable spirit of men who, however far away from us, are now welded by a common bond with their brothers in Budapest and in Prague. For they also asked only for freedom.

PRINCIPAL EVENTS
IN TIBETAN HISTORY

BIBLIOGRAPHY

INDEX

PRINCIPAL EVENTS IN TIBETAN HISTORY

Period of Independence under native kings and princes

ca.625   Song-tsen Gam-po (ca.613–50) becomes king of Tibet.

ca.641   Introduction of Buddhism. Building of Tsug-lag-khang (Cathedral of Lhasa).

763   Tibetans capture Ch'ang-an, capital of China.

ca.779   King Tri-song De-tsen (742–97) founds the first monastery of Sam-ye with help of Indian Buddhist teachers.

821   Treaty, surviving on stone pillar at Lhasa, fixes frontier between Tibet and China near present boundary of Chinese province of Shensi.

ca.838   Accession of king Lang Darma. Persecution of Buddhism.

842   Assassination of Lang Darma, followed by break-up of Tibetan kingdom into numerous small monastic and lay principalities.

1042   Visit of Buddhist saint from Bengal, Pandit Atisha, stimulates revival of religion in Tibet.

Period of Mongol suzerainty

1207   Tibetan leaders offer submission to Genghis Khan.

1244   Abbot of Sakya Monastery (Sakya Pandita) named as viceroy of Tibet on behalf of the Mongols.

1253   The Sakya Lama, Phagpa, appointed viceroy by Kublai Khan.

1260   Kublai Khan conquers China and establishes Yuan dynasty.

ca.1350   Chang-chub Gyaltsan of Pagmotru takes power from Sakya Hierarchy. Formal relations with Yuan dynasty maintained.

1357   Birth of Tsong Khapa, founder of the Gelugpa (Yellow Hat) sect.

Period of renewed independence

1368   Mongol Yuan dynasty evicted by the Ming. Tibet recovers complete independence.

ca.1481   Rimpung princes supersede Pagmotru family.

ca.1565   Princes of Tsang establish themselves as kings of Tibet.

1578   Lama Sonam Gyatso (1543–88), third successor of Tsong Khapa, given title of Dalai Lama by Mongol chief, Altan Khan.

1642   Qosot Mongol chief, Gusri Khan, invades Tibet, defeats the king and sets up Vth Dalai Lama, Ngawang Lobsang Gyatso (1617–82), as ruler of the country.

1644   Manchu Ch'ing dynasty replaces Ming dynasty in China.

1717   Dzungar Mongols invade Tibet and seize Lhasa.

Period of Manchu suzerainty

1720   Expedition sent by Emperor K'ang Hsi evicts Dzungars and establishes Imperial supervision over Tibetan Government.

1723   Withdrawal of Chinese (Manchu) troops from Lhasa.

1728   Civil War in Tibet leads Emperor, in fear of further interference by Dzungars, to send another expedition to restore peace. Tibetan Government reorganized and Imperial representatives (Ambans) stationed at Lhasa with a Manchu escort.

1740   Sonam Topgye of Phola, Chief Minister since 1728, given title of King of Tibet.

1750   Trouble at Lhasa after death of Phola leads to another Chinese expedition. Tibetan kingship ended. Authority restored to Dalai Lama (VIIth Dalai Lama, Kesang Gyatso, 1708–58).

1791   Nepalese (Gurkha) invasion of Tibet repelled by Chinese Army.

1855   War between Nepal and Tibet. No help sent by China.

1890   Anglo-Chinese Convention fixes frontier of Sikkim and Tibet.

1893   Tibetan Trade Regulations agreed with China, without Tibetan participation.

1904   British invasion of Tibet under Colonel Younghusband. Lhasa occupied. Anglo-Tibetan Treaty signed, to which Chinese are not a party. XIIIth Dalai Lama (Thupten Gyatso, 1876–1933) flees to China and Mongolia.

1906   Anglo-Chinese Convention secures Chinese adherence to 1904 Treaty, which it also modifies— without consulting Tibetans.

1908   Vigorous Chinese reassertion of authority, by diplomacy in Chumbi Valley and by force on eastern border.

1910   Chinese army of invasion despatched by the Viceroy of Szechuan, Chao Erh-feng, occupies Lhasa.
        XIIIth Dalai Lama takes refuge in India. He declares the independence of Tibet.

Modern period of complete independence

1912   Revolution in China and overthrow of Manchu dynasty. Tibetans drive out all Chinese forces from Tibet as far as Mekong River.

1913   January: Dalai Lama re-enters Lhasa.

October: Simla Conference, where British, Chinese and Tibetan plenipotentiaries meet on equal footing.

1914   March: Eastern section of Indo-Tibetan frontier (the 'McMahon Line') negotiated directly between British and Tibetan plenipotentiaries.

April: Chinese government refuses to ratify initialled draft of the Simla tripartite convention. British and Tibetan plenipotentiaries sign declaration making the convention binding on their governments and excluding China from all advantages under the treaty until Chinese government should adhere.

1918   Tibetans push Chinese to east of the Yangtse.

Tibetan advance halted by truce of Rongbatsa.

1919   Chinese proposal to reopen negotiations on 1914 basis comes to nothing.

1921   Mission of Sir Charles Bell to Lhasa establishes closer relationship between British and Tibetan governments.

1923   VIth Panchen Lama (Chos-Kyi Nyima, 1883–1937) quarrels with Dalai Lama and flees to China.

1930   Unsuccessful Chinese overtures through Tibetan Lama, Yungon Dzasa, for direct settlement with Tibet.

1933   Death of XIIIth Dalai Lama.

1934   Chinese Mission, under General Huang Mu-sung, allowed to visit Lhasa in order 'to condole on death of Dalai Lama'. Tibetans resist diplomatic pressure to accept Chinese suzerainty.

1937   Death of VIth Panchen Lama.

1940   XIVth Dalai Lama (Tendzin Gyatso, b. 1935) enthroned at Lhasa. Mission of Mr. Wu Chung-hsin makes further attempt to secure settlement with Tibet.

1943   Under pressure from both the British and Chinese Governments to allow passage of war supplies for

China through Tibet, the Tibetans firmly maintain their own neutrality.

1946   Tibetan Goodwill Mission visits India and China.

1947   Tibetan delegates attend Asian Relations Conference at Delhi.

August: Transfer of power to new national Government of India, which takes over rights and responsibilities of its predecessor towards Tibet.

1948   Tibetan mission, travelling with Tibetan passports, visits U.K. and U.S.A.

1949   Chinese Nationalist Government set up puppet Panchen Lama.

July: Tibetan Government expels Chinese Nationalist Mission from Lhasa.

September: defeat of the Nationalists. Communist Government established at Peking.

1950   January: Indian Government recognizes Communist Government of China. Communist threats to 'liberate' Tibet.

October 7th: Chinese Communist troops invade Tibet. Indian Government's protest met with reply that 'Tibet is part of China'.

Bibliography

Books Consulted

My grateful thanks are due to the authors and publishers of those books from which brief quotations have been taken.

Bell, Sir Charles: *Portrait of the Dalai Lama*, Collins, London, 1946

Chogyam, Trungpa: *Born in Tibet*, Allen and Unwin, London, 1966

Dalai Lama: *My Land, My People*, Weidenfeld and Nicolson, London, 1962

Ford, Robert: *Captured in Tibet*, Harrap, London, 1957

Gelder, Stuart and Roma: *The Timely Rain*, Hutchinson, London, 1964; *The Long March to Freedom*, Hutchinson, London 1962

Harrer, Heinrich: *Seven Years in Tibet*, Hart Davis, London, 1953

Holmes, Peter: *Mountains and a Monastery*, Bles, London, 1958

Migot, André: *Tibetan Marches*, Hart Davis, London, 1955

Moraes, Frank: *The Revolt in Tibet*, Stirling Publishers, Delhi, 1960

Patterson, G. N.: *Pekin versus Delhi*, Faber, London, 1963; *Tibetan Journey*, Faber, London, 1954

Peissel, Michel: *Mustang—a lost Tibetan Kingdom*, Collins, London, 1968

Richardson, H. E.: *Tibet and its History*, Oxford University Press, 1962

Sandbering, Graham: *The Exploration of Tibet from 1623-1904*, Thacker Spink, Calcutta, 1904

Snelgrove, David and Richardson, Hugh: *A Cultural History of Tibet*, Weidenfeld and Nicolson, London, 1968

Spencer-Chapman, F.: *Lhasa, The Holy City*, Chatto and Windus, London, 1938

Tieh-Tseng, Li: *The Historical Status of Tibet*, King's Crown Press, Columbia University, New York, 1956

Torbu, T. J.: *Tibet is My Country*, Hart Davis, London, 1960

Woodville, W.: *Tibet*, Royal Asiatic Society, London, 1891

Tibet and the Chinese People's Republic, Report by International Commission of Jurists, Geneva, 1950

Tibet and Her Neighbours, Hugh Richardson, Tibet Society, London

Tibet Today, Rev. Ngawang Thubtob, Bureau of His Holiness the Dalai Lama, Delhi

Tibet and the United Nations, Hugh Richardson, Tibet Society, London

Tibet and Freedom, Anon., Tibet Society, London

The Function and Status of the Dalai Lama in Tibet, Lois Lang-Sims, Tibet Society, London.

Chronology of the Tibet Revolt, US Joint Publications Board Research Services, Washington, 1959

Detained in the Norbulingka, Gyamtao Jaltsolin, *Pekin Review*, April 14, 1959

A Lhasa Diary, Shan Chao, *Pekin Review*, May 5, 1959

Index

American University, Washington, D.C., 215

barley, 26
barley beer, 122
Benchen monastery, 22
Brahmaputra River, 127
bullets, black market in, 124

Cape Comorin, India, 30
Cathedral (Chokhang), Lhasa, 21, 27, 56, 67, 92–93, 104, 132, 135, 138–139, 141, 152–153, 156–157, 166–167, 171–172, 178–179; Chinese attack on, 173–179
Chai Tsonkang café, 20–21, 125, 135, 141, 175, 184
Chambra, Miss (interpreter), 12
Chamdo area, Chinese invasion of, 36
chang, 214
Chang Chin-wu, Gen., 41
chang girls, 190
Chang Hwa-ting, Gen., defection of, 59–62, 214
Chapman, Spencer, 163

Che-la pass, 127–128, 196, 198
Chengtu road, 42 n.
Chenrezi (living Buddha), 33
Chiang Kai-shek, 91
Chiba, Major, 106, 129–130
Chime Youngdong, 22, 47, 189, 208, 215, 217; and downing of Chinese plane, 25–26; visits Dalai Lama in Lhasa, 27–28, 48–50; flight of, 92–93
Chinese Communists: ambush by at Tsona, 209–211; artillery forces of, 103; atrocities and executions by, 42–43, 53; attacks on monasteries, 41, 49–50, 216; "civilization" of, 20; "control" of by Dalai Lama, 51; defeat of at Happy Valley ferry, 198–201; fortifications in Lhasa, 134–137, 140, 157, 161–162, 174–176, 216; genocide by, 215–216; hand-to-hand fighting with, 141–142; "insulting" of by guerrillas, 47; invasion of Lhasa by, 40–41; number of killed in uprising, 180; reign of terror by, 187–188; see also Communist China
Chinese Foreign Bureau, 99

Chinese Hospital, 20
Chinese Military Area Council, 74–75
Chinese People's Liberation Area, 160
Chinese tanks, in Lhasa, 167–170, 175, 178–179
Chinese Transport Centre, 142–143
Choegyal (Dalai Lama's brother), 79, 110
Chokhang, *see* Cathedral
Chongan monastery, 185
Chopel Tashi, 131, 194–195, 209, 211, 214
Chou En-lai, 192
Communist China: "civilization" of, 20; Dalai Lama's opposition to, 38; invasion and occupation by, 20–23, 33, 36; strength of in central Asia, 42; *see also* Chinese Communists
Cyprus crisis, 159

Dalai Lama: power of, 22; "cooperation" with Chinese Communists, 23; escape route (map), 29; Chime's plea to, 28–30; appearance and personality of, 32–33; oral examination by monks, 33, 67–68; as God and King, 33; transmigration at death, 33–34; visited by Chinese delegation, 43–44; confrontation with Gen. Tan, 45; audience with Chime, 49–50; ordered to Chinese army camp theatre, 68; Summer Palace home of, 70–71; sister of, 74,

106, 110, 112; Chinese terms on "visit," 74–75; as "public property," 75; secrecy demanded by Chinese, 75–76; flight first suggested, 78; cancels Chinese visit, 82–83; assassination plot against, 83; non-violence policy of, 85; escape plans, 91; letter to Tan explaining absence, 95; meets with Freedom Committee, 98–99; second letter to Tan, 101; flight of, 103–121; offers to surrender, 105, 109; pressures on, 108–109; clothing and arms for, 111–112; sandstorm aids escape of, 119–120; climbs Che-la mountain pass, 127–128; protected by Khamba warriors, 151; reported death of, 182; learns of fall of Lhasa, 185; violence accepted by, 186; extreme illness of, 205–206; crosses frontier into India, 206–207; reception in India, 208; with government in exile at Dharamsala, 212–213; position of today, 213
Daly, Mrs. Catherine Sawle, 12
Dekyid Drolkar, 134
Dharamsala, India, government at, 212
Dhekyi-Wonang cinema, 154–160
Dinsley, Donald, 12
Dolma Lhaki, 145
Drepung monastery, 79, 131, 147, 194

Eisenhower, Dwight D., 159

forced labour camps, 41
Freedom Committee, 94, 96, 98, 114, 121, 129
Fu, Brig. Gen., 74, 76, 78, 89
Fuchs, Klaus, 159

genocide, by Chinese Communists, 215
Genyen (daughter of Jamyangling), 54, 97–98, 116–118, 123, 146, 167–168, 189, 191, 207–210, 214, 217
Gormo Rimpoche, 145
guerrilla warfare, 47; Chime Youngdong as leader of, 22–23; Chinese defection to, 59–63; "stamping out" of, 57; Tibetan losses in, 26
Gurgur, see Rupon Gurgur
Gyalyum Chemo (mother of Dalai Lama), 46–47, 78–80, 92, 96, 110–112, 116, 131, 213
Gyamtso Ling, 67–70, 72, 83, 93–94, 99, 109, 129
Gyantsen Chopel, 144

Happy Light cinema, 154–160, 181
Happy Valley, 127–128, 151, 187, 195, 197
Happy Valley ferry, Chinese defeat at, 195–201
Harer, Heinrich, 110, 126
Hsinhua News Agency, 201
Hugo, Victor, 154
Hungarian revolt, 161, 179–180, 217

India: Chinese invasions and, 37–38, 42; disbelief in, as to Lhasa conflict, 104; expected aid from, 91, 104; flight of Dalai Lama to, 109–121; "ignorance" of Tibetan struggle in, 159
Indian Consulate, Lhasa, 77, 131
International Commission of Jurists, 43 n., 215
Iron Mountain, 85, 113, 130, 137, 150, 164, 169

Jamyang (bodyguard), 73, 77, 83, 90, 93, 120, 207, 211, 214
Jamyangling, Tibetan noble, 54, 116–118
Jyekundo area, 22–23, 49, 51

Karzey Nyinrey Sargypur, newspaper, 41
Kashag, Tibetan cabinet, 37–38, 62, 76, 78, 90–91, 98, 105, 114, 154, 182
Kham, Chinese invasion of, 36
Khambas (Tibetan guerrilla fighters), 44, 47, 123; barricades raised by, 104; blocking of Chinese by, 80; deaths among, 50; destruction of Chinese cinema by, 181–182; and flight of Chime Youngdong, 92–93, 113, 126–127, 151; at Happy Valley ferry, 197–204; in Lhasa uprising, 141–150, 160–161, 175; at Monlem Festival, 70; as national monument, 169; number of, 52; re-

Khambas (cont'd)
cruiting among, 56; reprisals by,
51; revolution planned by, 43,
48–49; "secret army" of, 88;
secret notes from, 57–58; "stamping out" of called for by Chinese,
57; at Summer Palace, 100, 163–
164; Tibetan collaboration with,
58; at Tsangpo River crossing,
197–198, 201–204; uprisings of,
62
Khelenpa Suicide Squad, 129
Khrushchev, Nikita S., 159
kite-flying, 28
Kunchok (trader and guerrilla),
55–56, 77, 104, 123–124, 149–
150, 196, 199–200, 207, 209,
211, 214
Kusangtse, Gen. (Tibetan commander-in-chief), 11, 34, 36,
84, 112, 122, 165, 213
Kusung Depon, Gen. (personal
bodyguard), 73, 75, 79, 106,
118, 120–121
Kyichu River, 17, 56, 85, 99, 113,
127 n., 130, 137, 168, 187, 192

Lang-Sims, Lois, 35 n.
Lenin, Nikolai, 42
Lhamoi Latso, lake, 34
Lhasa (capital of Tibet), 17, 67,
76, 81; battle of, 139–160; Chinese Communist casualties in,
180; Chinese frontier incidents
and, 37; civilian deaths in, 179;
contrasts in, 19; fall of, 182–
184, 187; fires in, 170–171, 179;
mounting tension in, 100; mysticism of, 19; radio messages
from, 130; "return to normal"
announced by Communists, 193;
road to Chengtu, 42 n.; shelling
of, 133–134 (see also Summer
Palace); shops in, 20–21; as symbol of defense, 217; Tibetan
army in, 104; Tibetan demonstrations against Chinese in, 81–
82; Tibetan victories in, 176–
177
Lhasa cinema, 154–160, 181
Lhasa City Council, 69
Lhasa Radio, 158, 160
Lhoka, town of, 90
Lhuntse Dzong, India, 152, 187,
191–192, 209
Lingka River, 113
Ling-kor, sacred walk, 19
Lobsang Gampa, 114–116, 119,
129, 137, 150, 164–165, 214
Lobsang Tashi (Chang Hwa-ting),
59–62, 214
London Daily Mail, 159
Lubok Gate, Lhasa, 56, 135, 144,
156–157, 161, 174–175
Luishar (Foreign Minister), 11,
58, 76, 82, 86–87, 89, 114, 215
Lundok (priest), 77

"Ma," nurse, 54, 116–118, 167, 212
Macmillan, Harold, 159
Mao Tse-tung, 45, 142
Mary Taring, see Taring, Mary
Medical College, Lhasa, 150–151,
164–165; see also Iron Mountain

Medo-Gongkar, village of, 167, 189

men, sterilization of by Chinese, 42

Military Area Command, 95, 101

monasteries, Chinese attacks on, 41, 49–50, 216

monks, execution of, 41

Monlem Festival, 70

Moslem House, 173, 184

Nehru, Jawaharlal, 104, 159

New Chinese News Agency, 177, 180

New Delhi, India, 130

New Year, Tibetan, 21

Ngabo (Ngabo Ngawang Jigme), 13, 72–73, 78, 82, 87, 100–101, 105, 109, 146, 170, 182; mission to Communist leaders, 40–41; defection of, 40; as Secretary of State in Communist regime, 192–193

non-violence, doctrine of, 37, 85

Norbulingka, see Summer Palace

Paljor House, 144, 155, 157, 162–163, 174–175

Park-hor, Lhasa, 135, 171

Passang (servant), 117–118, 190–191, 208–209, 212

Patterson, George, 11, 159

Patung Ahnga village, 42

Peking, Seventeen Point Agreement in, 40

Peking Radio, 142–143, 158, 160, 166, 193

Peking Review, 129, 194

People's Liberation Army, 193

People's Republic of China, 40; see also Communist China

People's Volunteers, 85

Phakpala (monk and traitor), 55, 72, 75, 82, 95, 216; attempted assassination of Dalai Lama by, 83; murdered by Tibetan mob, 83–84

Phala (court chamberlain), 11, 43, 59–61, 75, 78, 81, 87, 91, 93, 95, 101, 108, 113–114, 118, 121, 215

Potala, government building, 17, 28, 30, 60–61, 70, 72, 85, 99, 104, 114, 123, 125, 131, 134, 136, 194; Chinese delegation at, 43–44; and Chinese frontier invasions, 37; Dalai Lama's room in, 32; shelling of, 144

Ragyapa, 84

Ramagan ferry, Lhasa, 113, 137, 187, 192

Rapten, Sonam, 12

Robinson, Heath, 196

Rupon Gurgur (policeman), 154, 156–158, 162, 178–179, 184, 212–214, 216

Sacred Inner Ring, 135, 171

Samdup Phodrang, 82

sandstorm, "miracle" of, 119

Sera monastery, 22, 35, 60, 72, 77, 85, 207

Seventeen Point Agreement, 40–41, 52, 72

Shagyari Street, Lhasa, 134–135, 138, 140, 157, 161, 174–176, 183, 216

Shan Chao (Chinese journalist), 84, 99, 104, 123–124, 142, 163, 183

Shasur (cabinet member), 82

Sho, hamlet of, 60, 125

Shukti Lingka (field), 123, 130, 137, 163–166

Sikkim frontier, 39

sterilization, by Chinese, 42

Stone Bridge, 74, 77

Suicide Squad, 129

Summer Palace (Norbulingka), 61, 70, 93–96, 130, 185–186; arming of guards at, 85; artillery surrounding, 103–104; demonstrations outside, 77, 90; isolation of, 80–81; shelling of, 106–107, 110, 122, 124, 129, 133–134, 146–147, 163–167

Surkhang (Wangchin Gyilek Surkhang), 11, 13, 57, 76, 82, 86–87, 89, 91, 107, 109, 114, 170, 215, 217

Szechuan province, 42 n.

Taktser, village of, 34–35

Tan Kuan-san, Gen., 43, 57–58, 71–72, 76, 82, 86, 88, 93, 109, 124, 129, 146, 216; addresses Women's Association, 59; reaction to Gen. Chang's defection, 62–63; orders Dalai Lama to theatre, 68–69; told of Dalai Lama's cancellation of visit, 87; threatens reprisals, 89; letters from, 94, 100; and shelling of Summer Palace, 133–134; in battle of Lhasa, 152–153; fails to use tanks, 169; appeals for surrender of Tibetans, 182

Tan Kwee (Tibetan storekeeper), 97, 146, 168–169, 189

Taring, Jigme, 55, 105, 112, 123, 134, 147, 163, 181, 213

Taring, Mary, 11, 55, 59, 71–72, 99, 105, 123, 130, 147–148, 181, 194–195, 213–214

Tasha Paran, Gen., 60–62

Thondup (City Council member), 11, 69, 104, 135–136, 138–139, 152, 157, 159–160, 171, 174, 176, 182–183, 212, 216

Tibet: Chinese ancestry in, 36; Chinese destruction and genocide in, 215–216; Chinese invasions of, 36–37; collaboration with guerrillas, 58; "coordination" of Chinese oppression in, 57; see also Tibetan people

Tibet Autonomous Region, creation of, 192

Tibetan government, dissolution of, 192

Tibetan Homes Foundation, 214

Tibetan monks, 41, 67

Tibetan New Year, 21

Tibetan people: fortifications by on Iron Mountain, 137; gathering of at Summer Palace, 77, 81, 90; hand-to-hand fighting with Chi-

Tibetan people (cont'd)
nese, 141; traitors among, 55,
67-68
tsampa (barley food), 26, 136
Tsangpo River, 62, 78, 113, 127-
128, 195-196
Tsepon Namseling (government official), 185
Tsering Dolma (fiancée of Kunchok), 56-57, 124-126, 148-149,
201, 209, 214, 217
Tsona village, 206, 209; Chinese
ambush at, 210-211
Turquoise Bridge, 46, 158, 161

United Nations, "postpones" Tibetan appeal, 39

Volunteer Guards, 85, 137, 150

Western countries, expected aid
from, 91
Women's Association, 56, 59, 72,
99, 105-106, 124-125, 144, 148
Wynberg Allen School, India, 214

Yatung, temporary government seat
at, 39
Yellow Wall, Summer Palace, 72,
96, 110, 113
Yutok village, 46, 57-58, 60, 76,
83, 142, 146, 160, 169